Praise for *The White Peril*

"*The White Peril* is the book I wish I had my whole life; it is astonishing, beautiful, courageous, luminous, heartrending, inspiring, fierce, sympathetic, provocative, necessary, unflinching, and, above all else, true. Braiding together a family history, a civil rights chronicle, and a moving account of his own coming of age under the ever-present threat of whiteness, Omo Moses has written an epic reaffirmation of Black diasporic life and a clarion call for justice. *The White Peril* is destined to be read and cherished."

—JUNOT DÍAZ, Pulitzer Prize for Fiction recipient and author of *The Brief Wondrous Life of Oscar Wao*

"In this captivating collection of stories, reflections, interviews, and sermons, Omo Moses provides readers a glimpse into the Black struggle from the son of one of America's most important leaders, Bob Moses. Part memoir, part poetry, part biography, and much more, *The White Peril* gives Moses's readers insights into what it was like to be a child of the Black struggle in Tanzania, Mississippi, and Cambridge. With unapologetic honesty and candor, he conveys both the challenges and the beauty of being raised to understand why committing oneself to the struggle for justice is not a matter of choice but one of fate and destiny. Moses shows us what it is like to live a life dedicated to the uplift of the powerless. For those who need to be inspired during these bleak days, this book is just what you need."

—PEDRO NOGUERA, the Emery Stoops and Joyce King Stoops Dean of the University of Southern California Rossier School of Education

"Intricately crafted, and a riveting read, this unputdownable whirlwind journeys through five generations of a Black family fighting for Black liberation, and a young man's fight to traverse the rocky distance between father and son. With sometimes lyrical, sometimes jarring prose, this moving memoir has achieved Omo's stated goal: 'to allow poetry to take root inside the story.'" Omo has granted us a glimpse into the psyche of young Black manhood and a window into the mind of his father, the brilliant visionary Robert P. Moses."

—LISA DELPIT, MacArthur Fellow and author of *Other People's Children* and *"Multiplication Is for White People"*

"*The White Peril* is searing, honest, vulnerable, profound, and undeniable. I loved it. In the distance between Omo's experience and mine, in the same place, at the same critical age, is the distance perhaps between black and white America. It is that distance that continues to test this country, to bedevil it, to confound it, to force people into all kinds of denial. I believe the way through that distance or perhaps across it are bridges . . . bridges built with love and truth simultaneously, that connect us. Though they don't make us the same, they allow us access to one another. Those bridges, if they can be made, look in my mind's eye precisely like *The White Peril.*"

—BEN AFFLECK, actor, writer, filmmaker, and CEO, Artists Equity

The

White Peril

The
White Peril

A FAMILY MEMOIR

Omo Moses

Beacon Press · Boston

BEACON PRESS
Boston, Massachusetts
www.beacon.org

Beacon Press books
are published under the auspices of
the Unitarian Universalist Association of Congregations.

28 27 26 25   8 7 6 5 4 3 2 1

This book is printed on acid-free paper that meets the uncoated paper
ANSI/NISO specifications for permanence as revised in 1992.

The language used in *The White Peril*, which is a memoir and
autobiographical in nature, reflects the author's decision on how
to write about and represent his lived experience.

Some names have been changed to protect people's privacy.

Text design and composition by Kim Arney

Robert Moses's account of voter registration drives in Mississippi and other
writings, as well as interviews from *Radical Equations: Civil Rights from
Mississippi to the Algebra Project* (Boston: Beacon Press, 2001);
Oral History with Amzie Moore, University of Southern Mississippi
Digital Collections; Eulogy for James Chaney; and lyrics from
Taba Moses are printed here with permission.

Library of Congress Cataloging-in-Publication Data is available for this title.
ISBN: 978-0-8070-0482-1; e-book: 978-0-8070-0483-8;
audiobook: 978-0-8070-1468-4

For Baba, Bob Moses, Mama, Janet Moses
For Taba
For Johari and Kamara

CONTENTS

AUTHOR'S NOTE

I wrote this book because I had to. I began writing it in eleventh grade in Karen Hawthorne's Intro to Creative Writing class—the only class in four years of high school that managed to get me to reach inside and share parts of myself. The intimacy of that introspection, which had been reserved for prodigious love letters, now found its way into the poems and short stories I shared with my classmates, into the free-writing exercises that began most classes, that in a stream of consciousness inevitably returned me to Tanzania, East Africa, where I was born.

I wrote this book in college when I took all the creative writing classes I could take, some of them more than once. I wrote more poems and short stories and kept returning to distant memories of Africa and not-so-distant memories of growing up in America. As my dream of becoming a great basketball player began to fade, I began to dream of becoming a writer. My professors encouraged me and honored me with the school's creative writing award. I started to realize that I was eventually going to write something. "I have at least one good story in me," I would tell myself as I visited local bookstores and imagined my book on display in the window.

When I left college, my dad gave me a book by Naguib Mahfouz called *The Harafish*. The writing was lyrical, the book was about family, about love, common people, the ordinary and enduring alley, about democracy, about generational change, about the cosmos. I cherished it and would share it with as many people as I could as if it was a way to know me, as my dad had shared it with me so I could better know him. I wanted to write about the things that Naguib Mahfouz wrote about as they pertained to my life, to allow poetry to take root inside the story.

I wrote this book in Mississippi, which is where I landed after leaving college. In Mississippi I encountered the powerful voices of my past, of America's past: the voices of freedom fighters and freedom singers, the voices of students growing from all that history—what was present in the trees, the architecture of towns and cities, in eyes and limbs. I wanted to understand and share those voices and connect them to the voices of my childhood. I interviewed my dad on a bench next to a pond. My mom in the kitchen over bottles of wine. My brother always at a bar.

I wrote this book while reading others: Junot Díaz's *Drown, The Brief Wondrous Life of Oscar Wao, This Is How You Lose Her*. Díaz became family with the Dominicans and Puerto Ricans I grew up with, and so I got to know him a bit and got a sense of how he unapologetically unleashed his voice and appeared on those pages. *We the Animals* by Justin Torres, who in his first line captured the urgency of youth, and in the remaining pages the short distance between love and hate that we all travel. In NoViolet Bulawayo's *We Need New Names*, the characters roamed and renamed and reinvented neighborhoods in Africa in the same way that the brothers I grew up with roamed and roared and reimagined the streets of Cambridge where we grew up.

At some point I got an agent, and she asked me if I was trying to write poetry, fiction, or nonfiction. Creative nonfiction is what I landed on, and it was decided that my first book would be a memoir. I went through as many titles—*UnAmerican, 44 for President*, something about laps around the sun—as the almost ten years it took us to get the proposed book sold.

I wrote to Sweet Honey in the Rock, I wrote to Bernice Johnson Reagon, I wrote to Curtis Mayfield, I wrote to 2Pac, I wrote to esperanza, I wrote to the Hot 8 Brass Band, I wrote to Keith Jarrett, I wrote to Abdullah Ibrahim, I wrote to Biggie Smalls, I wrote to Nas.

I wrote this for my kids so they would know their Dada.

I wrote this for my dad, Robert Parris Moses, knowing he would never read it, but that his kids would, and his grandkids, and his great grandkids, and so on and so on, so that they would always have a place to go to, to remember who he was, who we are, to hear his voice, to get a sense of where his voice came from and how what he had to say relates to these perilous moments we find ourselves in.

WILLIAM HENRY MOSES OBITUARY

William Henry Moses was my father's grandfather. This was found among his papers after he died in 1940.

It is Feb. 22nd 1935. The country is celebrating the birth of George Washington and I am preparing my obituary. The doctors say I cannot live long. I am flat on my back, cannot move an inch to the right nor the left, but fighting back at death to the bitter end, though I know he will win in the end. I have never prepared for death, I've been too busy preparing to live the life that might be given me on earth. Were I able, and my friends were willing, I would celebrate my funeral with a happy feast for my friends. But since I have saved but a little for a funeral, I write these words to cheer those who may not have realized the fullness of life.

They tell me that I was born Dec. 31st 1872. I am uncertain about my earthly parents, but I am reasonably certain of my ultimate creator who is without beginning of years. As I look back on these 62 years, I rejoice, like a strong man, having run a race, and won. I see myself in all stages, from a toddling child, to an old man, surrounded with children and grandchildren. I think I remember when I first walked, and when I recognized my mother, wearing a red striped dress. I lived with my grandmother five miles away. They carried me to my mother, before I was six, and I left the next afternoon and returned to my grandmother and told her, that I had been to Farmville and rode in the cow-catcher, and enjoyed my ~~exagerated~~ exaggerated story of adventure. Before I was ten, I was trapping rabbits, with bare feet, in frosty weather, and enjoyed it. My feet became wet in the first rains and snows of autumn, and the rain wet them until spring, until I was nearly a man. I was plowing at ten, and cutting wheat at fourteen, splitting rails, and ditching in mud and water up to my waist at sixteen. At seventeen I was asked to carry the corn to the mill, on my head, because the working teams were busy. I ~~slipped slipted~~ stole into the pastures, drove two young steers to the pen, lassoed and yoked them and hitched them and carried the grist to the mill and back, without the family knowing I had done it. At seventeen, I was hired to oversee a farm of several thousand acres, at the highest wages ever paid a colored man in my county (Charlotte Va.). When a student I worked in the mines of West Va. to make the money. The first day my hands became a blister from my wrists to the tips of my fingers, which bursted and dripped blood. But I kept at it, rejoicing with it, until I accomplished my end. I did not pity myself then nor now, but was glad to be alive, and too busy to complain.

Speaking of education, I never went to school, but a month, nor did I have a private tutor until I attended Virginia Seminary in 1892. I do not remember when I learned my alphabet. It seems like I always knew them. . . . I graduated from Virginia Seminary, without being called a brilliant scholar, but a hard student. Later, I became president of Nelson Merry College, and later I served as president of Guadalupe College in Texas, but I majored in teaching religion.

Speaking of religion; I have believed in God, ever since I have believed in my own existence, and was taught the descent of my mother and father. At first I was too afraid of God to love him. I thought it was awful for him to burn up the world, and any sort of people, I trembled at the falling of every star. After my father's death (at fourteen) I studied the Bible, and life, until I decided that God loved me, and would save me from unnecessary suffering and torment. When I went to school, I decided that the Lord wanted me to preach and major in showing people how to love him and each other.

Speaking of preaching, I was amazed, at what seemed to me the gross misunderstanding in preaching and teaching the Christian religion. So I majored in studying the Bible itself, rather than what most people said about it; and later discovered, that I was unconsciously following the trail of the most advanced Christian thinkers of all times. And I saw the importance of the darker races, taking the lead in helping to reset the Gospel, which was first delivered unto these saints.

I have spent the greater portion of my ministerial life endeavoring to awaken National Negro Baptists' consciousness to the importance of ~~leading~~ molding International Christian sentiment, for the mankind in general and the darker people in particular. Much of my early ministry was wasted, by endeavoring to be orthodox after the old school, of misguided people. In my later years, I learned how to distinguish between the distinctive teachings of Jesus, and that of all the other Bible writers, many of whom radically differ from Jesus, on the essence of religion. I've summed up my ministry of preaching, in a little booklet called "The

Five Commandments of Jesus." My dying request to the preachers of the world is study them carefully without prejudice. I hope the National Baptists Publishing Board will always be able and willing to print and circulate them.

In my poverty I gave five hundred dollars to help establish the Negro Baptists Publishing House, not to mention my time and strength to this day.

In my opinion I could have made money in the ministry, had I measured in money. In my first pastorate, I had a good parsonage; a brick suburban residence of twenty acres, with fruit and vegetables; work horses, thoroughbred mares and stallions, thoroughbred cattle; hogs and chickens; hounds and setters; later I started a half a dozen stores in Philadelphia and purchased a mansion on Broad St., a stone's throw from City Hall. But when my eyes became open on the true mission of a Christian minister I ~~gave all~~ flung it from my hands, and counted it as dung, when compared to the work in which I was called to major.

I've been called a fool, for not saving money for my family, after my death. Well, I've saved none, but I've used enough to keep my wife and children in comfort, every day they have been with me. Our six children are educated and honored in their day and generation. They may not be as good saints as I would like them, but they are as good as their father. My wife is known and honored, wherever I have spoken. I am leaving three sons, a successful lawyer, a gifted ~~architect~~ teacher of architecture; a baby boy who can hold his own in civil society, or anywhere.

I have three wonderful girls; one happily married, all of which have publicly entertained the leading people of the world, ~~from Broadway to~~ in America and Europe. I could have wished that my sons had been preachers and my daughters missionaries but God did not will it so. After all, preachers and missionaries are not saints, nor are people of other callings sinners above the rest.

During these sixty-three years, I have every reason to ~~enjoy~~ rejoice in the goodness of God and his people. I see myself at every stage of existence, and rejoice in the whole. My friends are many, from coast to coast. I should like to name them to each other, one by one, high and low, great and small. Among them President Hayes, Booker T. Washington, R. R. Morton, J. O. Fuller, A. M. Townsend, J. D. Chrinshaw, John H. Brauhaus, Miss Nanny Burroughs, Mrs. Maggie Pogue Johnson, N. W. Brown,

Thomas H. White, Mrs. Mary Hayes Allen, and thousands of others, of the younger generation, equally worthy of mention, are all my friends.

What a rich life has been granted me! I go to the closing day, satisfied ~~wh~~ with the Lord's doings with me. If there is anymore beyond, I welcome it, as an overflowing cup. ~~If not~~ I know not what awaits me as the sun of my life goes down. I've never known what a day would bring forth, but I have found each new day full of blessings. Every view of God and heaven I have had, is inadequate to my reason, and always will be; for it is written that I [sic] hath not seen, nor ear hath not heard, neither has it entered into the imagination of man, what God has in store for them that love him.

Should it please God to call us again from cosmic consciousness, ~~to his fold~~ into personal existence, to glorify him, as he has done; then so may it be. Or should it please him to glorify us with a glory which we had inseparable from him before the world was then may the future ~~continue to open up~~ reveal his presence in an ever increasing fullness, is in my prayer. For my life in this world has been so worthwhile to me that I loath to give it up, despite the fact that I'm expecting to live on, ever rolling the past up into the future.

CHAPTER 1

In the Distance
Between Us (I)

In the beginning, we inherited our parents' dreams (and their parents' dreams, and their parents' before them). The dreams they harbored for themselves. The dreams that bound them together—a dream for America that they were willing to die for, a dream for each of us.

.　.　.

"Don't ever do this again," Baba would say when he arrived.

It was the Fourth of July, 1992. I had just turned twenty and was a bull pacing in the gate at John F. Kennedy International Airport in Queens, New York, alone with the ticket agent who, like me, believed that Baba would arrive with my passport in the nick of time, who in her tight red uniform stood like a matador in the mouth of the jetway.

My summer basketball team, and my coach, and possibly gypsies from Andalusia, had already boarded the plane to Madrid. Most of my teammates had just met each other for the first time that morning. The gypsies had emerged from the narrative that Mama pieced together, that she'd wrapped us in like a patchwork quilt, stitching a story about America, its inception, the arrival of Africans here before Columbus.

Each teammate had arrived from their hood, from their homies, on the wings of a black boy's prayer—that our bodies could rise with the bounce of a basketball above the barbed wire of America's cages. Except the one white boy, who'd arrived from a suburban bunker, from *Leave It to Beaver*, from "I Have a Dream," his hair cut like a corporal.

I recognized Doremus. He was the only player who was shorter than me. We exchanged a head nod, a grin, half a hug. Removed, for a moment, the headphones barricading our eardrums. We had spent a week together back in high school at Five Star Basketball Camp in Honesdale, Pennsylvania, competing against the best basketball players in the country. The rest of our teammates were exceptionally tall, shared a similar journey—from a court in America, where generations of black men attempted to escape the circumstances of black life, to becoming good enough in high school to earn a Division 1 college scholarship (except for the white boy, who'd paid to attend Yale), to the precipice of three weeks in Spain, an ancestor of the Americas, where we'd compete against the best of Columbus's countrymen.[1]

Our coach, who had also played ball at Yale, was thin, with a narrow nose and bugged-out eyes. "Do you have your passport?" he asked each of us as we trickled into the gate. I had flown into JFK that morning from Cambridge, Massachusetts, had nodded on beat with my music the first few times he asked. And then I began rummaging through my backpack and emptying my pockets. And then I could see the passport on the mantle in our living room in Cambridge, where I had stood with a hand on it as if it were a Bible, reminding myself not to leave it there. I had just finished making a peanut butter and jelly sandwich and the peanut butter was chunky and I had laid it on thick and had had to return to the kitchen for a glass of milk to wash it down.

"Don't forget your passport," Mama had said.

"I won't," I grumbled. I was looking forward to a three-week break from her telling me to *clean up your room* at the crack of dawn.

At the airport, I found a pay phone and fed it the quarters in my pocket.

"*Polè*," Mama said. Which meant "I'm sorry" in Kiswahili, which meant she was really sorry. She didn't sound hopeful as she placed the receiver on the kitchen table. I began to wish I was someone else, any one of my teammates, even the white boy. And then, quite miraculously, I heard Baba's voice. He had just arrived home from his trip to Kentucky. I could hear them talking—Baba shouting something to the cab driver who had just dropped him off, and then a door slamming.

"Your father is going to get it to you," Mama said as if it wasn't something she'd been willing to do herself. Whatever rendezvous my parents had planned for themselves would have to wait. He would go to Boston's Logan Airport, attempt to give the passport to a flight attendant flying to JFK.

I called Mama collect periodically for updates.

"He has to buy a ticket to put the passport on the flight," she said.

"He couldn't put the passport on the flight," she said.

"He may have to get on the plane," she said, to deliver the passport to JFK himself.

"He's on the plane," she said.

·   ·   ·

Our coach was the last to board. "The next plane leaves in a week," he said. He wasn't optimistic, didn't possess the duende of the ticket agent who, for reasons unclear to me, was determined to get me on that flight.

"Your father's flight arrived," she said.

"He's coming from gate so and so," she said, a little deflated. She had a map in her mind of the distance he had to travel to reach our gate.

"Five minutes," she said to the flight attendant responsible for securing the door of the plane.

"Another minute," she said.

"Another minute," she said.

·   ·   ·

Baba appeared unlike I had ever seen him, huffing and puffing, his eyes unhinged, like he had reached the limits of his body. And then he hurdled, in a row of chairs, the distance between us, what fathers and sons accumulate, what we needed to transcend to make it back to who we were in the beginning, when he was a hand on Mama's belly and me a being in her womb.

I felt the impulse to tackle him, to tell him, for the first time, that I loved him.

"Don't ever do this again," he said as he relayed the passport and pushed me toward the ticket agent, who called to the flight attendant and raced with me down the jetway. The flight attendant pointed to the first open seat on the plane, which landed me in first class, and secured the door behind me.

"I won't," I whispered as I fixed my eyes beyond my reflection in the window.

·   ·   ·

The plane was an albatross, required every inch of the runway to become airborne, abort gravity. Methodically cut a diagonal path over the Twin Towers. I pressed my face against the glass as fireworks exploded and night became day. The anxiety of climbing forty thousand feet receded as my eyes became transfixed on the rainbows of shimmering light that rose and fell on the bosom of the Hudson River. It was Independence Day and the United States of America was celebrating its story about itself.

"Find the Moors," Mama had said, as if my life depended on it, when she learned I was traveling to Spain. She wanted to place my mind in the bodies of the Muslims and Jews and Christians who'd coexisted for centuries in Moorish Kingdoms along the Andalusian peninsula, to see and touch the descendants of African men who had conquered Europeans on the backs of elephants.

When we arrived in Madrid, we found our way to a train station and spent a day and a half on a train to the port city of Cadiz. The land was unremarkable: cattle field after barren cattle field. Each player had a bunk. There were four bunks in a car and not much room to fit anything else. I tried to write, to conjure Wimbledon, her black hair, her purple lips, the warmth of her body, the generosity of her hands, the crevices between her legs. Each word was unmiraculous, each sentence unable to evoke the intimacy of her embrace, returning me to the monotony of the wheels straddling endless silver tracks, straddling the arid earth.

I gazed out the window at the tumbleweed and dust as the music of Brother J and X Clan pummeled my eardrums. I listened to their invocation of the red, the black, and the green. A rare celebration of Africa, where I was born, in African American popular culture. Their lyrics were laced with a Parliament beat. It was infectious. An attempt to transplant adolescent black feet from the inside of America's cages into a narrative about African kingdoms.

The rap was an indoctrination. Beyond the chorus I didn't know what the fuck they were rappin' about. What was initially infectious, empowering, became monotonous. I removed the headphones and kept staring out the window, hoping something miraculous would emerge in the distance between us and the horizon.

In the distance between us and the horizon was the din of the train.

In the din of the train I found silence.

In the silence emerged memories of Tanzania.

Memories of me, a few years old, barefoot, attached to the dirt that became a road, that became a savannah, that stretched as if a barren cattle field, to the base of Mount Kilimanjaro.

Memories of Baba holding my hand as I learned to walk on the dirt road. Of our existence before we arrived in America.

. . .

For the next three weeks we became members of the People's United basketball team—a ragtag group of mid-major college all-stars—playing against men with full-grown beards from club teams, while also running a basketball clinic for dozens of their kids. Our sponsors put us up in a suite of rooms above a bar—the rooms were windowless, required imagination. The bathroom had a contraption that allowed you to wash your ass. We ate at the bar, mostly soup and steak—thin gray slabs of beef. The bar closed every day for siesta. Before siesta we taught in the camp and then practiced against each other, to determine the pecking order, who got to shoot first and second and last. Which left a lot of hours in the day, which felt like an interminable siesta, the sun crawling from one side of the earth to the other, the shadows cast by modest homes and midget buildings inching across the cobblestone street.

I purchased a power converter that short-circuited my clippers. I shaved with a razor and waited for the bumps to arrive on my jaws and in the creases of skin around my Adam's apple. I gave up on my appearance and turned the razor to my head, which led to repeated trips to the ocean to brown my scalp.

Cadiz shared the Atlantic Ocean with Africa. On the beach we meandered toward the waves, past women who bared their breasts, the hair between their legs, some shaven. At first we walked right into the Atlantic as if we hadn't seen what we had seen, allowed our bodies to cool off, feet first in the foam as the waves reached the sand and evaporated. The sight of public pussy was disorienting. I wondered what in Spanish manhood enabled niggas to let their chicas take off their clothes in front of other niggas. I was afraid of being naked. Began to have nightmares of me strolling the beach with my dick semi-erect.

We went to bullfights and witnessed the conjuring of Spanish machismo. A man on a horse stuck ceremonial pins in the bull's ass to get the bull animated. The bullfighter was judged by how close he shimmied to the bull's horns without getting gored. The stadium inhaled a collective gasp, exhaled: *Olé*. The matador turned his back to the bull and bowed. We witnessed their fearlessness and flamboyance, the matadors getting gored, the imminent death of the bulls—the certainty of life and death flamencoing inches from the matador's balls.

We discovered a club near a US naval base. We spent most of our per diems on taxis to and from the club—haggling drivers to come down on the price, to charge us the same number of pesetas to take us home as they'd charged to get us there. We haggled the local chicas with the same broken Castellano with which we haggled the taxi drivers. A few players got lucky, ended up fucking in a cattle field. I regretted not taking my Spanish classes, from middle to high school, more seriously. I regretted shaving my hair, which had chopped two inches from my machismo. Most of the chicas thought I was a marine and not one of the ballplayers. They called me *el toro*. I drank to soften my edges, to smile more. I loitered at the bar until the DJ played a hip-hop tune. It was usually "Push It" by Salt-N-Pepa, chopped and screwed into jagged techno. I tried to dance to that shit. It felt like stepping on broken glass. I was hoping they'd play a slow jam. Something that required a two-step, conjoined body parts, conjured body heat, the intimacy of space evaporating.

When I was homesick I phoned my cousin Khari, who my brother and I call Spice, asked him to check on my whip. I had left my car in his possession in our driveway on School Street. I had shown him the amp and subwoofer and CD changer in the trunk so he and his middle-class homeboys could ride around Harvard Square and pretend to be from the projects, rattling the professors and students and snow bunnies with their Bob Marley and Tribe Called Quest.

"Yo, what's up with Wimbledon?" he asked. I braced myself. He said she was at the basketball courts holding hands and kissing one of her girlfriends.

"There goes my rep," I thought.

"Who?" I asked.

There had been signs—all the girlfriend sleepovers, the time I caught her leaving Butchie's, the lesbian bar around the corner from my house. When we were seniors in high school she'd handed me a letter that one of her homegirls wrote her. I handed it back to her.

"Read it," I said. I wanted to hear the words from her lips.

"She can't sleep over anymore," I said when she was finished.

My rep had been earned on a basketball court like the machismo of the matador had been cultivated in the bullfighting arena. The court was a cage where we too could be conquerors. Burgeoning black manhood on display from colored generation to colored generation. Below the hoop, between the lines, battling each other for an ephemeral shot at glory. The possession of Wimbledon's fine Puerto Rican ass on the other side of the chain link—sometimes watching, her polished fingernails hanging from the fence until it was game over—conjoined to my coronation.

Idio mio! she would say when I got to her. She liked me when I was funky, a little wounded, enjoyed removing my armor, licking salt from wins and losses, returning me to flesh. I would lose myself in her body parts. Would write her monumental love letters about bathing together. Remained conflicted by all the other good pussy I imagined waiting for me on the other side of the fence.

"I'll marry her when I'm thirty," I whispered.

"I'll marry you now," she said. "I don't care if you're a basketball player."

"Word," I said.

· · ·

I went looking for the Moors with the white boy. I expected Morgan Freeman in a turban with a Kalashnikov beneath his djellaba. But the Moors were in the blood, the food, the architecture, the flamenco, the gypsies, the duende.

We learned that we were a short boat ride from Africa, that from the beach you could see the rock of Gibraltar. Land in Morocco.

We did a little sightseeing and discovered a statue of Columbus in town, and I understood for the first time that Columbus wasn't white, wasn't from *Leave It to Beaver* or a suburban bunker or "I Have a Dream," that he was from eight hundred years of Moorish rule in Spain.[2]

A small, inconsequential plaque enshrined the sliver of ocean from which he'd set forth, initiating the rape of the planet.

I found a postcard of the bullfighting arena and sent a note home. "Dear School Street," I began—"I'm doing all right. The girls are beautiful, and the weather is constantly sunny. The food tastes great and the beer goes down smooth. The competition is tough, but we haven't lost yet. We sign about 50 autographs a day, but we are not celebrated like the matador. . . . At the bullfight the matador stuck a thin sword between the shoulder blades of the bull while the bull's horns were inches from the matador's balls. . . . Eleven days and counting, I can't wait to get home. Love you all."

In Madrid we played in a tournament against the French, Italian, and Spanish Junior National teams. I scored 11 points down 10 with two minutes left in the championship game to defeat Columbus's countrymen.

I wished Baba was there as they handed our coach the trophy. Baba, more than anyone, was responsible for our arrival in that moment, for so many of my life's most precious moments. I wished he could have witnessed me down 10 with two minutes left on the clock. How I'd made the most of those precious seconds. I wanted him to know how good I could be.

How good I could be was in the distance between us.

It would be my last glorious moment on a basketball court.

W. H. MOSES SERMON: LIBERTY HALL,
120 WEST 138TH STREET, NEW YORK CITY

Published in *The Negro Word*, July 21, 1923

UNDERSTANDING THE TIME

Mr. Chairman, Sisters, and Brothers:

I am one of that large group of sympathizers with this organization who has not become an active member. It is my privilege, in addition to being a pastor in the city of New York, to be the field representative of the National Baptist Convention of the United States, representing my denominational group of nearly four million Christians, the largest group of Negro Christians in the world. In the last sixty days I have been in some twenty states, and everywhere throughout this country where I have been, North and South, East and West, during the trial of the Hon. Marcus Garvey I have not heard a single criticism even from those who used to criticize him and disagree with him throughout the length and breadth of this country . . . Whether you think it or not, don't let anybody fool you or fool themselves that the Negroes in this country or throughout the world want anybody to put Marcus Garvey in jail. Whether we are members (of the United Negro Improvement Association) or not, we want Marcus Garvey out. Because as long as Mr. Garvey is in, you and I are on the way in. He must come out.

[But] I am a preacher, I take a text, and I am going to take it now, because I preach every problem from the angle of Jesus of Nazareth.

I want to call our attention to this passage that is found in the First Chronicles, the 12th chapter, 32nd verse: "The men of Issachar had understanding of the times to know what Israel ought to do." I want to talk a little while about understanding the times and knowing what to do.

CHAPTER 2

The King of the Court

M y reign, if you wanna call it that, was short-lived, ended in 1995 when I was twenty-three, ended when Taba, my younger brother, helped move me off the George Washington University (GW) campus. It was the end of spring and my allergies, provoked by the cherry blossoms, were in full bloom. We drove home to the Port, to the neighborhood in Cambridge we'd grown out of. I was leaving college because my basketball scholarship had expired. I'd exhausted the first of my five years of eligibility allotted to student-athletes at the University of Pittsburgh, and then the remaining four years at George Washington. I was self-conscious about leaving the best conference in college basketball for one almost as good, about switching mascots from a panther to a colonial. My dream of playing in the NBA evaporated with the end of the scholarship. To Mama's cha-grin, I dropped out six credits short of a degree in math. I could have gone back but those six credits felt irrelevant to who I was, were in conflict with figuring out who I should become.

"You can always become a math teacher," Mama said.

"Fuck becoming a math teacher," I said.

• • •

My reign, if you wanna call it that, lasted a couple summers at best, was bound to the cracked asphalt of the basketball court in Corporal Burns Park at a bend in the Charles River, sometimes to the court in Colum-bia Terrace Park where the Dominicans and Puerto Ricans had landed when they migrated to this patch of earth. The best basketball players in

Cambridge, some of the best on the planet, laced up their kicks at Corporal Burns. I'd begun watching them in 1976 when I was four years old, when our family first arrived in America from Tanzania. I sat on the curb that lined the court (sometimes alone, mostly with Taba) for a decade, waiting for my turn to get in the game.

The court was a cage. The court was a stage. Where men appeared to defy gravity, to rise above the barbed wire that crowned the fence surrounding it. They knew the height and diameter of the hoop, the weight of the ball, the effects of the wind careening off the bank of the river—all of this knowledge informing a wrist, a finger, an arm. The men performed on weekdays after work, on weekends between the sun rising and falling. The men performed as if their lives depended on it. Calves coiled into fists, springing from rubber soles, legs jockeying for space below the backboard, anticipating the ball ricocheting off the rim, fingers pulling it out the sky, tossing it the length of the court, from hand to bounce to shot, swallowed by net—all in a twitch of muscle. Spectators congregated on the other side of the fence, rattled it as if to say *Amen*, to let them in the game, so they too could escape, if only for a moment, the circumstances barricading their lives.

Take his money, they said. *He can't handle the rock.*

Get the fuck off the fence and come an' get next.

I got next, make sure you got next!

Don't let that muthafucka talk you out your game.

On that court we saw Dip and Rudy, Pat and then Rumeal pole-vault niggas. Dip and Rudy would go on to the Big East, Pat and Rumeal to the cover of *Sports Illustrated*, to national championships, to the league. When we first arrived in America, Dip and Rudy were on their way to Providence College. Pat was in high school, would become the top-ranked player, would make Cambridge Rindge and Latin the top-ranked high-school team in the country. Dip was six four, could score as well as anyone on the planet—push jump shot, worked it if he needed it to from twenty feet, seemed to skip to his spots on the court, put his body on you to create room to shoot. He could get to the rim if he had to, could beat you in infinite ways. Rudy was built like a tight end, left-handed, could have been a pro in football, a pitcher in the major leagues if those had been the sports he'd chosen. He looked to throw a baseball pass to whoever was running the lanes after each rebound he snared. Grabbed most of the boards. Didn't shoot much. Put the ball in the hole when he had to. Dip went on to lead the Big East in scoring—dropped 50 on Magic. Scored 50, one on five for most of the second half, in a summer league game. Was the closest thing Cambridge had to Michael Jordan. A clip of Rudy throwing the ball from one end of the court into the basket to win a game circulated on Channel 56. Both Dip and Rudy were drafted into the NBA. Dip ended up playing overseas in places like Turkey. Would come home and almost drown in the wave of drugs that flooded the neighborhood in the '80s and '90s. Rudy would end up working the back of a garbage truck.

"I picked you because you could be good," Dip said when I was fifteen. "But you don't always play hard."

I didn't always play hard because I was never comfortable on stage. The stage fright had something to do with forgetting my lines in third grade during a speech in the Martin Luther King Jr. Elementary auditorium and before that and before that, the bitter seed of self-consciousness that accompanied becoming black in America.

Before the speech I practiced my lines with Mama and Baba every night for a week. They were proud of how I had begun to embody the words I had memorized. I remember them in the audience, wanting to perform for them. I remember reaching the stage and making eye contact with Marlon Godfrey, a classmate who knew me from running around the neighborhood. He smiled and then laughed, and when it was my turn to speak his face became a mirror, and in its reflection I could only see the boy he knew from running around the neighborhood and I struggled to remember the words I wanted to become. "One looks in the eyes of another to find oneself," John Mohawk said. I met John Mohawk in 2006 at a gathering Harry Belafonte organized with the Onondaga Nation. "You are on sovereign land; next time bring your passport and we will stamp it," Chief Oren Lyon said.[1]

The court was a sanctuary where black men and boys confronted who they could become in the eyes of America. Where generations of us prayed that the bounce of the ball would deliver us to the other side of America's cages. Which raised the stakes for winning and losing. I played hardest when the game was on the line. The desire to win or the fear of defeat almost always eclipsed my fear of personal failure, which made me a wildly unpredictable performer. Which was why I spent so much time in the Terrace trying to shoot and dribble myself into becoming good enough to control the outcome of a shot, of a game. Invariably, while I was practicing, someone I knew would honk from a passing car, attach fingers to the chain link, hoist a question, a critique, a memory over the fence. Some came inside the fence, to rebound, to shoot, to challenge me to a game of one-on-one, to attempt to knock me from my throne.

. . .

The drive with Taba, from DC to home, marked the end of a journey. I was ambivalent about being back. Cocaine had become crack. The corner had become something to live and die for. Many of the people we had looked up to—some parents, some of the older boys—were now fiends. The brothers from the neighborhood I'd grown up with had abandoned their hoop dreams, turned to the corner for a shot at America.

There were twelve of us—Moke and Fats, Colin and Dana, Dico and Daco, Hector and Alex, Ariel and Nando, me and Taba. Six sets of brothers, each within two years of each other, and within that three sets of twins.

When we reunited, we hugged and then wrestled. They were stronger than I remembered. I'd expected the years of elite college training to give me an edge, but it had made me softer. Their daily regimens of pushups and pullups conditioned them for survival. Each embrace led to beads of sweat, bruised flesh, exhausted lungs.

The drugs had divided the city. Kids from one neighborhood would eventually kill kids because they were from another neighborhood.

"O-O-Omo," Big Twin (what we called Colin) stuttered as he sized me up. "I'll—I'll bust your ass now in football. You—you—you had big legs. That's the only reason we couldn't tackle you." We watched the next generation of ballplayers run up and down the court in the Terrace. We'd played tackle football ten years ago. Who we were now was still chained to what we'd done on the playground or in the projects when we were kids.

Big Twin stuttered like his mother.

"I'll—I'll bust your ass now," he said again, challenging me to a game of one-on-one. I took the bait, took my slides and socks off so I had less of a chance of turning an ankle, and to let him know I didn't need sneakers to beat him.

"I don't give a fuck," Moke said from the sidelines, "no way you're gonna beat me barefoot." When we were kids we'd collided every day. The collisions were how we embraced each other.

. . .

I spent most of that summer dribbling by myself in the street against imaginary defenders.

"You can still play ball," Baba had said when it was game over.

I struggled to detach myself from what I had hoped would be waiting for me on the other side of the chain link.

Wimbledon was long gone.

At home my body remembered.

Her in the crevices of my room.

Us in each other's skin, in time stuck like molasses.

What I missed, what I needed was her companionship, how she'd bridged the distance between my stepping off of and back onto the court, between who I'd been and who I wanted to be.

We'd met in tenth grade while Taba and I were dribbling in the street, between the headlights of the passing cars. Wimbledon was with a girlfriend, on her way home to Newtowne Court to giggle and sleep; lingered because she knew Taba, which made it easy for me to say hi, for her and her girl to get in Mama's car and ride with us through an empty parking lot, her in the driver's seat, Taba and her girl in the back seat, me in the passenger's seat coaching her on when to press and release the clutch as I put my hand on hers and helped her move in and out of first gear. We bucked and bucked until she learned how to simultaneously ease off the clutch and onto the gas. She had dark skin, hazel eyes, long black hair, a free spirit. She was born in Puerto Rico on the day her mother's older sister was hit by a truck. She was given her aunt's name. Her mom, who was short and fair-skinned with strawberry hair, had been a coffee bean picker. When she was young she'd toiled in the sun until the day the farmhand, who was from a lower caste, offered her water. At that moment they fell in love. Her family abandoned her, and she abandoned him after bearing his fourth child and relentless abuse. She and the children flew into Logan Airport and moved into the projects across the street from the penny candy store with the man who became Wimbledon's stepfather. Wimbledon and her older sister would become off-limits to the other men and boys in the neighborhood. I saw their family driving once, the two girls in the passenger seat below their stepfather's outstretched arm, their mother in the back seat.

After the driving lesson, we drove Mama's car home, parked in our driveway, and returned to the porch and then to the street with the basketball as Wimbledon and her girl continued home. Taba and I watched as they giggled around the corner and then her girl came back and gave me Wimbledon's number as Wimbledon returned to the apartment in the projects, back to her mother, back to her brothers strung out on heroin, back to her older sister who had been the senior class president, who'd left for a naval base in San Diego to get out from under the outstretched arm of her stepfather as soon as she'd graduated from high school.

·   ·   ·

Dico and then Daco—who now lived on the second floor of our family home with me, Taba, and our sisters, Maisha and Malaika—joined me on the porch. Dico had moved in when I was fourteen so he could continue to go to school in Cambridge after his family got kicked out of the projects when Daco got caught hustling. Daco would move in a couple years later. Upstairs was like a community center. Other brothers moved in and out. Also joined us on the porch, on their way to the square or to a corner to flip whatever was buried in a cheek or a sock for a fistful of cash. Their bodies America's oldest form of currency. On their way to wounded, incarcerated, commodified.

The rhythm of the bouncing ball and the passing cars were a metronome for boyhood. Summers spent meandering out a front door with nothing but a plan to find each other. Our bodies like magnets, converging into nascent waves, fomenting as we rolled up and down sidewalks, as if the distance between the sun, rising and falling on the concrete, was ours and ours alone. Our time was now stamped by police cameras attached to poles in the projects, by the passing cars, which returned us to the porch steps, to our beleaguered breath, to the precipice of manhood.

Babu, our mother's father, also lived upstairs. He moved in when he was ninety-five. I was twenty-one and was driving home from George Washington for Thanksgiving break, when I saw the sign for the Vineland exit on the New Jersey Turnpike and something told me to get off the highway and go see him. I hadn't seen him in years. I drove instinctively through the lowlands of South Jersey, navigating the few memories of visiting him when we were kids, past the chicken coops and barren pastures, and arriving, remarkably, at the brick house he'd built with his hands at the edge of a three-acre plot on a dirt road. The curtains were drawn. He stumbled through the dim light from the bed to the door, back to his bed. He reached for my hand as I sat next to him, smiled as if an angel had arrived at his doorstep. He was decaying alone.

"How are you?" I asked. He asked me to pour him a shot, pointing to a bottle of 151-proof Bacardi rum and the damp glass next to it.

"Not so good," he said.

"It's my medicine," he said. I asked if he wanted to come home with me for Thanksgiving.

"Naturally, it will be a miracle if I survive," he said.

He moaned quietly the entire drive home, slapping the sides of his legs to wake them, keep his blood circulating in the bumper-to-bumper traffic that stretched the distance between the Vineland and Cambridge for five excruciating hours.

"Only for a few days," he said.

"Daddy?" Mama said when we arrived on her porch. She didn't say much more than that. They would have five years with him upstairs in Maisha's old room to work out their relationship.

· · ·

While I'd been away at college, Taba had hung a heavy bag from a beam in his room and attached a speed bag to it. Sometimes we hit the bag together. Hard enough and long enough to fuck with the house's foundation.

He said that I was a civilian and that he was a soldier. The distance between civilian and soldier was the beginning of the distance between us. I didn't shoot dice, didn't belong on the corner, didn't feel the need to carry a heater, would never be prepared to shoot niggas. I felt estranged from this pursuit of America.

"I'll fuck you up," he said, for all the times I'd bullied him when we were kids. Now that I'd left college, he was eager to establish a new pecking order.

The first time we boxed, it was just me and him and Maisha there. Maisha sat on the porch and watched as we stood in the street and circled each other. Taba boxed with the flair of the matador. My repertoire was a one-two punch. Maisha had watched us tumble in and out of laughter and tears as kids. I'd always been bigger and dominant. We were the same size now. His punches landed a centimeter from my face as I bobbed and weaved. I still had the longer arms. I faked a 1 and landed a 2 on his chin and his knees buckled. Instinctively I reached out to grab him. Walked him to Maisha, whose face reflected her disappointment that we still needed to throw punches to express how we felt about each other.

By the end of the summer he'd grown a centimeter taller than me. "No face," we said as we took the gloves to the corner. He landed his fists on my face anyway, with flair. Niggas flooded the mouth of the projects to watch. "Taba can beat Omo! Taba can beat Omo!" Big Twin celebrated, as if something fundamental to who we all were had shifted, as Taba knocked me from my throne.

As I walked back to the porch and upstairs into my room and closed the door, I was ashamed that I had allowed how Taba and I felt about each other to become entertainment for niggas.

. . .

"You can be whoever you want to be," my eighth-grade teacher had told me, and meant it, as she attempted to wrap me in America's flag. She thought I was exceptional. It's what was normally sold to little white boys and to a lesser extent little white girls—that white, and red, white, and blue was a measuring stick, that there would always be a measurable distance between them and niggas and the rest of the planet.

In eighth grade we watched, along with other schoolchildren across America, as the space shuttle *Challenger* exploded on the television set in our classroom. Ronald McNair, the second black man in space, and Christa McAuliffe, the mother who would have been the first teacher in space, died. Theirs are the only names I remember. We watched as the countdown began, as the rocket boosters smoked, the platform shook, the arms attached to the platform broke, and flames erupted. I could wrap my head around how McNair had ended up in that cockpit, strapped to 2.8 million pounds of thrust, to unshackle himself from the United States of America, to float in space, to have an unobstructed view of the planet. But I wondered what had propelled Christa McAuliffe to abandon her child on earth.

"We have liftoff," command control said. We could hear the cheering in the control room as gravity was momentarily aborted and human bodies twisted and turned as they surfed a wave of American exceptionalism that, in seventy-three seconds, turned to plumes of smoke. The spacecraft's cockpit command center, unhinged from wings and jet propulsion, became a ballistic missile. Reached sixty-five thousand feet, the astronauts probably alive, possibly conscious while they fell for almost three minutes before they made impact with the ocean and their bodies shattered into pieces. I wondered about those moments in particular, before consciousness was severed from their bodies, as the classroom became soundless and "you can be whatever you want to be" joined the great silence of the universe.

· · ·

"Come to Mississippi," Baba said in the hotel room, after we had just lost to Ohio University in the first round of the NIT Tournament, which was the tournament you played in if you almost made the NCAAs. Gary Trent gave GW 26, 10, and 6. I didn't start that game but had started most of the season. Coach Jarvis put me in for a few minutes because Baba and Taba had traveled across the country to be there. We had won twenty-one games that year, had beat UMass when they were the number-one-ranked team in the country. The coaching staff and players were disappointed we hadn't been invited to the NCAA tournament. I thought I was ready for it to end. When I got in the game, I dribbled the length of the court like it was me alone at the Terrace and nailed a three-pointer. And then Coach Jarvis returned me to the bench. And then it was game over.

"You can still play basketball," Baba said. He remained a pillar of logic. He ordered pizza, kept his George Washington University sweat jacket zipped, collar popped. He and Taba and Wimbledon, wherever she was now, had been my fan club. Either Baba or Taba had come to every tournament game I played in. I gifted Baba each watch I was given for participating in the NCAA tournament, knowing he would continue to lose them. Back in high school, I don't think Baba had believed that basketball would get me a free ride to college until Stanford flew us out to tour their campus. Taba and I had shared the dream, the ten years on the curb at Corporal Burns Park waiting for next, the years spent on the court attempting to shoot and dribble myself into Dip and Rumeal. Baba came to watch me play when the stands were already full.

"Play ball, Cambridge!" he said in high school. And then "Play ball, GW!" in college. From tip-off to the final horn.

"How come your dad keeps saying that?" my teammates would ask.

"Play ball," he said—to remind us to keep our head in the game, to remind us that the game was a game.

"Yo, we saw your dad on TV," my college teammates said. Baba had worn the GW sweat jacket when Peter Jennings had interviewed him on

ABC Nightly News about his Algebra Project. He had begun to divide his time between Cambridge and Mississippi to grow the Algebra Project, now a burgeoning national initiative to ensure that all kids had access to algebra by the eighth grade.

"Math literacy is the key to citizenship in the twenty-first century," he said. He thought of the Algebra Project as an underground railroad off some white boy's plantation.

"If your friends don't get this algebra, they're going to end up in jail," he said.

I couldn't just play ball.

Baba wanted black America to master mathematics like they had mastered basketball and music. He'd even come to DC to meet with Coach Jarvis and me about creating a math and basketball camp. We couldn't see or understand the role he envisioned us playing in liberating America.

The game wasn't just a game.

"Come to Mississippi," Baba proposed in the hotel room in Ohio. It was as far as we got to talking about who he wanted Taba and me to become. Taba sat on the corner of the bed. His skin was darker than mine, nose flatter, broader. Strangers still took us for twins.

"What's next?" Taba asked me. Back in high school I used to drag him out of bed at six in the morning to help me train. To run up stadium steps, run in circles around a track. To dribble and shoot on vacant courts for exhausting hours. For countless one-on-ones. He beat me once and ran home to celebrate. *My brother this, my brother that*, he would say with pride. We shared the disappointment that I wasn't going to the league. We'd hoped my success on the court would be a way for both of us to escape some white boy's plantation.

"Come to Mississippi," Baba said.

There wasn't room in the hotel for commemorating the end of a journey, the distance we'd traveled.

For licking wounds.

For *I love you*.

"Come to Mississippi," he insisted.

The broken bones, the chipped ankles, pestled knees, lacerated flesh— all from a decade and a half of pounding my body against bodies, against asphalt, against fences—suddenly felt present. I didn't want to go anywhere. I wanted to linger in sweat, let the sweat calcify, become a sarcophagus.

. . .

"You can always be a math teacher," Mama said.

Mama stood in the driveway as I stuffed the Maxima—her gift to me—with all the shit my life had accumulated. We were both disappointed. If it were up to her, I would be returning to college to get my degree. In her mind the deal for gifting me the car was that I would graduate. When I'd been a freshman in high school, I'd told her she didn't have to worry about paying for me to go to college.

"Bet," she said.

"Easy money," I said. The Maxima was the reward for the basketball scholarship.

"I don't know why your mother agreed to that," Baba said.

The car had been a crown. Our reign mysogynistic. Taba and I would scrub and polish the car religiously on Sundays in the driveway—Armor All and a toothbrush for the rim's cavities. Until iridescent. "Middle-class motherfuckers with good jobs don't have whips like this," my friend Danny had said. But niggas who sold drugs in the park and niggas on their way to the league did. Taba and I drove the Maxima in circles around the projects—shirts off, tinted windows down, sunroof open. Moss-like hair beneath arms, punctuating lips.

"Don't be a rooster," Mama said.

It felt like a rite of passage. Parading burgeoning black manhood. We weren't interested in middle class—we wanted Trump status, to possess model bitches.

. . .

"Don't forget your classes," Mama says.

I place a fat leather bomber jacket in the trunk, which I know I will never wear in Mississippi.

I stick the basketball behind the headrest in the rear window. For the next decade I will dream—sometimes it will feel more like a nightmare—that I have one more year of eligibility.

I leave the math books in the closet in my room upstairs. In college I'd struggled to decipher their hieroglyphs. Single sentences could take weeks. Each book a black hole. I felt microscopic in the expansive math library stacks. I had decided to major in math because there wasn't a creative writing major and, even though Baba would never admit it, I knew he would be proud of me.

"Don't forget your classes," Mama says again as she helps move my clothes into the back seat. She could be relentless.

"C'mon, Ma, give me a break."

"You can always become a math teacher," she says.

"C'mon, Ma, give me a break."

"You give me a break," she says.

"No fuckin' way I'm gonna become a math teacher."

. . .

We were seven, nine, eleven, and thirteen when Mama applied to the medical schools at Harvard, Boston University, and Tufts. *What alternate careers are you considering if you are not accepted at a medical school?* was one of the questions on the Tufts application.

"Family nurse-practitioner, public health/nutrition, or pediatric nurse-practitioner," Mama replied.

How do you spend your free, unscheduled time? they asked.

"The little unscheduled time I have is usually spent with the children, swimming, or reading. I recently have taken on a series of sewing projects," she said.

Why have you chosen Tufts?

"At Tufts, I feel that I will have the opportunity to deepen my understanding of the role of nutrition in the treatment of disease and in the maintenance of optimum health. I have also chosen Tufts because of what I perceive as its historical commitment to the delivery of health care to underserved populations. Tufts can certainly be proud of its role in the improvements of health care in the Delta area of Mississippi."

They asked her to talk about the people that had been influential in her life.

"Three people," she said, "have etched indelible engravings on my spirit and mind." She began with Bibi.

Foremost among these is my mother, Jessie Ardalia Stenhouse Jemmott, who distilled from her childhood in South Carolina in the early 1900s a deep pride in the herculean efforts of her parents to raise a family of seven children in an environment that rewarded Black effort with a pittance. Their poverty corroded neither their spirits nor their ingenuity: Grandma took in washing and Grandpa taught music, ran a one-man taxi service, and hired himself out as a tinsmith. Jessie left home in her mid-teens to seek her fortune in the kitchens of the affluent of Shaker Heights, Cleveland, and struggled her way to an RN degree from the Harlem Hospital School of nursing in 1929. I am heiress to the fund of wisdom born of Jessie Ardalia's quiet, personal struggle and triumph, which are reflected in her firm, yet kindly gaze and her unbent shoulders. She taught by example the meaning of family loyalty and personal integrity. She turned our having very limited financial resources into an opportunity to foster within us self-confidence, thriftiness, and creativity. Her priorities, which ranked the health of mind, body, and spirit over the acquisition of the trappings of material success, strongly influence my decisions about how I should spend my personal resources. She taught me the value of hard work, of having clear goals, when necessary, of sacrificing immediate rewards for the attainment of long-range goals, and of not permitting circumstances to whittle away my pursuit of what I deemed to be my purpose in life.

And then she wrote about Babu.

Daddy, Joseph Jemmott, is an enterprising immigrant from the West Indies who has spent the majority of his eighty years learning whatever skills he has needed to be self-reliant: He has been a master men's tailor, a carpenter, radio-TV repairman, construction worker, gardener, and auto mechanic. Daddy lives a quiet life on a patch of land in New Jersey in a five-room house which he designed and built himself. During my own studies, I often reflected on his tenacity and the nature and breadth of his learning experiences. His unrelenting quest for knowledge instilled in me an appreciation for learning.

And then Uncle Richard.

My maternal uncle, Richard, was the driving force behind the expansion of my worldview beyond the sidewalks of the South Bronx in NYC. A conscientious objector for religious reasons during WWII, he challenged us to apply the tenets of our spirituality and morality to those beyond the circle of our family and our people. It was through Richard that I spent my eighteenth summer with the American Friends Service Committee in a work camp in rural Mexico, and it was through his example that I was able to glimpse the richness inherent in living a life dedicated to service.

· · ·

Bibi was proudest when Mama graduated from Boston University's School of Medicine in 1986. She prodded me to force my way through the phalanx of white professional photographers to capture the moment that Mama received her diploma. The Pentax 1500 that hung from my neck belonged to the Cambridge Community Art Center, which was a darkroom in the basement of the projects where I learned to roll, load, and develop black-and-white film. It was magical, standing above the bins of chemicals below the dim red bulb as images were revealed on what had once been blank white paper. My picture of Mama receiving her diploma sat prominently on the desk in her office at the MIT Medical Center, which was around the corner from our house. It was the only building on campus that Taba and I didn't have to worry about getting kicked out of.

"You here to see Dr. Moses?" her assistant would ask. I would smile and she would smile and I would keep walking. In the midst of Mama's plaques, her periodic dictations, pictures of the four of us, the hinging and unhinging of jacket and stethoscope, were remnants of an umbilical cord, the comfort of a womb.

I came to visit her frequently that summer in an attempt to return my wounded body to her. To return to who we had been before she'd gone to medical school, before we'd moved next door to the projects, before Taba and I outgrew her spankings, when we'd been comfortable holding her hand.

"I miss Wimbledon," I confessed.

· · ·

Pictures of Wimbledon, letters she'd written, were all packed into an Air Jordan shoebox, along with other love letters, nude Polaroids, the postcard I'd sent from Spain, Bibi's birthday cards, a note from Spice, other memories made while parked along the river.

"*Birches at Lakeside*," read the front of the card Bibi had chosen for my twenty-second birthday. *Hello Omowale, thinking of you and hoping "all is well." It was nice talking to you, I had a wonderful birthday. I learned that you will be coming home for a few days before Thanksgiving, will talk to you again. Love, Bibi.*

There was a card that Baba had made from eight and a half-by-eleven-inch paper, folded into fourths:

> *To my son Omo from Baba, I remember with my heart how I held you in the years before you turned two and how, as you approached that magic age you perched in perfect balance and pitch off my shoulder, off my back, off my chest. I still hold you, ever so close, in my mind's eye and wish you that same perfect balance and pitch as you perch off of Life.*
>
> *To Our Omo, Happy Birthday. To live simply, in touch with ourselves and the world around us, to water the love in our hearts despite the cultural cloud that darkens our planet, is perhaps the greatest gift we can give to ourselves and others. Find time to laugh and revel in life's miracles. Love Mom.*

The box itself had come with the sneakers I'd worn my senior year in high school when we won the state championship; it traveled with me from high school to college and is now behind Baba, who is sitting in the driver's seat.

Mama presses her face against my cheek, wraps her arms around me. She loves me the most when I am coming or going or wounded.

The tailpipe of the Maxima carves a line in the pavement as Baba struggles with the clutch and the car bucks out the driveway.

And then it's just me and Baba.

It is fall in New England and the leaves are dying.

We are beginning again.

Baba had insisted on driving first. I clench my teeth, am not sure the Maxima can withstand him shifting its gears. The car is on its second clutch.

"Put your seatbelt on," he says, both hands gripping the steering wheel. I had hoped the drive would bring us closer. By the time we reach Western Avenue, just blocks from our house, the silence is galactic.

Baba was surprised I had agreed to join him in Mississippi to work with him and Taba on his Algebra Project.

THE KING OF THE COURT · 25

When I was five or six, Baba would confront me, at home on days I preferred to be outside, with Cuisenaire rods and Unifix cubes.

"I don't have to do anything I don't want to do," I would say, ignoring his questions.

"That's not true," he would say. But I knew it was, even as I couldn't bear waiting any longer and finished whatever lesson we had started. He would say I took up a lot of his time. That I took up the time he would have spent teaching Taba.

The time he would have spent teaching Taba math is in the distance between us.

We drive toward the Charles River. The river is where our family landed in America. Western Ave. cuts a diagonal path to the bridge that straddles the polluted water. In the rearview mirror is a flyer advertising an offer of $150 a day to be an extra in a basketball film being shot in Boston. I had second thoughts about going to Mississippi then.

"The Algebra Project can do that," Baba had said, eyeing the flyer and matching the offer.

I feel unsettled. When I was playing college ball, people in the neighborhood had gone out of their way to say hello, offer some sort of congratulations, ask a question about a game, offer an opinion, wish me well, attach themselves to my potential. What I had and hadn't accomplished had begun to feel like a cage. I want to talk to Baba about that. The river represents a horizon. On the other side of it I imagine I can become a stranger. I want to tell Baba about Corporal Burns Park. The endless days, elbows wrapped around knees, waiting for next. The thousands of missed shots, the stage fright, the fear of losing, and the fierce desire to win. What it felt like becoming the king of that court, if only for a precious second, about scoring 11 down 10 with two minutes to go to defeat Columbus's countrymen, about the money and model bitches. I need to talk to him about that. About what I had hoped to possess and accumulate. About America's cages. About what's buried in the Air Jordan shoebox.

When the light turns green I snap my seat belt in place. The car lurches forward and then roars into second gear with enough torque for third, and we stay roaring in second as we approach the bridge. It is still morning and the sunroof is open. On the bridge the sun slaps me in the face, shimmies on the water. I can see Peabody Terrace, the high-rise apartment complex that had been our first home in Cambridge, still towering above Corporal Burns Park at a bend in the river. I turn to the speckling of woods, the Blodgett Pool where we swam miles of laps. The oceanic distance traveled in those lanes now imperceptible in the rearview. On the other side of the bridge we follow the signs to the highway. I begin to have second thoughts again. Even the cops know me on that side of the water.

———————

W. H. MOSES SERMON

UNDERSTANDING THE TIME, *continued*

WE have taken up the collection. Now let us sit here and understand it. I want to remark in the first place that this passage of Scripture is a practical definition of prophecy. Prophecy is understanding a time to know what to do. And it is not something that is confined to fortune-telling, it is not the foretelling, it is the telling forth what God is doing in your day and generation. . . . The men of Issachar, back yonder in David's time, understood the times. They understood that they are in a pivotal period upon which centuries and decades turned. And we are in a pivotal period upon which centuries and decades will turn.

CHAPTER 3

Out of Africa

W e belonged to the earth. Our skin bathed in the red dirt that formed a path in front of our home in Tanzania, that spread as if an ocean toward the ivory caps of Mount Kilimanjaro.

We were one, three, and five. Maisha, who was born in 1970, was first. Mama said she was born with her eyes wide open. That when she saw her she knew that she and Baba had had nothing to do with what they'd created.

It's so clear, when they handed her to me, I don't know if they had bathed her or not, here was this baby, I'm looking at her, and she's looking back at me, and these weren't the eyes of a baby that was dazed—she was looking. It was almost as if she was reading me.

Maisha was the only one of us who remembered her birth. She remembered a place filled with light. . . . *And they were telling me it was time to go but I wasn't ready because I couldn't remember what I was supposed to do, it was like I felt I hadn't prepared as well as I needed to. I remembered I had done this before, and other times had been easier, or I had been better prepared, so I didn't want to go but they were telling me, now. And that's it, that's my first memory. And then I don't remember anything for a long time.*

"I saw and named each of you before you were born," Baba said.

Maisha Vuyiswa—life, joy;

Omowale Johari—the son who comes home, a precious stone;

Tabasuri Watabiri—the wise one, forecaster.

"When I saw you, you were red," Baba said to me.

Mama told me that Maisha had predicted each of us. "And of course I didn't believe her at first. She was very clear about you, and then with Taba she kept telling me, 'I'm not sure, I'm not sure, you have to wait, I'm not sure,' and then she said it was a boy. And then with Malaika, 'It's a girl.'"

"I knew you were gonna be a boy," Maisha said. "I knew Taba was gonna be a boy, but by the time we came here to America I wasn't, I was starting to doubt my knowingness, so I had a strong feeling Malaika was gonna be a girl but my feelings got in the way and so I went back and forth, and Mama used to ask me and I'd be, 'Yeah I think she's gonna be a girl,' but before I knew. With you and Taba I knew, I just knew.

"And Mom tells the story about—we had these neighbors in Same, I think it was a white family, and the father went into town one night on his motorcycle and hit a pothole and the motorcycle went into the air and he died, and so she said something like, when he was passing by, or when I heard the motorcycle, I made this comment that 'He's going and he's not coming back,' and I don't—she remembers that—I don't really remember that."

"While your mother was pregnant with you, her body became hard like stone and she became confrontational," Baba said. Mama said that, unlike Maisha, I had punched and kicked in her womb. Mama was determined to keep her cool when she gave birth to me, like the women from the village who gave birth with dignity and in silence, unlike when she had given birth to Maisha, when she screamed. Mama drank tablespoons of castor oil to accelerate my arrival, sat with her legs elongated, heels fixed to the patio, arms at rest on the limbs of a chair, determined to greet each wave of contractions with silence.

"Georgia," Baba said to Mama. *Georgia*, her sobriquet.

"I'm OK," Mama said as she slowly inhaled and exhaled.

"It's time to go to the hospital."

"I'm OK."

"Georgia . . . Georgia," Baba said. He had found our neighbor, Mwalimu—*Teacher*—Temu, and borrowed his Volkswagen bug. Mwalimu Temu was the only one within a couple miles who owned a car. Baba hoisted Mama from under her arms, placed her in the back of the bug, and rode with her the slow unpaved miles to the hospital as my head began to crown. The nurses helped carry her up the white cement steps and onto the available bed as she began breathing as they had practiced.

"Mama Mwalimu," the nurse said. *Mother Teacher.* "I don't know what you are doing, but you need to stop, this baby is already here."

· · ·

"One of the things about you," Mama said, "you cried, you cried a lot when you were a baby. You'd light up the night. I don't think it was colic, it lasted too long. Cry, cry, cry, cry. Inconsolable. At one point I felt that . . . I was concerned about you being vulnerable. Emotionally vulnerable—not weak, but vulnerable. I stayed home with you longer than any of the other children. I didn't understand. And in response your dad just walked you for hours and hours and hours."

"When you were born, your mother couldn't placate you," Baba said, "And Bibi wouldn't. You'll have to ask your mother about that."

Bibi had spent a year in Tanzania when each of us was born.

"And so they would hand you to me. I would walk with you in my arms along the road and we would listen to one of Aretha's albums Bibi brought from New York."

When darkness fell, each night for the first year of my life, Baba took me in his arms and we rolled like a wave, back and forth on the road in front of our home for hours, in the wake of Aretha's voice, lacing the pitch-black distance between the patio, and the mountain, and the cackling hyenas, my eyes bedazzled beneath the stars, infinite constellations ornamenting the boundless arms of our creator.

I remember returning to the sound of Aretha's voice years later—"Bridge over Troubled Water," "Respect," "Love the One You're With," and then as much of her music as I could get my hands on. The vibration of her voice instantaneously returning me to the warmth of Baba's arms, stars strung like lanterns above our heads, in the distance between us and our creator.

Baba Olatunge, a teacher in the secondary school, found Baba putting me to sleep one night and gave him Paramahansa Yogananda's *Autobiography of a Yogi.*

"He said I would need the patience described in the book to raise you," Baba said.

"God is the ocean," Paramahansa Yogananda said in *Journey to Self-Realization,* "man is a wave. As man is a part of God, so is he never truly apart from Him. I am the ocean of consciousness. Sometimes I become the little wave of the body, but I am never just the wave without the Ocean of God."

Baba would say that the Civil Rights Movement that rose and fell on the shores of Mississippi in the '6os—that bound him and Mama together, that carried them to the shores of Africa, that gave birth to our family—was an "ocean of consciousness, protest, rebellion, organizing," and that the people in the movement were the waves.

. . .

"I remember the mongoose," Maisha said. "There were mongooses in Same that were getting the chickens, and Dad stayed up all night to try to catch them. I remember being scared that he was out all night. I remember the snakes—they used to go and watch the snakes, the big cobras and everyone would be standing around in a circle, and the snake charmers. Ohh, I hated that, 'cause I used to think that the snake was long enough to catch us, that you could never run far enough away."

I remember dirt of road, trace of scent, contour of face, women towering beyond six feet, knees crowning head, arms and legs carved like ebony, beads, concentric circles fanning from neck to breast, babies curled in cloth, draped along spine of back, heads crowned with calabashes of water.

. . .

"We would go outside and play and you were sooo fascinated with these ants," Maisha said, "and you always wanted to step in them, so mom would say, 'Stay away, it's gonna hurt, it's gonna sting,' but you still wanted to step in the ants, and I was like, 'No Omo, no you can't step in the ants,' so one day I was like—part of it was feeling like, always being responsible for you—I had this deep feeling of responsibility, I was three when that happened so you had to be one, and on this day I was like, 'I don't want this responsibility, It's OK, fine Omo, go ahead, step in the ants'"—she laughed—"and so you did, you stepped in the ants and that's the part, I remember up to there, and then Mom said she just heard this screaming, and she ran out and they had just crawled all over you biting you."

I remember Hamisi's cropped hair. His presence in our lives. He was a boy from the village who Baba took in, who became an older brother.

I remember loitering in the shade beneath the thick branches of the tamarind tree. Peeling its fruit from the ground, pulling the seeds from their shells with my teeth, sucking the pulp until my mouth puckered. The boys, about Hamisi's age, climbing its trunk, draped over its branches like pythons. I remember wandering alone in the distance between the tamarind tree and home. "It could have been a mile," Mama said.

"When we moved to Kibaha, you used to leave the house and walk down the hill with your pillow and come into my classroom," Mama said. "By the time we were in Kibaha I had enrolled you in a little nursery, it was like a little day care, and you would come down and be so angry and upset and you would sit in front of my classroom door, and you would just fume and sputter and spit.

"Your little day care—if I didn't get there on time you would, you had figured out what the long way home was, so instead of walking straight you would walk to the tamarind tree—if you can imagine a three-year-old, instead of taking Bishop Allen to School Street, taking Mass. Ave. to Main to Cherry to School Street."

I remember holding Baba's hand by the side of the road, waiting, watching travelers continue on their journeys, our journeys momentarily colliding.

I remember standing next to Baba on a makeshift basketball court, the boys who knew only soccer attempting to dribble the ball with hands as Baba taught them the game.

I remember Baba letting go of my hand as he released our chickens from their coop, my thick legs attempting to keep pace with neck and beak, wings without lift, becoming quick and strong enough to catch those flightless birds, hold them upside down by their feet.

· · ·

Taba was born less than two years after me. Baba said that he had wanted Mama to wait longer before having another child. That I needed more attention. That he knew what it was like to grow up with an older brother very close in age. He and Uncle Greg were a year apart and had fought like Taba and I would fight.

Uncle Greg, and Mama not waiting longer to have another child, was in the distance between us.

The Tanzanians called us Wa Negro—from the tribe of African Americans. Europeans were Nzungu or Mwazungu. They called each other Mweupe, light. Mweusi, dark. Or Maji ya kundu, brownish reddish. There were over a hundred tribes in Tanzania, many with their own language: Wa Chaga, Wa Pare, Wa Gogo, Wa Kiswahili—the most refined Swahili.

Mama and Baba had arrived in Tanzania in 1969 among the first wave of black American expatriates. Like their comrades, they had thought they could become something other than American. That their children could become children of Tanzania. Their journey to Tanzania began in 1967 when Baba, despite being five years older than the draft age limit, received a draft notice to fight in the Vietnam War. He believed this was politically motivated—*Part of a broader right-wing offensive to decapitate the movement.* Another attempt to take him out. After the assassinations of JFK in '63 and Malcolm X in '65, he had made a list of who could be next. The list included Martin Luther King Jr., Robert Kennedy, James Farmer, Bob Spike, and Stephen Currier. Within two years, four of them would be dead.[1] He borrowed money from Uncle Greg and rented an apartment in Montreal. He became a night watchman, a department store salesman, a paperboy, a janitor. He also packed food on trays at the airport, sold ads in a telephone book.

"I almost lost it," he said.

He befriended a West Indian couple, Vony and Suga, whose four children adopted him as Uncle Bob. Vony and Suga were running the operation selling telephone book ads. He was drawn to their youngest child, Craigie, and enjoyed watching him play in the courtyard. Craigie would come up to his apartment and they would hang out. He said it made him think about having his own kids. When the world's fair arrived in Montreal in the spring of 1967, Vony and Suga gave the kids to their Uncle Bob and they spent the summer exploring, with fifty million other people, *Man and His World*, which featured ninety pavilions of exhibits from nations around the globe.

"It was the kids that saved me," he said.

Baba said that the real reason behind the choice to go to Africa was so he could do family instead of more movement. Mama was his comrade then and his only contact to his family in the States. She made several trips to visit him. It was on one of her trips that they realized they loved each other. The first time they got married was on April 20, 1968, in Montreal. Vony and Suga helped to get the papers together. Baba used his mother's maiden name, Parris. They were fugitives. Bibi and Uncle Jerry, Mama's younger brother, attended the wedding.

Mama learned about a Yugoslavian freighter in Brooklyn that she and Baba could stow away on, that would take them to Africa. Bibi stood with them on the deck of the freighter docked in Red Hook, snapped a picture of Baba incognito, face concealed in beard, eyes covered with dark shades, Mama in his lap. It is the only picture we have of them together—in love, on the battlefield—from before we were born.

Mama got sick as the freighter rolled across the Atlantic. She would spend most of her honeymoon in the cabin. From the deck she saw schools of fish leaping from waves, fins becoming wings as they glided over the surface of the water, momentarily escaping whatever lurked below.

The freighter took them to Morocco, where she and Baba continued to smuggle their bodies across borders. Their luggage piled on top of a taxi, a Peugeot, with the luggage of three other passengers. They traveled from Tangier through the desert into Fez, the driver chewing on a stick to remain awake during those indistinguishable days and nights, occasionally sleeping on a cape in the sand. They traveled from Fez to Algiers,

Algiers to Tunisia,

Tunisia to Libya.

Miraculously, they reached the train that arrived at the Aswan Dam in Egypt, took a boat into Wadi Halfa, Sudan, and then Khartoum, the capital. The plan was to take a boat from Khartoum into Uganda, across Lake Victoria into Mwanza, Tanzania, but war between Muslim and Christian, between blue-black and red-black Ugandans, obstructed land and sea. They traveled into Tanzania by plane instead.

"We were declared Prohibitive Immigrants at customs," Baba said. Without a return ticket, without working permits or money, they became the property of Lufthansa airlines. Lufthansa offered to fly them to either Germany or Egypt. David Du Bois, the stepson of W. E. B. Du Bois, was in Cairo and offered them residence. The plan was for them to get papers there and then return to Tanzania, but while in Egypt they were in a terrible car accident and Mama's foot got split wide open. They stayed nine more months in Egypt while her foot healed. Mama sucked on lollipops to quit smoking, learned the art of cooking, refused the veil as a mare might her hackamore.

They became embedded on Radio Cairo.

Insurgent broadcasts critical of America's domestic and foreign policies reached Bill Sutherland, who had the ear of Tanzanian president Julius Nyerere, who himself made the arrangements to bring my parents into his country.

"We believe that only evil, Godless men would make the color of a man's skin the criteria for granting him civil rights," President Nyerere said. He came from a village in the rural part of the country, was one of twenty-five children of Nyerere Burito, the chief of the Zanaki people. He had become Tanzania's first president in 1964. His rise to power was driven by anti-colonialism, anti-elitism, and anti-aristocracy. He replaced "God Save the Queen," the British national anthem, with "Mungu ibariki Afrika," *God bless Africa*. He attempted to unite the country's 120 tribes and made Kiswahili, or Swahili, the national language. He attempted to develop the country through *Ujamaa*—collective work and responsibility. He wanted the traditional African village to be the building block for Tanzanian society. The people called him *Mwalimu*, the great teacher.

"We, in Africa, have no more need of being 'converted' to socialism than we have of being 'taught' democracy," he said. "Both are rooted in our past—in the traditional society which produced us." While the villagization of Tanzania dramatically expanded access to health care and education, virtually eliminating illiteracy, it failed to result in economic independence.

Mama and Baba and other black expats were valued as resources to help build a country that was attempting to find a balance between individual freedom and collective responsibility.

"You need socialists for socialism," Baba said.

They were appointed by the government to teach math and English at a secondary school in Same, a village near the Kenyan border, in the shade of Mount Kilimanjaro.

· · ·

We were torn from the road. From the red dirt that stretched to the base of Mount Kilimanjaro, transplanted onto America's glacial concrete.

We would learn that our home in Same, like most of the homes of African American expatriates in Tanzania, had been searched by soldiers and police. That it had been reported that blacks from America had arrived by boat with guns and were headed to President Nyerere's village in the build-up to the Pan-African Conference to be held in Dar es Salaam in 1974.

We would learn that in 1975 President Jimmy Carter was offering amnesty to the citizens who had refused to fight in the Vietnam War.

We would learn that we'd been denied Tanzanian citizenship, that the political climate had shifted, that we couldn't become Tanzania's children.

"We're going to visit Bibi," Mama said.

It was 1976. We were six, four, and two, and Malaika getting ripe in Mama's belly, when the plane left the surface of the earth, its wheels folding into its guts. The engines roared like a pride of lions. We took off down the runway like a tortoise at first, and then a cheetah and then an albatross, wings abruptly rejecting gravity. Taking off felt like the car trips we'd made to the Indian Ocean, five, six, or seven of us in a vehicle yo-yoing on dirt and rocks until we reached the paved road, black and smooth. And then the plane was floating. On our way to forty thousand feet like on our way to the beach, the ocean's waves crashing on our toes, turning us upside down, pulling us toward its stomach, coating our bodies in salt then abandoning us on the sand. We treated the plane like the road. Inspected the arms of each chair as if a bush or an anthill, ran up and down the aisle unaware that an umbilical cord had been severed, that we were being delivered to the other side of the planet.

We landed in Nairobi and took off again.

We landed in Paris and took off again. Remained between the surface of the earth and the sun and moon for twenty hours.

We landed in the South Bronx, unaware that we had reached the shores of hip-hop.

We stayed there, at Bibi's, for three weeks—it was spring and wet and cold and the earth was covered in cement.

"*Karibu*," Bibi said. *Welcome.* She lived in a five-story walk-up, in the same one-bedroom apartment that Mama and Uncle Jerry had been raised in. Where Bibi and Mama had shared a bed until Mama had graduated from college. We slept on the couch and the living room floor. Each morning Bibi made grits and eggs and kielbasa, singed oatmeal and sweetened it with Carnation milk.

"*Hapana!*" *No*, Mama said, the first time Maisha and I reached for the kielbasa. "We are vegetarians."

Mama and Baba became militant about what we ate, didn't want us poisoned by America's white sugar and white bread and soda and hormone-injected animals. Would try to raise us like we could still be Tanzanians. And then Bibi placed fat chips of kielbasa right onto our plates and their grease bled into our hominy.

"In my house we eat kielbasa," she said.

We licked the plates clean. We would be carnivorous at Bibi's, vegetarian in the rest of America.

Uncle Jerry, who was tall and dark like the Maasai, gave us toy guns, turned us on to *Sesame Street* and Tonto and the Lone Ranger. And then

Mama pulled the plug. The screen became an infinitesimal dot. And then Taba and I practiced shooting each other like cowboys and Indians. It would be ten years before we lived with a television.

Outside was unobstructed gray and unmalleable.

We put on socks, wore shoes and sneakers to protect our feet. Met Baba's younger brother, Uncle Roger, and his children, Chris and Freddy, walked with them on streets, around corners. The streets were full of cars. Freddy had been bit by one. Patches of grafted skin were visible on his arms and legs. Freddy was older, more talkative than Chris, who was shorter and heavier, wore thick glasses. Each looked like a Moses, with thick eyebrows and deep-set eyes.

We landed in Bigfoot—what Uncle Jerry called his four-door Lincoln that roared like a jet engine, that got ten miles per gallon. Mama called it a gas guzzler. Uncle Jerry called himself the Groovemaster, or Gerald "Fingers," and had played bass with King Curtis at twelve years old and with Ray Charles, Aretha Franklin, and Roberta Flack as a teenager. He founded a band called Jerry Jemmott & Souler Energy. When I am a man, I will watch him perform at the House of Blues in Chicago. He will stalk from one side of the stage to the other like a caged tiger.

A U-Haul trailer hitched to Bigfoot's chrome fender hauled what little luggage we had and the sheets and towels and utensils Bibi had given us.

"We had a hundred dollars" when we landed in America, Mama said.

We landed in Peabody Terrace, at a bend in the Charles River in Cambridge, Massachusetts. Uncle Al, Baba's friend who'd grown up with him in the Harlem River Houses, met us in the mouth of the alley in a bronze Mercedes. He had made the arrangements for Mama and Baba to come home. He appeared fragile as he unloaded from his car boxes of secondhand clothes, pajamas, other things people thought we might need. As a child, he'd survived a bout of rheumatic fever. Mama and Baba appeared indebted. In addition to the clothes, Uncle Al had raised over ten thousand dollars from people who knew Baba from his work in Mississippi. *I began writing people and asking for donations for Bob Moses and his children, there was no money for plane tickets, for housing, medical care, all kinds of things.*

We landed in an alley. The alley began on Putnam Avenue, sloped, plateaued, then sloped again to Bank Street. A pair of silver poles, capped like fire hydrants, prevented cars from entering at each end. The alley led to three walkways, each separated by a square patch of dirt that was embroidered by a chain that threaded the wooden posts in each of its corners. The walkways led to our door—17—and others—16 and 15—which all led to identical lobbies with mailboxes and buzzers and another door that required a key. Our apartment was on the second floor above door 17, one of five hundred units that housed 1,500 people in low-rise buildings and three twenty-two-story cement towers.

Before the bulldozed trees and amputated street the landscape had been fields of grass, a dormant factory, autonomous two-flats with independent views of the river. Josep Lluis Sert had built Peabody Terrace in 1962 to provide housing for Harvard students with spouses or families. Instead of barricading the river, he designed the complex to be porous, to encourage students and neighborhood residents to share its plazas and walkways and consider themselves a community. To the builders, who didn't live within its abrasive gray skin, it was a miracle of modern design.

"Prison-like," the locals said, noting that the balconies were crates, the windows cages, and so much cement. "Like projects," they said. Mourning the loss of their unobstructed view of the river.

•   •   •

Maisha and I fixed our bodies to the kitchen floor next to the radiator at the base of the window overlooking the alley, protesting our arrival. The apartment was a box, cramped beneath seven-foot ceilings, absent the warmth of the sun. The kitchen had enough room for a table, an electric stove and oven, sink and fridge. The floor was tiled, slow to welcome the warmth of our bodies. Maisha's body was thinner than mine, ostrich-like, two years taller. A crescent scar the size of a fingertip hung from the corner of her eye. An iron had fallen on her in Tanzania.

"*Kuja*," Mama said. *Come.* We pressed our faces against the window in an attempt to see where the alley began and ended. We searched for remnants of Tanzania in the bank of infertile dirt that rose from the asphalt below. Nothing grew except shadows, stubborn blades of grass, a black-coiled fence where the dirt plateaued, gripped a sign delineating *Harvard University Property*. We were here because Baba was returning to Harvard, after almost twenty years, to finish his PhD.

"*Karibuni Chakula*," Mama said. *Dinner is ready.* It was the only Kiswahili we responded to.

After dinner Mama tried to fit us in her lap—all three of us, and Malaika now a melon inside her belly. There wasn't enough room.

"Omowale," she said as I stood at the edge of her fingers.

"Tell us about when we were born," Maisha asked. Mama and Maisha did the remembering—about Pretty Girl, our pet goat that became a neighbor's meal, about the army of red ants that marched up my legs with their teeth as I danced on their heads, about Brandy the chimp at the zoo that smoked cigarettes.

"Tell us about *nyoka*," Maisha said. *About the snake.* It was her and Mama's story, not mine, not Baba's. About the venomous green mamba that had found its way into my bed.

"You start," Mama said. The story was more Maisha's than hers.

"You were sleeping," Maisha said years later. "Taba and I were playing, . . . Dad had these notebooks, these composition books, and he used to do his notes for teaching. We were playing with something, we were drawing or writing so we needed to get another notebook and so we went to the room and the notebook was high up on the shelf, so I got a chair. . . . I was standing up and Taba was on the chair next to me and I'm reaching trying to grab this notebook and I look over on the wall and—so the bed is against the wall and in the corner, and there's a window—like say the window is maybe here—and then there's a bed in the corner, and I look over and I see this green thing on the wall and I'm like, 'Oh, there's a branch in the room,' 'cause it seemed, there was a big bush in front of the window, so I thought—it looked exactly like a branch, so that was my first thought—and then I stopped and was like, 'How could a branch just be suspended on the wall like that?'

"And as soon as I thought that I looked over and the head was coming out from the wall and circling, it's the illest thing, it's like this wire, you know, just suspended in space over the bed, and your head was that way, and so its head was at the foot of the bed, so it was turning around coming toward you, so I just started screaming—'*Nyoka! Nyoka! Nyoka! Nyoka!*'"

"I heard this screaming," Mama said, "I was in the kitchen and Baba was in the garden. Baba came racing with a *jembe*"—a garden spade—"and I grabbed Taba and he grabbed you and gave you to me and pushed us out of the room."

"And then Dad and Mom came in," Maisha said. "And Dad grabbed you—I think she grabbed Taba, he grabbed you—and then gave you to her and pushed us all out of the room, and then—this was in Kibaha, this wasn't in Same, and so the house in Kibaha had a patio, and so he grabbed you and pushed us out, and we were sitting here, you were crying—Taba was, I don't know what he was doing—so Dad closed the door and he got a *jembe*, a hoe, and he hacked the snake up, and he cracked a hole in the floor he hit the floor so hard. I think I remember going back in and the pieces were moving."

"The snake came after me," was all Baba said.

He was our hero then

.   .   .

The rest of our belongings arrived at Peabody Terrace in boxes shipped from Tanzania. Baba carried the boxes into the living room where the curtains Mama and Bibi had sewn muzzled the balcony window's light.

"*Kuja,*" Mama said. *Come.* "*Maisha na Omowale, kuja.*"

"English is for here," Maisha said. "Kiswahili is for Tanzania."

Mama unwrapped the ebony Maconde statues covered in newspaper. Generations of men and women and children were carved, one on top of the other, in the dense, black wood. Each sculpture represented a village of people. Some were taller than others—one almost five feet, and heavier than any of us. The slit where the wood was parted flowed vertically, like a widening river. Its scent reminded me of the red dirt road. In my mind's eye I could see the ebony men who had carved the wood, who had appeared unannounced at our doorstep, bartered, then became invisible within a few steps inside the dense, black night.

Mama polished the sculptures with lemon oil as they took root like baobab trees next to the milk crates that were both containers and stools, next to the couches she and Bibi had made from upholstery fabric and pillow forms.

Nyumbani, ni hapa. "We are not going home," Maisha said, when the Maconde statues arrived. We began shedding the parts of us that couldn't become American, the clothes, the words and inadvertent ways of seeing and knowing that had no translation in English language as Mama and Baba continued to try to raise us as if we could be Tanzanian.

"*Kuja,*" Mama whispered. *Come.* And we gathered around her as she placed a map of the world on the kitchen table, straddled the distance from Africa to America with her fingers.

"You can fit a hundred Americas in Africa," she said. It was our introduction to her counternarrative, her insistence that Africa, not America, be our point of reference for life on the planet.

Within days of the Maconde statues' arrival, Mama placed a book on the kitchen table that had been a gift from a professor. The book would sit like a sumo wrestler, sometimes on a milk crate in the living room, sometimes on the floor, other times on the bookshelf, always present as its photographic images took root in each of our minds. Its images belonged to America, to the birth of Jim Crow, marked the end of our journey out of Africa and the beginning of our journey into the United States of America. On the cover a black man hung from a tree branch. Inside was page after page of scorched, mutilated black bodies among crowds of proud white faces. It was an introduction to places like Mississippi and Alabama. A recognition of the systematic lynching of black people across generations, not limited to America's South.

"I don't want to go to war," Taba would say, conflating the images of lifeless black bodies with the Vietnam War that Baba had avoided.

I wondered why neck muscles couldn't prevent spines from snapping. What the men and women thought as they approached the end of the rope.

What was their last thought?

Were the kids alive before they were thrown into the fire?

I wondered where they'd traveled after they left their bodies—the cosmic distance their lives straddled, from before they were a being in a mother's womb to beyond breath, exhausted at the end of a rope.

I wondered why white mothers had taken their babies to witness the killing of black children.

W. H. MOSES SERMON

THE AGE OF PROTEST

Everybody in the world is telling what they want, while the world is in a position to straighten out things, and we are not the only folks with a protest. White folks are not satisfied. A whole lot of us have grievances. We are just kind of clubbing them up and adjusting ourselves and all of us, white and black and everybody else, are throwing them in and coming to a common understanding as to what we should do. Now I am talking about preaching. I know a lot of you kind of feel that we preachers are responsible for much. (*Laughter*) But I am saying that the man who understands his time is the man upon whom God has poured out His spirit. And He said this, this matchless Leader of men: "And it shall come to pass in the last days," saith God, "that I will pour out my spirit upon all flesh." (Not on some, on all flesh, sons and daughters, preachers and laymen—upon all flesh.)

CHAPTER 4

Freedom Fighters

ROBERT MOSES'S ACCOUNT OF VOTER REGISTRATION
DRIVE IN MISSISSIPPI IN 1961, FEBRUARY 1963
(CARL AND ANNE BRADEN PAPERS, 1928–2006;
ARCHIVES SOUND HOLDINGS, AUDIO 443A/18–19)

00:00.28 Robert P. Moses

My name is Robert Moses and I'm a field secretary for the Student Non-violent Coordinating Committee [SNCC]. I first came south in July of 1960 on a field trip for SNCC. Went through Alabama, Mississippi, and Louisiana gathering people to go to the October conference. It was the first time that I met Amzie Moore and at that time we sat down and planned a voter registration drive for Mississippi. I returned in the summer of 1961 to start that drive. We were to start in Cleveland, Mississippi, in the Delta. . . . However, we couldn't. We didn't have any equipment. We didn't even have a place at that time to meet. So we went down to McComb at the invitation of C. C. Bryant, who was the local head of the NAACP there, and we began setting up a voter registration drive in McComb, Mississippi.

00:01:06 Robert P. Moses

What did we do? . . . Well, for two weeks I did nothing but drive around the town talking to the business leaders, the ministers, the people in the town, asking them if they would support ten students who would come in to work on a voter registration drive.

00:01:27 Robert P. Moses

We got a commitment from them to support students for the month of August and to pay for their room and board and some of their transportation while they were there. The project began August 1 and lasted, as it turned out, through December, not just through the month of August. We began in McComb,

00:01:57 Robert P. Moses

canvassing for about a two-week period. This means that we went around house to house, door to door, in the hot sun every day. Because the most important thing at the beginning was to convince the local townspeople that we meant business. That is, that we were serious, that we were not only young but that we were people who were responsible. What do you tell somebody when you go to their door? Well, first of all you tell them that, ah, who you are, what you're trying to do, that you're working on voter registration and you have a form that you're trying to get them to fill out. Now the technique which we found best usable, I think, was to simply present the form to them and say, "Have you ever tried to fill out this form? Um, would you like to sit down now and try and fill it out?" and then psychologically as they were in the process of filling out a voter registration form,

00:03:08 Robert P. Moses

they have to complete a gap to go and imagine themselves as being at the registrar's office. As you know, in Mississippi currently you have to fill out a form which has about twenty-one questions on it and, aside from routine questions, has on it a place where you write and then interpret some section of the Constitution in Mississippi. And finally a section where you write and describe the duties and obligations of a citizen in Mississippi. Now when we did this for about two weeks and finally began to get results—that is, people began to go down to Magnolia, Mississippi, which is the county seat of Pike County, and attempt to register. In the meantime, quite naturally, people from Amite and Walthall County, which are the two adjacent counties to Pike County, came over asking us if we wouldn't accompany them and conduct schools in their counties so that they could go down and try and register also. And this point should be made quite clear because many people have been very critical of going into such tough counties so early in the game.

00:04:35 Robert P. Moses

The position was simply this: that farmers came over and were very anxious to try and register and you couldn't very well turn them down. One, just from the human point of view, they had greater needs in those counties than in Pike County, where we were working.

00:04:52 Robert P. Moses

And secondly, from [the] psychological point of view, where the whole problem in Mississippi is pervasive, pervaded with fear. The problem is you can't be in the position of, of turning down the tough areas. Ah, because the people then, I think, would simply lose confidence in you. So we, we accepted this.

· · ·

We have been down this road before, tunneling through Massachusetts and Connecticut—the Mass Pike to 91 to 84 to 95 to 278 through Brooklyn to the Verrazano Bridge to Staten Island to New Jersey. On each trip Baba had been adamant about being the one to drive us out of Massachusetts, taking us west and eventually south, away from the coast and into the blood and guts of America. The first trip had been in the fall of 1991, my sophomore year of college, a couple months after Mama had bought me the Maxima. Baba didn't think I was ready to drive the eight hours to DC by myself and insisted that the family drive with me part of the way so that I wouldn't face the perils of the road alone. He insisted Taba drive me in the Maxima until we reached the Verrazano Bridge, while Mama and Malaika would ride with him in the Dodge Caravan in front of us, cutting in half the number of hours I would spend behind the steering wheel, the number of state lines I was responsible for crossing.

The Verrazano Bridge was the long way to George Washington University. Less traffic, fewer trucks, more highway, fewer highway patrolmen. Baba paid the tolls, kept the map, flirted with sixty-five, and that was it. The first time we passed him he was going fifty and then he punched the gas and stormed up next to us and waved to Taba to move over and slow down. Taba and I laughed it off, began to drive slow enough to let cars come between us.

"Stay behind me and keep up," he said when we got to the next service station. We didn't say anything until we got back in the car.

"Dad's crazy."

We lost him behind an eighteen-wheeler. We flanked it and then ran neck and neck with it for a while and then punched the gas all the way to the tollbooth at the foot of the Verrazano Bridge.

We parked on the side of the highway. Mama got out of the Caravan first, smiled, and shook her head, started acting like I was going to college for the first time. She and Malaika hugged me. Baba acted like we hadn't just dusted him, gave me his gentle hand, an envelope with a couple hundreds.

"Have a great year," he said.

"We gonna kill 'em this year," Taba said. Every new season was the year we were gonna kill 'em on the court.

They watched as I strapped in and took off. It felt good to have my hands back on the steering wheel. The Maxima had less than twenty thousand miles then, was symbolic still of the money and status I hoped to accumulate. They waved, returned to the Caravan, became invisible in the mirror as the distance grew between us.

. . .

The Maxima, which has sixty-three thousand miles on it, is no longer a jewel in a crown but has become simply a vehicle to get from one place to another.

Baba and I are greeted by welcome signs on America's highway. Each state line demarcating the jurisdiction of each state's constitution. A jigsaw puzzle of laws forming the United States of America. I interpret each sign as a window into the country's schizophrenia.

When I was growing up, the slogan on Massachusetts's welcome sign was "The Spirit of America." I learned many years later that the name of the state had been the name of a people. Additional Native names sporadically appear on signs and disappear in the side mirror as we linger at fifty-five miles per hour. Their randomness, and the redundancy of the uniformed men who patrol America's highways, intentionally obscures that all of this is Native land.

The plan is to drive straight to Atlanta, make a pitstop at Malaika's, who is a student at Spelman College, then continue to Mississippi. I'm worried the Maxima won't get us to Mississippi with Baba's knuckles wrapped around the steering wheel. The tip of his pinky is missing. He'd slammed it in a car door a decade ago while he was somewhere in Jersey—I remember Mama on the phone with him in the kitchen in Peabody Terrace, gasping as if someone had died. Mama wanted to know if he could find the rest of it. It is my first memory of him being vulnerable.

I take the atlas from the glove compartment, begin grinding teeth, calibrating hours and miles to distract me from the road crawling. At fifty-five miles per hour, it feels like we will always be approaching Connecticut.

I start to tell him we've been down this road before, that I'd done this leg of our journey a hundred times, even yawn to unhinge my jaws, but the words get stuck, attached to all the other words I've been waiting to share with him, all the history we're tunneling through on America's highways.

America's highways remind me that the land was once wilderness and belonged to the earth before the arrival of Columbus. Belonged to a consciousness that recognized the earth as our mother, as the mother of "unborn generations."[1] As we pass through what had been Nipmuck and Pequot land, I turn the pages in the atlas, tracing with a finger miles of highway zigzagging north and south, east and west, scaled to inches. In the inches are the generations (of Chinese immigrants) it took to connect one side of the country to the other, at first through the transcontinental railroad. Mama said we could have chosen more railroads instead of more highways. But that would have meant fewer cars that society be driven by something other than the extraction and consumption of the earth's resources.

"Who's the 'we'?" Baba asked. Who chose cars over trains, who drew the state lines that denied the sovereignty of Native nations, who patrolled America's borders now decorated with Native names?

Colonials, John Mohawk said.

Settlers, Robin Wall Kimmerer said.

Baba doesn't do small talk. With each mile, conversation feels less and less probable. Baba sits upright as if he is meditating. His eyes on the horizon. I imagine on some past or future battlefield. Every now and then I turn to look at him. His eyes, like his mother's, could be light brown or greenish, somber, conveying a deep sensitivity. His eyebrows are thick. The hair on his face grows between manicured and jungle-like, obscures his lips. He'd let me cut his hair for the first time in 1993, seventeen years after we'd arrived in America, for a *New York Times Magazine* photoshoot.

The *New York Times Magazine* article made the connection between the voter registration Baba had done in Mississippi in the '60s and the emergence of the Algebra Project. The cover photo attempted to frame him and black students and math in the space between our (not-so-distant, rural, Jim Crow, undemocratic) past and our (tech-addicted, metropolitan, not-so-democratic, not-so-distant) future. His eyes were wide open and boxed into one of the rectangular graphic overlays that, together, resembled a train of batteries, framing his face and the figures of four students from the Mississippi Delta, two boys and two girls, seated around him. Baba imagined the Algebra Project as some sort of underground railroad toward participatory democracy as he gazed into America's future.

"Algebra for All, Algebra para Todos" was the Algebra Project's slogan.

Baba understood that America's public education system would have to deconstruct itself, that families and communities would have to organize themselves to ensure that all children were prepared to take algebra by the eighth grade. That the work required to achieve algebra for all, algebra para todos was at the heart of democratic participation.

"Do your best," he had said when I asked how he wanted his hair cut. I shaved the beard from his face. Left him with a goatee as if he were another kid in the neighborhood. It was the first time I could remember touching his face. I pressed my fingers into his cheek to make his skin taut, so that each strand of hair became erect. Nudged his head back so that his Adam's apple was exposed. He closed his eyes, didn't give any instructions. I stepped back and held him in my eyes for uninterrupted seconds. Moved in close enough to feel him breathe as the clippers began peeling layers from him. He pressed his lips together and held his breath as I clipped the hair from his nose. It took two hours to unmask him. It was the closest we had been since Tanzania.

·   ·   ·

Silent minutes become a silent hour as we drive toward Connecticut.

"My mother taught me how to live in silence," Baba would say. I had inherited their quiet. In this way we are crippled. In this way we are comfortable.

He said his favorite memories of her were of them on cold winter evenings, each of them with a book they had just borrowed from the library, seated in the living room of their Harlem River Houses apartment.

"Her death freed me to go south," Baba would say. Baba, who had begun working on his PhD at Harvard, left school then to take care of his father. He said that he had been clueless at Harvard when the sit-ins started in

1960, that the picture in the *New York Times* of the four black North Carolina A&T students sitting in at Woolworth's lunch counter woke him up. The sudden death of his mother from cancer in 1958 and the emergence of the sit-ins two years later were stitched together in his mind, as if the two events had occurred simultaneously.

"They hit me powerfully in the soul as well as the brain," he said. That those students looked and felt like he looked and felt and were doing something about it.

Louise—Baba's mother—was just forty-three when she died. She and Pop had recently returned from their only vacation when she was hospitalized. Pop and Baba and Uncle Greg and Uncle Roger adored her.

The men in my life, she would say.

"The prettiest thing on 111th Avenue," Pop said. Louise had been fifteen and making plans to go to college when Pop, who was ten years older, "snapped her up." Baba believed that Louise's mother had allowed her to get married so young because she had been born out of wedlock and Louise's mother had since remarried. Louise gave birth to Uncle Greg and then Baba before she was twenty. Uncle Roger would be born six years later.

Pop worked as a janitor at Harlem's 369th Armory. Baba said Pop felt "shortchanged," turned to alcohol as a remedy for the circumstances of his life. Baba said:

> I think my father was kind of trapped by the Depression and in terms of his own education, though I don't know whether he really had a goal to continue his education after high school. His two brothers both—one became a professor [and] actually started the Architectural Department at Hampton, and his oldest brother became a lieutenant colonel in the United States Army . . . and then his boss at the armory. Pop talked about the man in the street. He was a kind of philosopher who liked to visit, and I was a kid who liked to hang. And so if he said, "Are we going to go see a dog about an elephant?" I went. He was fun to talk to. He helped me understand how to read people. He was always talking to me about the person we had just talked to. And he had a way of thinking about whether people lived up—whether what you saw was what was there and whether what you heard was what was real.[2]

Pop wrote to his boys after Louise had died, remarking on their life together. "Dear Boys," the letter began.

> Louise and I had a beautiful twenty-seven years of happily married life, to which union was born Gregory, Robert, and Roger, my sons, but her boys. . . . She was proud of each of her brood from the day the first one went to kindergarten [until the last] entered college. Though at times it was hard, particularly on her keeping three children in a school, but never did she complain. Her home was her castle. She was the spirit behind [apartment] 211D.
>
> Petite would not describe her, for she was big boned, with enough flesh in the proper places to make her absolutely feminine and intriguing to look at. She was proud at all times, straight as a rod, shoulders well back, head high, and she had a funny little walk. I liked to watch her coming and going. What color the eyes? Gray, everyone said. But they didn't see the big eyes that ogled off into space, that would change their hues so that you couldn't distinguish the different tints. . . . In an era of tints and dyes she was a natural. Her grays made her young and stood her apart in a crowd. Did you know that mother had freckles? I did, because I counted them. They were hard to spot beneath the golden brown skin.
>
> Always the little smile, the delicate laugh, the musical voice, that was so soft and low, you had to listen closely at times to understand. Her perfume, Abiano, was part of her, an aroma that only she could wear. Little were her needs but they had to be the best, whether clothes, books, music, wine or friends. Crowds and confusion upset her, she had to be handled like she was a delicate rare flower. I can see her now, jumping for joy, clapping her hands, and dancing like a little girl, because she had received a present, maybe only a trinket, but if it was something that she valued, it would find its way into her shoe box vault with her treasures. Three pairs of baby shoes, first-grade Valentine, and birthday cards, things made by her children, belts, wooden plaques, copper engravings, or maybe just a stone from camps. They were her priceless things.

Louise had been forty when Baba helped her get her first job. He was working at the NYU library and arranged a desk job for her there. "It was a long trip downtown for her but it gave her a life outside of the home."

A new life had opened, the magic carpet was going to work, the future looked bright. Not a home in the country, but a co-op apartment in the city, near the shows, art galleries, Lewisohn Stadium. Asking not much of life, just the comforts of a job well done, maybe in later years, travel.

Her forty-third year was to prove to be the twilight of her life, that would bring forth her strong endurable character, her heritage, that she passed to you. "Why me? Greg. Why me?" Ten minutes later she shed her last visible tear.

The next six months was an eon. . . . Just the two of us again, no bubble, but life, laughter and sorrow taken in stride. Remembering the past through plotting and planning the future, yet living each day, for the joys thereof. As the funny little walk changed to be a proud limp, the delicate flower became a sturdy oak . . . a woman in every sense of the word, a mother whose prime interest was her family and her home.

Her fight for three weeks to stay in her nest with "the men in my life" was heart-rending. . . . The light went out of her eyes and the smile left her face when she told the doctor, "I'll stay." You boys and I knew the vigilant week that followed, where for twenty-four hours a day Mother had one of "her men" by her side, each thinking his own thoughts and praying his individual prayer. It was fitting that her firstborn was to be by her side. That her second was to say, "Sleep sweets in thou quiet room," and her baby was to walk alone into the wee hours of the night, and come back a man.

The melancholy ride through Harlem, down Seventh Avenue, the churches, YMCA, theaters, bars, the people coming and going about their ways, was no longer a part of me. Central Park was different. It was like a sunrise at high noon. . . . The grass looked so green, the trees so tall and still, here and there the tweet of a bird, and the squirrel that ran along the side of the road. I must have gone into a dream, for Louise and I were taking that long-planned ride in a horse-drawn hansom through the park. The thousand and one memories that we enjoyed and shared with our children and the world. The whispered secrets that were only for our ears. . . . I came out of my haze looking at my "Doll in Blue." She must have been proud of her crew. For you boys arranged what I still like to remember as Louise's last party, where no one was allowed to cry but her mother and sister. The enchanting organ music that she loved, the oration by Rev. Moore her pastor, her son curling her hair and reciting poetry. The many friends from all walks of life who came to say "Hello." . . .

So we come to the crossroads of life again and I think we are all due a bow for the last year and a half for trying to evaluate our collective and individual problems. Though we [will] be going our separate ways. May we always go then together.

"Skeets," as the first to walk, so you are the first to make the big step in life, marriage, and seem to be well on your way in your chosen profession. May you someday be a guide to us all.

"Bob," your training in philosophy will open many wearied and varied doors for you. Do what you have to do. Just remember the world is your high-chair now, keep your balance.

"Roger," you had more to gain or lose in the past year than any of us. I watched you very, very closely and at no time was I ever worried. You were taking things in stride, making the proper decisions at the proper time. I believe you have discovered the spoon in sterling silver, and you can shape it like you will.

What about me? I'll get along, for one reason: "I'll never be alone," and if you worry about my seeming effort to go nowhere, remember the words of the poet.

"They also serve who only stand and wait."

Baba said that Pop lost it when Louise died, that he was picked up by a patrolman who said he'd been impersonating Gary Cooper, that he would spend months in Bellevue Hospital. Baba came home from Harvard and took a three-year contract teaching math at Horace Mann, a Manhattan prep school. He and Pop got an apartment together. Baba did a stint as Frankie Lymon's tutor. Saw black America then, was awakened to the idea that Harlem was part of an "urban black archipelago." That his father's struggles, Harlem's struggles, "exemplified the economic and emotional situation of many blacks in the cities" across the country. "Until then, my Black life was conflicted . . . moving back and forth between the sharply contrasting worlds of Hamilton College, Harvard University, Horace Mann, and Harlem. It made me realize that for a long time I had been troubled by the problem of being a Negro and being an American.[3]

"From the first time a Negro gets involved in white society, he starts repressing, repressing, repressing. My whole reaction through life to such humiliation was to avoid it, keep it down, hold it in, play it cool."

Baba saw Pop's "man in the street" reflected in the *New York Times*'s image of the four students' dignified, sullen faces at the Woolworth's lunch counter.

Baba went to visit Uncle Bill in Hampton, Virginia to see firsthand what was happening in the South. "I had never wanted to go south," he said. When he saw students picketing a Woolworth's store there, he joined them. "I felt a great release," he said. This experience led him to volunteer in the Southern Christian Leadership Conference (SCLC) office in Harlem, which was run by Bayard Rustin. "I asked Bayard if I could go down and work with King, and Bayard said, 'Well, I'll send you down to Ella Baker in Atlanta.'"

. . .

"Welcome to Connecticut," the sign reads. "Still Revolutionary. The Constitution State."

The sight of the welcome sign puts me on edge. I had gotten my first speeding ticket in Connecticut while driving back to college. The state trooper approached the car with his hand on his gun. Most of them would do this, would show up with their hand on their heater.

"Driver's license and registration," the state trooper had said as I instinctively turned down the music. "Put your hands on the steering wheel." Beyond my hands on the steering wheel the highway was flat and straight, visible on the horizon. Every now and then a truck passed, rallied the wind, rattled the car. Life was still ahead of me, something I was in pursuit of. Something I believed I had the power and time to define my relationship to. The state trooper's presence reminded me that there were forces opposing whatever future I envisioned for myself. The state troopers became "storm troopers" then.

I realized that this could happen again and again—in New York and New Jersey and Delaware and Maryland. That I had little to no control over when, where, and how I got detained. I armed myself with a radar detector on subsequent trips to level the playing field.

Fuck it, I said. I pushed ninety, sometimes a hundred, once a hundred and five. Shaved an hour and a half from the eight hours it normally took to drive from Cambridge to DC. Anticipated the storm troopers in the breaks in the median, at the bottom of long hills, above or beneath bridges, their radar guns cocked. The radar detector had its own language—stochastic red lights and beeps and whistles, like R2-D2 and C-3PO, warning me of the storm troopers in pursuit. Each sound spiked my adrenaline. Placed my head on a swivel, eyes darting from the road to the breakdown lane to the median as the storm troopers camouflaged themselves in unmarked cars, matched miles per hour, glared into my tinted windows before moving on or unleashing their shock and awe. I tucked the tickets in the glove compartment, punched the gas, shifted gears from slow, to middle, to passing lane. Mailed the $300 tickets to Mama.

Between 1986 and 1995—from my freshman year in high school to my departure from college—the stretches of highway that I traveled between home and school were among the front lines for the "war on drugs," first launched by President Nixon in 1968, part of the backlash against the Civil Rights Movement and antiwar demonstrations, an attack on hippies and black people.

"You understand what I'm saying?" confessed former Nixon domestic policy chief John Ehrlichman in 2016. "We knew we couldn't make it illegal to be either against the war or black, but by getting the public to associate the hippies with marijuana and blacks with heroin, and then criminalizing both heavily, we could disrupt those communities. We could arrest their leaders, raid their homes, break up their meetings, and vilify them night after night on the evening news. Did we know we were lying about the drugs? Of course we did."[4]

The war on drugs was expanded by Presidents Reagan, Bush, Clinton, and Bush Jr. as laws and policies were created that made it easier for storm troopers to detain black bodies now predestined for prison. The details about the federal government's complicity in fomenting the tidal waves of cocaine that crashed on our streets and flooded our neighborhoods in the '80s have emerged in the decades since.

Baba saw this coming.

If your friends don't get this algebra they're going to jail, he would say.

Dad's crazy, we said.

I was ten the first time I was detained. I was riding through Peabody Terrace at night on a bike that a Harvard police officer assumed was stolen. The bitch was black. The bitch was Mama's age. Told me to put my hands against a tree. I gripped the bark. She began moving her hands down my legs. Up my shirt. I began crying then.

·   ·   ·

Taba said that Baba had sung freedom songs when the two of them had first driven to Hollandale and Indianola in the Mississippi Delta. Baba had begun taking Taba with him on his trips with the Algebra Project to get him off the streets, if only momentarily, and out of the scope of the storm troopers. Taba was approaching nineteen then. They'd stared each other down in Taba's room when Baba found out he was hustling. Taba allowed Baba's tears and fists to land on his body. Baba sent him back to Tanzania for a couple weeks and then he and Mama began wrestling with what to do next.

Taba said the Tanzanians had welcomed him like he was a son returning home, unlike the other African Americans he traveled with, who they treated like strangers. He said men held his hand and walked him around the neighborhood and marketplace. That the boys rode him on the backs of scooters, made him promise to send them CDs of the latest hip-hop when he returned to America.

Mama and Baba would never agree on what to do with Taba. Mama blamed herself, said if she hadn't gone to medical school she would have been around when we were hanging from corners. Baba blamed me, said if I hadn't quit the swim team when I was twelve that Taba would still be a swimmer.

Quitting the Bernal's Gators Swim Club remained in the distance between us.

.   .   .

"Welcome to New York," the sign reads, "the Empire State."

I want to hear Baba sing freedom songs too, to know that other person locked in his body.

.   .   .

We switch seats in New Jersey, where "Liberty and Prosperity" is the state slogan.

"Put your seat belt on," Baba says as we approach the Mason-Dixon line, that mythical line surveyed between 1763 and 1767 to resolve a border dispute between Pennsylvania, Maryland, Delaware, and Virginia. The line, which was marked with large stones every half mile, came to represent, at least on paper, the distance between human property and freedom, for free and enslaved Africans. Part of the mythmaking was the mistaken belief blacks couldn't be enslaved in the North (most free states had some enslaved Africans, according to the 1840 census) nor captured and returned to bondage in the South. The idyllic American pursuit of "liberty and prosperity" was bound to the coffles of enslaved men and women marching hundreds of miles south and westward to fuel the economic and geographic expansion of the United States throughout Native lands. Africans and African Americans were valued for their labor, while Indians were valued for their land, John Mohawk said.[5] In 1850 Congress passed the Fugitive Slave Act, the progeny of the compromise between "free" and slave states at the birth of the Constitution: that enslaved Africans, for the purpose of representation, for the purpose of forming a more perfect Union, would be considered three-fifths of a human being. Which gave slaveowners the right to retrieve their human property anywhere in the United States. Which, on the eve of the Civil War, became the fuse that led white boys to point their guns at each other and pull the trigger.

"My seat belt is on," I say. The car automatically straps us in at the shoulders.

"All the way," he says. He wants me to also manually strap myself in at the waist, is concerned with my safety on America's highways.

I try to get out of first gear smoothly, to model for him what's possible with the clutch, show that we don't have to buck into second and third, and then I rip into fourth and glide to fifth.

"Watch your speed," he says as I reach the passing lane.

"Stay to the right," he says.

In DC the AC begins pushing hot air. We roll windows down and the wind streams in, muffling the music. By the time we reach South Carolina, the wind coming into the car is heavy and wet. Sweat gathers on Baba's forehead, threatens to trickle into the corner of his eye as he sleeps. I manage a ten-mile run of a hundred miles per hour while he sleeps, and the highway lamps arrive in grenade flashes as I attempt for a moment to fast-forward the history we are tunneling through. The Confederate flags become more frequent, and then ubiquitous. Dixie Gas becomes more frequent. The Confederate flag a brand of petrol, part of the state apparatus. The gas is eighty-nine cents a gallon. The service stations seem isolated, dim-lit, some invisible from the highway. We have less than a quarter tank of gas and my bladder is full. I hold out for a Shell or Chevron. Don't want to get caught with my dick in my hand by the side of the road. On the road are more Cracker Barrels and Shoney's. We are knifing across the Black Belt of America—a swath of land that extends from Mississippi to Alabama, through Georgia, the Carolinas, and Virginia, and in the other direction to Texas, named for its thick, black, nutrient-rich topsoil, for the density of black hands and feet that worked it from slavery through the 1960s. Counties in which formerly enslaved Africans significantly outnumbered the white population. Counties that elected formerly enslaved Africans to local and state offices during Reconstruction. Counties that gave birth to Jim Crow, where white terrorism took root and flourished.

In the distance between the Mason-Dixon line and the Black Belt is a reckoning with the fantasy that I harbored of who Taba and I would have been in 1960s Mississippi, and before that, and before that. The sheer vastness of the land is humbling and provides a stark frame for the daily acts of courage required to survive, to preserve humanity, to create and protect family, to resist, to liberate oneself and lead others to freedom.

· · ·

When Baba headed south in the '60s he arrived in Atlanta at the office of the SCLC, which at that time was led by Ella Baker (the executive director) and Martin Luther King Jr. (the president). The SCLC had been founded in 1957. Baba said that it was unheard of at the time for a woman to be leading an organization of male pastors. The Student Nonviolent Coordinating Committee (SNCC) office was contained within the SCLC office. SNCC had been founded in 1960. Unlike King—who, Baba said, was as melodic in person as he was in the pulpit, and who wanted to be sure Baba wasn't a member of the communist party—Ella took an interest in him, asked who his people were. It turned out she'd had something to do with the cooperative in the Harlem River Houses that had enabled his family to sell milk and in so doing keep milk on their own table.

It was Ella who gave Baba a list with names of local leaders that included Amzie Moore (head of the Cleveland, Mississippi, chapter of the NAACP and local business owner); who put him on a Greyhound bus to look for young people who had been part of the sit-ins in Alabama, Mississippi, and Louisiana and invite them to participate in the "first Southern Black Conference of SNCC." Baba said:

They put me on a Greyhound bus. I take off. Talladega, Birmingham, Clarksdale, Cleveland, Jackson, Shreveport, New Orleans, and Biloxi, Gulfport, Biloxi, Mobile, back to Atlanta. So I'm a scout, right? I'm also somehow representing this very militant sit-in organization. There's an expectation. So at the bus stop in Atlanta, they're [members of SNCC] watching to see where I sit when I get on. So I sit up front until we get to the Georgia line and I go back. So when the bus hit Anniston . . . the Highway Patrol guy comes on, but I'm in the back. He can't tell me from anybody else, right? When I go to Clarksdale, right, Aaron Henry sees me off, and they're watching where I sit. I sit up front, but nobody else is on the bus then.

I spend several days there [in Cleveland, Mississippi], and . . . Amzie was the first one who really begins to take me in. . . . Amzie is the one who tells us what we should do. I mean, he really is the one that says. . . . He's sitting on—he's compiling the information about voter registration in the Delta. And it blows my mind, because I've been to all the schools, and we're talking about, you know, the Iron Curtain; people are giving lectures at Horace Mann, and everybody—*oh, these people have to vote over there in Eastern Europe* and everything, and no one, nobody ever said anything about this congressional district in Mississippi which is 80 percent black in terms of eligible voters [and which] has never sent a black person to Congress. So it just blows my mind. And Amzie is plotting how he's—how we're going to . . . And he sees the sit-in movement and the youth energy. He's the only one on that whole trip who really sees that the energy is there now to take on Mississippi, right in the Deep South.[6]

·   ·   ·

I was nineteen when I lived in the South for the first time. I spent the summer before my sophomore year at GW in Alpharetta, Georgia, with Rumeal—who was twenty-five and playing basketball for the Atlanta Hawks—in the mansion he'd bought there, just outside Atlanta. Rumeal's journey had begun in Jamaica, and before that and before that. The public's story about him began with his mother abandoning him in Cambridge, and then becoming homeless, and then being adopted when he was a teenager.

"Take it to the hoop," he said as he refereed my eighth-grade championship game. He could see that I needed to be more aggressive.

"Meet me at St. Mary's," he said when I was in high school, so that he could begin passing down what he'd learned about the game.

"Good luck," he said before we won our state championship.

"We're the only ones doing this," he said when he would pick me and Taba up at 6 a.m. to run on the track at MIT.

"She's beautiful," he said when he met Wimbledon, "but you better watch what she eats, you know the Puerto Ricans start getting fat when they're thirty."

"Don't let them fuck up your jump shot," he said, about the athletic trainers at Pitt who would sculpt my body and fuck up my jump shot during my freshman year there.

"He's a good coach, but he'll leave you," he said about GW's Coach Jarvis, who'd left him when he was a junior in high school to coach at Boston University. Rumeal arranged for Jarvis to watch us work out when he was coaching at GW and I was thinking about transferring from Pittsburgh.

"Game over," I said the first time I beat him, that summer before my sophomore year. We were the only players in the gym at Georgia Tech. He was waiting for me at the three-point line. I stood ten feet behind it and became giddy with laughter before I launched the ball in the air. I knew the ball was gonna go in. The laughter was a wave of emotion that rose from the past eight years of trying to become as good as him.

"I want to be the moon," he'd said when he spoke at our high school graduation.

"When you're in the league," he would say, affirming his belief in me that I could follow him onto the biggest basketball stages.

We never talked about his version of his story, what it meant to be abandoned, homeless, adopted.

His mansion stood on a partially manicured, partially wooded ten acres on the edge of Forsyth County. Forsyth County had been known as a "sundown town." Sundown towns are municipalities that remain all-white through local laws, intimidation, or violence. The term came from signs posted that "colored people" had to leave town by sundown. Sundown counties and sundown suburbs were not restricted to the Southern states, with New Jersey and other Northern states being described as equally inhospitable to black travelers. Forsyth County had expelled blacks in 1912. In 1987 five thousand white nationals and members of the Forsyth County Defense League had marched to keep them out.

In the mornings we walked his two-hundred-pound Tosa Inu dogs (Japanese mastiffs), or raced his thousand-dollar bikes up and down Alpharetta's red hills. We rode the bikes before the sun was strong. Every redneck smiled and waved, said hello and good morning. At first, I was startled, ignored them, and then started waving too—to each car and person, which was exhausting until I was no longer conscious of it. And then someone yelled NIGGERS from a pickup truck and tried to run us, in our florescent Lycra suits, off the road.

While our days were spent on the court or in the weight room at Georgia Tech University with other pros and elite college players, our nights were spent at Magic City, the mecca of naked black women. Rumeal would give me a fistful of twenty-dollar bills, tell me to put the key to his Mercedes or Porsche on the table to entice the girls to climb onto it. To dance, untie strings lining a crevice, as bodies thumped along with speakers. I was hypnotized by the constellation of bejeweled vulvas and navels and nipples. I thought I was gazing into my future. As niggas shot fists of cash to the ceiling. As asses clapped like thunder. As it rained Lincolns, Hamiltons, Jacksons.

· · ·

"What was it like down here in the sixties?" I ask Baba.

"You had to know when you were safe and when you weren't," Baba says.

"Watch your speed," Baba says.

It is the last mile to Malaika's house and at this point there isn't a CD I own that I want to listen to. My skin is salty. I want to wash the last twenty hours from my body. Baba asks if Taba and I will be bringing our dogs to Mississippi.

"Eventually," I say.

"Taba would have been an excellent veterinarian," he says.

"Me too," I say. As if I could have delivered the Rottweiler pups the way Taba had. The first Rottweiler Taba and I ever saw had been on the baseball field in Peabody Terrace. It scared the shit out of us. *I want one of them*, we said. *Why not a Great Dane?* Mama had asked. *Pussies*, we whispered.

"No," Baba says. "Taba would make an excellent veterinarian."

"If I want to be an excellent veterinarian, I could be an excellent veterinarian," I say.

Malaika lives with Monica, her best friend from high school, and with Xavier—the first Rottweiler that Taba and I had owned, that we had convinced Mama to buy when we were in high school. Taba and I had named him after Professor X, the leader of the X-Men. And then we purchased a female, Kaya, and bred from the two of them a half-dozen Rottweilers. I'd watched from the top of the basement steps as Taba delivered both litters. We sold some of the pups and gave the rest to friends, except Tyson, who was the pick of his litter and who we named after the heavyweight champion of the world.

Malaika is in her third year at Spelman College in Atlanta, is a dancer in a troupe of African dancers, her hair between afro and conked, her thighs thick like Dad's and mine, like Louise. She lives in a Victorian-style house Mama bought her. The mortgage is less than a dorm room. "Everyone should have a house," is what Mama says. Xavier moved in with Malaika to make sure the house never gets broken into.

It's good to see Xavier again—his muzzle is graying; he smells washed. He turns in circles and rubs his body against my leg and wags the nub of his tail.

In the morning Malaika tells me she wants to talk and hands me a letter. I stand against the wall in her room as the door closes and she begins telling me how fucked up I was, how I'd shaved in her room and never cleaned up the hair on her dresser afterward, how I'd barely spoken to her for four years, how she felt about me fuckin' around with one of her friends. I knew that that was where it was headed. *Gimme a break*, I say to myself. *I waited until she was in college.* As if that mattered. When I was playing ball on national TV, I had grown accustomed to people moving around me a certain way but am beginning to get a sense of what life will be like now that I'm no longer on stage. Malaika cries a little, like she had already cried about this a lot more.

She asks if I want to keep the letter and I say "yeah" and ask if she wants me to walk Xavier. She says yes and hands me a leash and a bag for his shit and I say, "I don't need it," and she says, "It's the law now," and that he still chases cats and squirrels. And I say, "OK," because I know this is about her authority, that Xavier is her dog now.

He wags his stump when I call him. I attach the leash to his collar and we head out the door. I remove the leash when we reach the sidewalk because Taba and I trained him to obey our voices. Taba and I will always be his masters. Xavier sniffs and salivates, marks scent after scent from tree trunk to pole to tree trunk to patch of dirt. Walking in his footsteps returns me to a familiar rhythm—to a time when I felt clearer about my purpose.

Maybe Atlanta is south enough, I think, as far as me and Baba need to go. I could park the Maxima in Alpharetta. Become a version of who I had wanted to be. Attempt to turn my mind and body into Continental Basketball Association or overseas material. Spend days playing, exercising, eating organic, taking care of Rumeal's mastiffs. Spend nights stargazing in Magic City. Except that Rumeal was no longer an Atlanta Hawk. He was traded to the New Jersey Nets and then the Charlotte Hornets and then the Portland Trailblazers and eventually the Los Angeles Lakers. From contract to contract. From team to team. From plantation to plantation. Inevitably out the league. On his way to becoming incarcerated.

. . .

The sign downtown reads "Welcome to Jackson, Mississippi, the Best of the New South." The sun has fallen. Downtown is remarkably empty—I can make out active train tracks, railroad crossings, a pocket-sized skyscraper, its eighteen floors mostly unoccupied. I had slept most of the drive there, from Atlanta through Alabama and into Meridian. We park in front of the Standard Life Building, where the Southern Initiative of the Algebra Project has an office. In 1929 it was the largest concrete reinforced building in the world. It remains the tallest building in Jackson. Next to it are the four hundred abandoned rooms of the King Edwards Hotel. Both pillars of past prosperity. There isn't a person on a sidewalk, only a few cars in the street. A statue of Andrew Jackson. Confederate monuments safeguarding a not-so-distant past. I wait for Baba in the car as he goes to get from Dave Dennis the keys to the apartment that we will be staying in. Dave runs the Southern Initiative of the Algebra Project and has an office on the tenth floor. I'd seen Dave for the first time on *Eyes on the Prize*, the landmark documentary series about the movement. It was 1987. I was in eleventh grade and our family—Mama, Baba, Maisha, Malaika, Taba, the dogs—sat in the upstairs hallway in front of the thirteen-inch color TV and watched the national broadcast of Mama and Baba and their comrades in black and white on the battlefield. As we watched, Mama moaned as if the billy clubs and firehose blasts on screen were landing on her body. The clip of Dave delivering the eulogy at James Chaney's memorial caused my body to shiver. He was my age in the clip, with pale skin and mosquito eyes, appeared beet red in that black and white footage. "I don't grieve for Chaney," Dave said,

> because the fact I feel that he lived a fuller life than many of us will ever
> live. I feel that he's got his freedom and we are still fighting for it.

But what I want to talk about right now is the living dead that we have right among our midst, not only in the state of Mississippi but throughout the nation. Those are the people who don't care, those who do care but don't have the guts enough to stand up for it, and those people who are busy up in Washington and in other places using my freedom and my life to play politics with.

As I stand here a lot of things pass through my mind. I can remember the Emmett Till case, what happened to him, and what happened to the people who killed him. They're walking the streets right now. . . . I remember back down here, right below us here, a man by the name of Mack Parker and exactly what happened to him and what happened to the people who beat, killed him, and drug him down the streets and threw him in the river. I know that those people were caught, but they were never brought to trial. . . . And I can remember down in the southwest area where you had six Negroes who'd been killed, and I can remember the Lees and all these particular people who know what has happened to those who have been killing them. I know what is happening to the people that are bombing the churches, who've been bombing the homes, who are doing the beatings around this entire state and country.

Well, I'm getting sick and tired! I'm sick and tired of going to memorials! I'm sick and tired of going to funerals! I've got a bitter vengeance in my heart tonight! And I'm sick and tired and can't help but feel bitter, you see, deep down inside and I'm not going to stand here and ask anybody here not to be angry tonight.

This is our country too. We didn't ask to come here when they brought us over here, and I hear the old statement over and over again about me to go back to Africa. Well, I'm ready to go back to Africa, baby, when all the Jews, the Poles, the Russians, the Germans and they all go back to their country where they came from too, you see. And they have to remember that they took this land from the Indians. And just as much as it's theirs, it's ours too now. We've got to stand up.

Stand up! Your neighbors down there who were too afraid to come to this memorial, take them to another memorial. . . . Make them register to vote and you register to vote. Go down there and do it. Don't bow down anymore! Hold your heads up!

We want our freedom now! I don't want to have to go to another memorial. I'm tired of funerals, tired of 'em! We've got to stand up.

The car is quiet again when Baba returns with the keys. Music muted. Windows down. We've arrived at a crossroads. Baba seems tranquil, wading in memories he'll never share, where the wounded parts of him have been abandoned. The blood on his hands.

The Maxima idles in front of railroad tracks.

"Put your seatbelt on," he says.

"I'm all set," I say.

"Put your seatbelt on."

"It's my car. I don't have to put my seatbelt on." I begin to laugh. I become giddy as my body begins to shake loose all the words I had buried in silence.

"Do you know where you are?" he says. "Do you know where you are? This isn't a joke! All they need is one thing to jam us up! You think they don't know that we're here?"

"I'm not tryin' to hear that shit! Ever since we got in the fuckin' car you been tryna' tell me what to do!"

"Let me out!" he says as he struggles with the door.

"Let yourself out."

"Let me out the car! Let me out the car!"

"Let yourself out the fuckin' car."

He recoils as if my words were clenched fists landing on his body. As if he doesn't recognize me. We idle there. His foot on the clutch and the brake, the Maxima between gears. We stare at each other. Eventually his eyes return to the road. He sits upright and begins calculating something. Fixes his eyes on what's in front of us. Begins to march deeper and deeper into himself. Into the bunker that allowed him to confront America's storm troopers. It will be easier for us to confront America's storm troopers than each other. He struggles to find first gear. And then we lurch across the tracks and keep lurching like we always have. Descend into pitch-black silence. Will remain there, with fresh scars and old wounds. We turn off the main road, and the streetlights become sporadic and then there are only headlights, occasional high beams, and the stars and the moon, and then bends in the road and more darkness, insects, big moths, Spanish moss, and, beyond that, maybe hyenas.

W. H. MOSES SERMON

RELIGION OF THE NEGRO

You know we preachers have been talking about revivals. We want a revival of religion. Well, most of us preachers would not know the Holy Spirit if we met it in the road. (*Laughter*) I mean to say we talk about a revival of religion. Most of us do not know our Bible when we see it. . . . Don't think that God runs nothing but churches. Don't think that the Lord is in business, taking up collections and ordaining preachers. Don't think that a revival consists of nothing but a "Glory Hallelujah." How the Spirit expresses Himself depends altogether on the circumstances. If the conditions are not such as would justify rejoicing but protest, then the Spirit expresses Itself or Himself in the spirit of protest.

———————

CHAPTER 5

Becoming Black

We were six and four when Maisha and I watched the black boys from our kitchen window as they eased their way through the alley in Peabody Terrace in cut jeans, canvas sneakers, mesh shirts hanging from muscles coiled to limbs, hair picked high and cropped low. The boys appeared twice our age, were warped like sticks, galloped like giraffes. Were hunters and hunted, armed with homemade slingshots. A gale of name-calling, laughter, barks, and whistling. History in pursuit propelled them through the alley toward predictable outcomes. They had names like Jay, Frankie, MB, AB. Some were black like crows, brown like dirt, brown like sand. They were from the Coast—what we called the Cambridge neighborhood that hugged the bend in the Charles River from Corporal Burns Park to the River Street bridge. They were grandsons and great-grandsons of men and women who had migrated from the South or the Caribbean. They lived in homes that their parents had purchased or inherited. Weathered three- and six-flat apartments scattered between Western Avenue and River Street—the blackened leaf of the Coast's otherwise white fan. They were from the Putnam Gardens Housing Project adjacent to the Martin Luther King Jr. Elementary School, across the street from Peabody Terrace.

I watched them clip a bird's wings once with their slingshots. The bird was black like them, with yellow-accented wings that opened as they cocked their rubber bands and released their rocks. Became barbarians. Gravity claimed the bird, one wing working furiously as the boys cheered and raced up the fence—a beating heart and broken wing suddenly at their feet. The severity of it would linger for a pulse—unsure of what to do with what they'd done; what wasn't dead but could no longer fly. They would leave it for the cats, or to drag itself under the guts of a car. They would uncoil their own wings after scaling the fence again, leaping from the top, becoming airborne.

Maisha and I remained on the kitchen floor to protest our arrival in America. A week would pass before we would go outside and kick the bank of dirt in the alley. It turned to smoke. Nothing grew but the stubborn blades of grass. The sign above our heads—"No Loitering"—was next to the sign that read "Harvard University Property." We were waiting for Baba. We were aliens. The black boys too. We could feel them now. The glass from the kitchen window no longer in the distance between us. Our spines pressed against the chain link. Their cadence was suddenly unfamiliar. Raised my skin. The sound of their words and limbs vibrating in the air, carving a path in the wind as they raced by. We watched as they became invisible in the slope of the alley. Reappeared momentarily, raced across the street, disappeared again behind the brick building at the mouth of Corporal Burns Park.

When Baba arrived with Taba, we walked together out of the alley into Corporal Burns Park. The decaying brick building at the entrance of the park had been a clubhouse. A boxing ring remained inside its caged windows. Between its sagging ropes was where the JDs once pummeled each other. Now it was padlocked, just another wall to piss on, trade insults and punches in front of. *JDs* was the label the Harvard students gave boys in the neighborhood they perceived to be juvenile delinquents. The JDs were born with names like Bruno, Jimmy, and Mark, names engraved in the brick with pocketknives or other sharp objects. They were shades of white. Skin white like snow, like pigs, like canaries. The great-grandchildren of Scottish and Irish immigrants who had worked in the now dormant or demolished factories along the banks of the Charles River.

On the other side of the clubhouse, I was momentarily blinded by the sun as it caromed off the surface of the river. I could hear other children in the park racing on their big wheels, parents calling their names, balls bouncing, balls hitting walls and rackets. Corporal Burns's basketball courts became visible. The courts were a watering hole. I could see silhouettes of men gathered like wildebeests and lions, alligators and gazelles. Taba and Maisha and I gathered around Baba like chicks. Walked the edge of an unmarked field where two of the JDs played stickball.

We stopped and watched as one of the boys threw and the other swung. A square drawn with chalk on a flag post indicated the strike zone. The flag post eclipsed the height of the fence that was crowned with dormant floodlights. The batter swung again and missed, cut a circle in the air. Stabbed the dirt with his mop stick to regain his balance. Chased the ball as it rebounded off the post, from a tuft of grass to a tuft of grass.

"Don't give me that shit no more!" The boy pointed the mop stick toward the sky, returned it to his shoulders, spit in the dirt as he waited for the next pitch.

"Home run! Home run!" he yelled.

We turned to watch the ball that he'd hit sail over the clubhouse; he ran as if the field had bases—a finger suspended in the air.

"That coulda been foul."

"Fuck you that was foul."

"Great swing," Baba said as the boy turned for home.

We continued walking. I could see the bodies of men stretched into thin shadows on the floor of the basketball court.

I was struck by a smell like tamarind, carried in the wind. I saw flat black pods, rotting on the asphalt around the trunk of a black locust tree, evoking Tanzania. I reached for one but there was nothing to peel, no pulp to suck, no boys hanging like pythons from the tree limbs.

To the right of the trees was the picnic area where the JDs hung from the slabs of cement tables and benches—Marlboros in fingers, Budweiser cans in fists. Beyond them was the cage, the black, coiled fence that wrapped around the park's two basketball courts and a tennis court. Music pumped from speakers hanging on the chain link. Clouds of ganja drifted in the air. We stood at the height of Baba's hips and watched as the ball moved from hand to hand to asphalt to air to hoop. It was immediately familiar. When I was two, Baba and I had spent a week in Zanzibar. I'd watched as the students he coached dribbled a basketball between poles in the dirt. Each basket was celebrated. A byproduct of some divine intervention. Baba said to get to Zanzibar we'd driven and taken a train and then a boat. That there'd been hippos in the ocean. That I had slept like a cub, growled in my sleep, pressed against his skin like a hot water bottle. That I had been a great companion.

My bad or *Good play* or *Common rookie!* the men at Corporal Burns said. *Take his money.*

He can't handle the rock.
Come an' get it.
I got next, make sure you got next!
Don't let that muthafucka talk you out your game.
We had arrived in Black America.

.   .   .

We were seven and five when Taba and I began exploring Peabody Terrace on our own. Our routine became taking a right out the door and up the alley, another right before the poles in the mouth of the alley, toward a thin walkway that was a shortcut to the field beneath our apartment's balcony.

"Go around," Baba had said the first time we approached the fence. We had walked with him down the alley, past our door, past doors 16 and 15 on our way to the underpass. The underpass led to a brick patio and then the sloped field beneath the balcony of our apartment.

A thick elm tree was rooted at its apex.

"Go," Baba said, and the three of us raced. Baba ran as slow as he needed to for me to win as Taba tried to keep up.

"Again," Taba said.

.   .   .

"Go around," I said, the first time Taba and I stood at the fence by ourselves.

"Go around," I said to him again, now halfway up the fence myself, unsure if I could make it over the top.

"Wait for me," he said as he began to climb too.

"Go around," I said, now at the top as I struggled to get over the twisted spikes of wire that crowned the fence.

"Wait for me," he said, now halfway up the fence as I grinned, passing him on my way down.

"Go around," I said. He knew if he did, he'd lose me.

"Wait for me," he said from the top.

I began walking to the field, was gonna take off when he made it to the other side.

"Wait!" he said. His shirt stuck on the fence.

"Wait!" I said as he struggled to unhook it. I ran toward him and climbed and for a moment we were eye to eye as I untangled him.

"Go back down," I said, but he wouldn't. He slowly worked his body over the spikes and then I began climbing down and jumped, this time turning in the air, falling forward, grinning as I took off across the field.

"Wait!" he said.

"Come on!"

The field was empty. I had hoped to find Imran there. He shared a journey like ours. He was from Kasur, a small village in the province of Punjab, Pakistan. Was nine when he was uprooted and transplanted to Peabody Terrace, was a teenager when I met him. "I didn't see another Pakistani until we moved to Canada five years later," he'd tell me, many years after that. He called the sloped field a football field. When we became friends he would tell me to meet him on the gridiron. He was often there by himself, shimmying with the NFL legends he attempted to embody. He didn't mind playing with me, a kid half his age, half his size, seemed to prefer it. He showed me how to line up, which *hike* meant *hike*; drew pass routes in the dirt with a stick.

"Jim Plunkett!" he'd say, most of the time he wanted to throw long.

"Ahmad Rashad!" he'd say while running under the ball.

"Earl Campbell!" he'd say as he pretended to bulldoze the Cowboy defensive line.

"Tony Dorsett!" he'd say as he stiff-armed the wind, his lean body mutating with each possession.

I ran across the grass, along the brick path, down the steps and into the courtyard. I ran until I couldn't hear Taba calling me, found satisfaction in controlling the distance between us. Usually I hid in a bush. Waited to pounce, to roll in the dirt, to square up like a cheetah. Days like this became a blur of stalked and stalking. When I didn't want to be followed, I would pummel Taba with his middle name—*Watabiri, Watabiri, Watabiri,* or *Wata*. He would always cry. Sometimes he would hit or bite. I was much stronger than him then.

"Go home," I would say.

Taba found me in the courtyard between two of Peabody Terrace's towers, at the tables in front of the convenience store. We sat catching our breaths within eyeshot of the river; strips of rose-colored clouds stretched over the dormant smokestacks in the distance. He smiled, wiped where the tears had cut a path in the dust on his face. There was a hole across the front of his shirt where it had gotten clipped by the fence. We wiped the scratch across his abdomen with spit to make sure he was finished bleeding.

"Let's climb it again," he said.

The courtyard was empty.

We walked toward the river; the sun was falling, turning the air orange. Rowers skirted the surface of the water like bugs. A man yelled, "Pull!" at the rowers through a bullhorn. We turned away from the river onto a field that ran parallel to the water.

We stuck close to the hedges. I would imagine the hedges were bushes along the dirt road in Tanzania. We grabbed sticks. Poked between branches. I told Taba we were looking for *nyoka*.

We searched with our sticks from leaf to leaf. We found dog shit. I told Taba that the dog shit was a lion's, that the ashen branches we found were the bones of a gazelle. We watched a rabbit dart across the grass. I told him that it would become dinner for nyoka coiled somewhere, longer than a school bus, big enough to swallow us whole, like the python the villagers had pulled from a tree, left in a cage, fed goats. Discarded wrappers became evidence of shed skin, the snake's existence. We found smaller, less nefarious things—an ant or bug, lots of worms. Attempted to catch bees in flight. Lured them to the end of our sticks and placed them in spider webs. Sometimes we would watch them wrestle with the silk threads. Sometimes a spider descended.

Beyond the hedges was the basketball court. The sound of black men playing ball. We tossed our sticks and walked, as if the fence was a wormhole, from the dirt road in Tanzania back into the heart of black America—the sound of niggas rappin' from scorched buildings, of hip-hop's primordial beats blasting from boom boxes hung on fences.

"Rapper's Delight" came out in '79. Mama was amused, said the shit won't last. "The Breaks" would come out in '80. "That's the Joint" in '81. "Planet Rock" in '82. We would have a record player by then, would spin those songs and *Space Cowboys* until the needle broke.

A game was in full swing. A man in a velvet sweat suit strutted like a rooster. His gold chains hung like an inverted plume to his stomach.

I'm gonna make you a star, he said as he stalked the sidelines with his chicks.

We found a seat on the court's curb. I had given some of the players the names of my favorite NBA stars—Dr. J, Chocolate Thunder, Mo Cheeks, Ice

Man, World B Free, Tiny. The play rose in intensity as the men approached
game over. A bucket didn't count if a foul was called. Brothers would hack
with impunity. Each call was protested.

Who got next? echoed on the sidelines when it was game over. A dozen
brothers sat on the curb of the court, unfolded their wings, released their
knees. Losing meant drinking beer and spanking dominos with the Bajans.
A half dozen balls were shot in the air. Some ricocheted toward us. Taba
and I would bounce the balls and pass them back. If we were lucky we'd
get a shot off.

· · ·

Taba and I found Imran on the other court with the men who weren't good
enough to play with Dip and Rudy, with the black boys whose game and
bodies were not developed enough to play with the men.

"Let's play horse," Imran said. "Can you spell? H-O-R-S-E. It doesn't
matter."

We swung the ball from our hips to reach the rim. Imran, who was
approaching high school, was happy about the appearance of competition.

"Tiny," he said, struggling to dribble the ball between his legs and
make a layup.

"Twice between the legs," he said when he finally did it.

"Cousy!" he said, dribbling with his head to the ground, attempting
a sky hook.

"Chocolate Thunder!" he said, his back to the basket, bulldozing
shadows.

"Dr. J!" he said as he leapt from the foul line.

"Ice Man!" he said as he launched a finger roll from the foul line. "One
more letter and you will be horses," he said.

"All of yous are horses," Bruno, one of the JDs, said from the other side
of the fence. He was tall and thick, every part of his body heavy. A fist was
wrapped around a can. He'd left the picnic area where the rest of the JDs
were drowning in Budweiser. Some were Imran's classmates. Sometimes
we sat with Imran on the outside of their circle.

"Ah you sure you don't know the ayatollah?" they would ask him. We
were over a hundred days into the Iranian hostage crisis.

"I am from Pakistan," Imran would say. Even Steve, who was from New
Mexico, had a picture of the Ayatollah Khomeini taped to a dartboard in

his room next to an American flag. Tried to impress us with the number of darts he could land in the ayatollah's eyes.

"Let me see if I can make it," Bruno said, motioning for Imran to throw the ball over the fence. We waited as he sat his beer in the grass.

"How do you spell *ayatollah*?" he asked.

"Too many letters," Imran said.

Bruno took off his shirt.

"He used to go to my school," Imran murmured to me. "He's still in love with my sister."

Bruno heaved the ball over the fence. The ball landed a few feet short of the hoop. Bounced over our heads.

"Give me a fuckin' *A*," he said. "Ah you sure you don't know the ayatollah?"

"I am from Pakistan," Imran said, returning the ball.

"Ain't you muslum?"

He was. Imran inspected every pastry in the convenience store for lard.

"I don't eat lard," Imran said.

"Give me a fuckin' *Y*," Bruno said.

"Last shot," Imran said.

"I need a refill," Bruno said, returning to the picnic area and taking the ball with him.

When Imran tried to get the ball back and returned ruffed up and empty-handed, Taba walked to the other half of the court and enlisted the black boys. We followed them into the picnic area where Bruno and the tallest black boy squared up. They swung at each other and then rolled on the ground and the tallest black boy wrapped his lanky arm around Bruno's thick neck and squeezed until Bruno began turning purple, until the other black boys were able to unhinge the two from each other. And then Bruno gasped for air and threw up the beer and the pink and purple things he had eaten.

Which established in our minds a natural hierarchy.

The black boys were on top, the local white boys in the middle, and the sons of Harvard students, for whom the fences were erected, languished, momentarily, at the bottom.

.   .   .

Taba and Imran and I stood on the other side of the chain link, on the sidewalk that bordered Memorial Drive. Behind us were the courts, the picnic area, the baseball field, Peabody Terrace's three high-rise towers. We had been instructed not to cross Memorial Drive unless with Mama or Baba, or on Sundays, when the drive was closed off to cars.

"Is this Peabody Terrace?" Taba asked, looking out across the river.

"It's all Peabody Terrace," Imran said. We began to gather rocks as we walked along the sidewalk and hoped they would land in the water as we threw them over the drive as hard as we could.

We returned to the brick path that led to the courtyard, past the third tower, convenience store, second tower, up the steps adjacent to the first tower, to Imran's football field.

Most of the field was shadow. A handful of boys tossed a football. The boys were happy to see Imran, needed more bodies.

I watched them throwing, catching, running. Imran just Imran. Ordinary among misfits. We were all from somewhere else, had a story that didn't belong to Harvard. Imran waved. Said that I was on his team. Most of the boys were twice my age. Steve hiked and blocked. I waited behind the quarterback as Imran ran routes, got stuck, slowly pulled himself from the grass.

The quarterback gave me the ball on fourth down. I was afraid of getting tackled. I searched for a hole, accelerated, and wiggled for my life past outstretched hands into the end zone.

"Touchdown!" Imran yelled, pumping a fist in the air.

"Jim Brown!" he said.

Baba found us there. He didn't call for us, just walked to the edge of the field and waited. Taba and I walked behind him through the underpass and up the alley.

"What happened to your shirt?" he asked Taba.

We were lathered in dirt, stained the color of grass.

"We climbed the fence," Taba said.

———

W. H. MOSES SERMON

NOTHING RIGHT TODAY

There comes a time when the Spirit of God takes the form of protest, and anything besides protest is a mockery of God and a mockery of justice. What are you going to say Glory Hallelujah for, when somebody is beating your boy? That is the spirit of the devil. Somebody has taken your homeland and is dominating the whole earth, and is not associating with you and does not want you to associate with yourself. And you stand grinning. Any spirit that makes you submit to that is the spirit of cowardice and the spirit of the devil. We have got to get a new kind of Holy Spirit here. That is all. I mean the spirit of protest. There is a spirit of love, there is a spirit of justice, there is a spirit of fair play, the spirit of a fair deal for everybody . . . , there is a spirit of protest; and the man who stands for that, the Spirit of God is upon him, and he has proclaimed the era of opportunity. He will pour out his Spirit upon all flesh.

Everybody will see, will find out what is right, and what is wrong and what is truth. And you have never seen so many folks in your life trying to straighten out the world as now. I mean white folks and black folks. I mean all sorts of folks. The world knows this world is not running right. Hardly anything is running right. Talk about great cities like New York, London, and Paris: and men living like devils in hell, can hardly get bread! Working from dawn to sunset and cannot get a decent livelihood! That is not right.

CHAPTER 6

Cookie and the Dust

ROBERT MOSES'S ACCOUNT OF VOTER REGISTRATION DRIVE IN MISSISSIPPI IN 1961

00:05:29 Robert P. Moses

Ah, we worked out a plan first whereby some of the students, John Hardy and two other students, who had just come off the Freedom Rides,[1] went into Walthall County to begin work.

That was about the middle of August. At about the same time I accompanied three people down to Liberty in Amite County in our first registration attempt there. One was a very old man and then two ladies, middle aged. We left early morning of August 15; it was Tuesday.

00:05:55 Robert P. Moses

We arrived at the courthouse about ten o'clock. The registrar came out.

00:06:02 Robert P. Moses

I waited by the side waiting for either the farmer or one of the two ladies to say something to the registrar. He asked them what did they want, what were they here for, in a very rough tone of voice. They didn't say anything; they were literally paralyzed with fear.

00:06:24 Robert P. Moses

So after a while I spoke up and said, "Uh, they would like to come to register, to try and register to vote." So he asked, "Well, who are you, what do you, what do you have to do with them, are you here to register?" So I told them who I was and that we were conducting a school in McComb and that these people had attended the school and that they wanted an opportunity to register. "Well," he said, "they'll have to wait," because there was somebody there filling out the form. Well there was a young white lady there with her husband and she was sitting down and completing the registration form. Um, when she finished then our people started to register, one at a time. In the meantime a procession of people began moving in and out of the registration office: the sheriff, a couple of his deputies, people from the office next door, people from the tax office, people um, from, who do the driver's license, looking in, staring and moving back out, muttering. A highway patrolman finally came in and sat down in the office. And we stayed that way in sort of uneasy tension all morning. The first person who filled out the form took a long time to do it. And it was noon time before he was finished. When we came back I was not permitted to stay in the office but had to leave and sit on the front porch, which I did. We finally finished the whole process about four thirty. All of the three people had had a chance to register. This was at least to fill out the form. This was a victory because they had been down several times before and had not had a chance even to fill out the forms.

00:08:19 Robert P. Moses

On the way home we were followed by the highway patrolman, who had spent the day in the registrar's office, office of Carwile. He tailed us about ten miles or about, very close—about twenty, twenty-five feet behind us all the way back

00:08:37 Robert P. Moses

towards McComb. At one point we pulled off the road and he passed us and circled around and came back and we pulled up as he was passing us in the opposite direction and then he turned around and followed us again. Well, finally he blew us down and I got out of the car. Asked him what the trouble was because the people in the car by that time were very, very frightened.

00:08:59 Robert P. Moses

He asked me who I was, what my business was. And told me that I was interfering in what he was doing. I said I simply wanted to find out what the problem was and what we were being stopped for. He told me to get back in the car. As I did so I jotted his name down. He then opened the car door and pushed me and said, "Get in the car, nigger," and slammed the door after, after me. He then told us to follow him in the car and he took us over to McComb where I was told that I was placed under arrest. They called up the county prosecuting attorney. He came down and he and the highway patrolman then sat down and opened up the law books and looked through to find out a charge. They first charged me with interfering with an officer in the process of arresting somebody and then found out that the only person arrested was myself and they changed the charge to interfering with an officer in the discharge of his duties. The county attorney asked me if I was ready for the trial I said, "Could I make a phone call?" He said yes, so I picked up the phone and called Washington DC—the Justice Department—because I'd been in communication with some members of the Justice Department, particularly John Doerr, and I'd received letters saying, delineating, those sections of the Civil Rights Acts of 1957 and 1960 which guarantee protection to people who are trying to register and to anyone who's aiding other people in trying to register. And he had also indicated that if we had any trouble we were to call Washington or the nearest office of the FBI. So I called him, collect. The people in the office were rather astonished at the, at the fact that the call went through, and then they began to get fidgety. Well . . . I explained to Mr. Doerr exactly what happened in their presence and told them, uh, told him that I thought we were being intimidated simply because the people had tried to go down to register.

00:11:08 Robert P. Moses

Well, we had the trial right after that; I was found guilty of this charge of interfering with an officer, and the judge and the county prosecuting attorney went out, consulted, and came back and I was given a suspended sentence, ninety-day suspended sentence, and fined five dollars for cost of court.

· · ·

We drive by a handful of schools on our way to Brinkley, the middle school where we'll be working, one of ten middle schools in Jackson, Mississippi. Taba and our cousin Spice flew in last night from Cambridge. Taba is in the passenger seat in the Maxima with me. Spice is with Baba in a rental car.

With each school we pass I wonder how many Algebra Project class-rooms it will take to bring about the changes in Mississippi, in America, that Baba and his comrades had been willing to die for in the '60s. It had been one thing to organize sharecroppers to demand the right to vote. From my short stints helping in Algebra Project classrooms when I was in college, it seemed like a whole other thing to get students to make a demand (en masse) for a high-quality education. That what a student had to confront in making that demand—themselves, their peers, their teachers, their cul-ture, the school building, the public education system, America's past and present economic arrangements—was a lot to try to wrap a middle school head around. That, unlike a "Whites Only" sign, it was difficult to put a finger on what needed to be confronted and how.

Baba would describe what needed to be confronted as sharecropper education. Which always needs explaining. Most people don't know what a sharecropper is. A sharecropper is what enslaved Africans became af-ter emancipation, around the time Jim Crow was born, when they were forced to remain on or return to the plantation. Baba defines sharecropper education as "a certain group of people got a certain type of education to do a certain type of work," a reality as entrenched in Massachusetts as in Mississippi. Mama calls it caste in the classroom. Which also needs explaining—most people associate caste with an Indian in India forced to clean up shit for a living.

Most of the schools we pass are adjacent to large grass fields inscribed by running tracks. Women walk around them briskly with sticks, appear serious about getting their hearts beating. The sticks, I realize, are for fighting off the packs of wild dogs that roam the neighborhoods and fuck on the edge of the road and in the middle of the field. I have already seen them get stuck, big dog mounting little dog, conjoined, pulling and yelping, trying to extract big dog penises from little dog vaginas while the rest of the males nip at their heels, bite each other for a turn. Cookie, a student at Brinkley, will tell me, "The only way to get them unstuck is to pour hot water on them."

We drive on Beasley Road, where the asphalt is fresh—the Maxima glides like it still has less than twenty thousand miles on the speedometer. The trees that line the road, draped in Spanish moss, evoke an older time when the land had been wilderness, swamp. My understanding of what dif-ferentiates city and suburb and country feels irrelevant here. The ranch-style fences and vast untamed fields and solitary oaks bleed into enclaves with names like Woodhaven and Woodcrest and Woodlee and manicured lawns with long driveways with fleets of cars and cavernous houses. I see brothas in robes and slippers collecting newspapers. I stare as if they are from another planet. The image is alien to my black experience.

An old airplane hangar houses crop dusters, sits on the corner of Beasley and State, which runs parallel to the train tracks. It is not clear to me where the planes take off from and land. The hangar has the same Delta insignia of the plane that Taba and Spice and the dogs arrived on. Mama says that Delta began as a fleet of crop dusters. That crop dusters were used to spy on them in the movement. I find it hard to imagine Delta Airlines beginning on a strip of dirt in a Mississippi field. I wonder if one has something to do with the other.

We drive across the train tracks, Baba and Spice leading the way, and then we drive next to each other, nudge Baba a couple more miles per hour as we follow the tracks downtown. In the rearview the tracks continue toward Memphis. The tracks carry excruciatingly long freighters with endless arrays of flatbeds, hoppers, tankers, and boxcars that haul shit from one side of the country to another. I begin to see firsthand America's industrial and agricultural bones.

"What we doin', yo?" Taba asks. The idea that we are on the road together, will always be on the road together, remains unspoken.

Taba and Spice arrived last night at the Jackson International Airport on different flights within an hour of each other. Taba swayed side to side, feet pointed outward as he moved forward in a more pronounced version of my stride, moving past security, past the blues bar and gift shop, and then down the escalator where the bags arrived. Men wearing red caps greeted Taba like he belonged to Mississippi. They wore shorts and buttoned short-sleeve shirts, appeared swole, some as thick as oak trees, offered to help with his luggage.

"Yo, what up," Taba said to them, as if they smoked, shot dice together.

"Y'all twins?" they asked Taba and me. "Who older?"

Spice was slightly pigeon-toed from when we were kids and he got hit by a bike and spent most of a year immobilized in casts. I could see this in his stride as he loped toward us in the baggage claim, how his body had absorbed that bike, the stunted athleticism. He and Taba and I were all cousins because we'd grown up in Cambridge among a village of almost all black parents, most of whom had at least attended college, who had decided to wrap their arms around each other's children. Most of the children were boys and around the same age. Maisha was the oldest. Spice was a birdwatcher then, had a poster of birds on his wall at home, went places where he could find them, listen, sound like them. In high school he replaced the posters of warblers and owls with Malcolm X and Bob Marley and joined a crew of boys who had become Jamaican and militant. Cloaked in essential oils and medallions, adopting creole accents, chewing on root sticks and rap lyrics, growing dreads. They raised their fists in the air as if a high school common room in Cambridge could be a corner of 1960s Harlem. The snow bunnies, what we called the white girls, loved them. The love was reciprocated. There was more to it than bottomless blow jobs—the entanglement of black male parts and white female parts.

Something had happened to Taba and Spice's luggage back in Atlanta and so we stood outside of the airport and waited with Baba as he sat in the rental car with the windows down, blasting a CD of a lecture of one of his gurus: *Dear students, from all over, and friends, I know many of you have had wonderful experiences, today, and that's what you should remember, that in meditation depth is the principal thing. Every day's meditation must be deeper than the previous day, then you will reach God quicker—*

Outside was an oven.

—but until, your mind gets used to intensity of meditation, it will not appreciate long meditation—

Taba took his shirt off first, and then we were all standing on the curb in wife beaters.

I hope that this will be an example before your mind, that whenever you can, four times a month, or even once a month, if you can take several hours off, and intensely meditate, you will feel yourself closer to God, Christ, and the Masters, than ever. . . .

I opened the passenger door of the Maxima, which was parked behind Baba, and turned the music up to quiet the gurus.

The heat unleashed Spice's dreads from their kufi.

"When the dogs comin'?" he asked. Tyson and the two puppies would arrive on the next plane from Atlanta.

"What did they say about the luggage?" Baba asked.

"It's on the plane with the dogs," I said.

When the dogs and the luggage arrived and we made it to the apartment, Taba and Spice dropped their bags and inspected the rooms—bare walls and thin carpet and beneath that the house's concrete foundation. We would sleep on sheets on the floor. Taba set up the PlayStation in the living room. I turned up Biggie Smalls. Soon I was kickin' both of their asses in Battle Arena Toshinden. Spice took his ass-whuppin' seriously. I had discovered Paul Masson, a potent cognac, at the liquor store gas station on the corner. We drank it with orange juice. Spice had smuggled weed on the plane, in his dreads or between his cheeks or under his balls.

"The dreads are more than dreads," Spice said.

"The smoke is more than smoke," Taba replied. The dogs were visible through the glass sliding doors, their muzzles hitched to the cement patio on the lip of the backyard. On the screen the fighter Spice had picked kept sayin', "I never give up," as my guy shanked her with a long spear.

"*Gariyaa!*" my guy said.

"Yo, if you didn't have that fucking spear I'd fuck you up," Spice said.

"Pick him. I'll pick her," I said, so that they would know it wasn't just the long spear kickin' their ass. Spice's dreads appeared unlike any dreads we'd seen before, poking out to the sides, some up like antennae, some threaded across his forehead, a few hanging from the back. In the haze of smoke and Paul Masson he confessed that the dreads in the front were more like a cap, that underneath was bald. He showed us what he was talking about, said that he'd begun losing his cabbage in college.

"All that fuckin' chlorine," Taba said, "you shoulda quit swimming when we did."

"*Gariyaa!*" my guy said.

Baba came in the living room to tell us what time he was leaving to go to Brinkley in the morning. He was excited that we were together in Mississippi. He would never admit it, that he had spent our lifetimes preparing and recruiting us to join him on the battlefield.

"*Gariyaa!*" my guy said.

"I never give up," Spice's girl said.

.   .   .

I continue to count the schools we pass, as Taba and I drive behind Spice and Baba. Watkins Elementary is situated on a corner across from the "Good

Hands Man"—a large parking lot where the Good Hands Man hand washes cars, sells T-shirts and legal insurance, will hawk bootleg CDs and fake Jordans from China as local markets become global. Powell Elementary sits on Livingston Road, past the mobile police station on the corner. The houses here are more modest than the ones we passed on Beasley Road (still suburban-looking to me), fewer cars parked in shorter driveways, the grass less green. Sturdy women walk with their sticks around the school tracks. Children burst from a convoy of school buses. We continue to drive parallel to the railroad tracks. There is a bar at the railroad crossing named The Crossroads. There is also Bully's, a family-owned soul food restaurant, just before The Crossroads. Taba, who has been traveling with Baba to Jackson for a year now, will take us there for lunch, and Bully will serve us with a big fat gun on his hip as he guards the cash register and his sisters and his wife, who cook and serve the food, who appear part Pocahontas.

Taba can see the head of a freight train coming and says, "Turn," so that we avoid the railroad crossing, which is how Baba ends up behind us. We turn again, drive between the pine-tarred pillars of a small rickety bridge on which the train tracks run. It doesn't look capable of holding the freighter. A farmer sits on the corner next to a steel barrel that ejects smoke, has erected a roadside market where he sells fruits and vegetables and coon and possum and muscadines, boiled peanuts and peanut brittle. *Coon* and *possum* are written on cardboard—will arrest my eyes every time we drive under the bridge. Eventually we will stop on that patch of dirt, buy muscadines and peanut brittle so that we can lay our eyes on the skinned vermin.

We pass a creek where Cookie, as he will tell us, played with all his classmates when they were little, caught frogs and crawfish and moccasins; and then a nine-hole golf course with carts and black men in white shoes and shorts—it is the first time I've seen black people play golf; and then we turn again, pass the Christ Missionary and Industrial College with a placard saying it was founded in 1897. It is one of many examples, like the Rosenwald schools erected across the South, of institutions that were built to move formerly enslaved Africans off the plantation and into society.

The street ends and we idle at the corner, face a row of three identical shotgun shacks. Each has two sets of three cement steps, a combined porch, and doors for two units. Each apartment is the width of a hallway, with rooms lined up one in front of the other. We turn left on Ridgeway and Baba follows us into the Brinkley Middle School parking lot next door to the shacks, which feel like they belong on a plantation. The proximity of the school to these remnants of a plantation illustrates the short distance that black America has traveled from enslaved Africans.

"Let's get a move on. We're going to be late," Baba says.

It is a hundred degrees in the parking lot. A hundred more in our Timberlands. What we have only perceived of as "history" is suddenly perpendicular behind us. We will have the rest of our lives to attempt to reconcile the remarkably short distance we have traveled from America's cotton fields.

Brinkley, like most public schools in Jackson, is 90-something percent black students and mostly white teachers and administrators, with a white principal. The doors are red, the AC high, and the contrast in temperature abrupt, like stepping from a sauna into an igloo. My skin is still perspiring. I tug on my shirt—the air is damp and cold between my shirt and skin. I feel the urge to go back outside, take my shirt off, bake in the heat. Khari and Taba and I have done this Algebra Project ritual at other schools before— introducing ourselves to the principal, the teachers, the guidance counselors, security guards, the janitors—and Taba has already done it at Brinkley.

The principal, Mr. Acton, strides out of his office, swallows our hands with his. He is a lumberjack with thick glasses. We follow him into his office. Baba and then us. Baba is the captain. A picture of the first President Bush hangs in Acton's office. "You see that," Baba will say. Mr. Acton is a descendant of those southern Democrats that became Republicans. He looks like he could belong in the crowd of images from the book of lynching that Mama planted on our kitchen table in Peabody Terrace when we arrived in America. He is gracious, with requisite Southern hospitality. The school is his plantation. We begin talking about the role the Algebra Project could play in the building. Baba and Taba have been working with the students here off and on for the past two years. Mr. Acton seems conflicted, begins talking about boys needing mentors, that they are going to build a canoe this year like the Tunica, Quapaw, Chickasaw, Ofo, Natchez, Houma, and Choctaw. Chop the wood and cut it out and cook it and sand and stain it. Put it in the water and float with it. I struggle to make the connections he has made between the descendants of Africans and Indians. Between canoe building and what it will take for "his boys" to be successful. It sounds like the canoe will be put on display in the lobby, that a handful of boys will make it and float with it. He talks about a bluesman who is teaching the kids the blues. That the bluesman and the kids have gigs singing the blues in schools across the country. That maybe we should collaborate. He and Baba seem to be on the same page about this, but I don't know what the fuck they're talking about. Am clueless about the mechanics of a school building, what the blues has to do with the manufacturing of quality students. I extrapolate there is a woman named Kay who Baba has recruited to teach the kids how to develop math dances. I want to see this. Taba and I were breakdancers when we were the students' age. We would count how many windmills we could do while holding our balls. Baba is excited about the collaboration, wants kids to perform what they're learning for other kids. It sounds like they have found some money in the school's budget for Kay. "The AP has been a blessing for our school," Mr. Acton says. He is happy to have us. And then Baba gets down to business, begins talking money to help the Algebra Project pay me and Taba and Spice (there will never be money in the school's budget to pay us), about turning the old unused science room into a math lab, about preparing the entire eighth-grade class to take the state's Algebra 1 test.

"Even the kids in special education?" Mr. Acton asks, chewing on Baba's vision. Baba is more serious now as he leans forward, his eyebrows start to furrow.

"We need to raise the floor," he insists.

Mr. Acton doesn't respond. He will leave the school at the end of the year.

·　·　·

"My name is Omo, or Omowale," I say. We begin introducing ourselves in Mrs. Byrd's eighth-grade classroom. There isn't anything yet to distinguish Mrs. Byrd's room as an Algebra Project classroom, except the students. Baba and Taba have been working with them since they were in sixth grade. Most are happy to see my father. All of them are happy to see Taba. Baba has the students rearrange their desks in groups, asks each of us—Spice, Taba, and me—to join a group. The students introduce themselves, share their names and something about themselves. Baba asks them to do it again if they don't speak up, or clearly. We stand up when it is our turn.

"Omo what?"

The Dust, a student who'd laughed when I'd first sat next to him, starts laughing again. And then I begin to say that I grew up in Cambridge, and he raises his hand and I stop talking and then he says, "Never mind," and the rest of the class starts laughing.

"OK, OK," he says when Mrs. Byrd says, "Antonio." "I'll try to pay attention."

Later, when Cookie and I become friends, he will confess that he and Dusty were born on drugs. "I know what he's dealing with," he will say—about the struggle to keep their bodies still, string thoughts together.

"You Taba's brother?" the students ask.

"Mmm hmm," some of the girls say.

"Yeah."

"And cousin?" they ask Khari.

"Yeah."

"What you call that?" they ask, pointing at his hair.

"Dreads," Khari says.

"You Mr. Moses's sons?"

"Yeah," I say.

"Where you from?"

"Cambridge," I say.

"Near Harvard University," Spice says.

"Boston," I say.

"New England," Spice says.

"You from New England?"

"Where's that?"

"How come you talk like you from England?"

"They from NEW England, god dammit!"

"Antonio!" Mrs. Byrd says.

"How come your name's like that?"

"I was born in Tanzania?" I say.

"Where's that?"

"Africa."

"You African?"

"Yeah." The class erupts again.

"You're African too," I say. They grow silent.

"Ooooo," they say, like someone got punched in the face.

"You got me fucked up," Dusty says.

"Antonio!" Mrs. Byrd says. "Come here. Now!"

"I ain't no African."

"You from Africa?" they ask Khari. He shakes his head.

"How come you ain't from Africa too?"

. . .

The hallway floods with students every fifty-five minutes. Waves of bodies are released from desks and chairs, become a current of ebony and red-boned skin. We are baptized in their receding flesh, as if wading into a restless ocean. Some students surround us, put their hands on us.

"What up, yo!" the boys say, mimicking our East Coast accents, attempt to teach us their handshakes, initiate us into their neighborhoods.

"You Mr. Moses's son?" Tasaunda asks me, wraps her arms around my waist, presses her ear to my stomach, darts off to her next class.

"How come you got that good hair and your brother don't?" another girl says, giggling.

Within seconds the hallway becomes silent, empty beach, except for the stragglers, what the tide left behind. Mrs. Edwards stands in front of her room at the end of the hallway, arms folded against her chest, the walls amplifying her raspy voice. She instructs the stragglers to begin alligator-walking from her doorway to the end of the hallway. Their bodies become parallel to the ground, a hand and foot reach forward simultaneously, their asses rising with each step.

"Keep your rears out the air," Mrs. Edwards says. Most make it as far as the next classroom before collapsing.

"Get up," she says. The kids begin alligator-walking again, collapse at the next classroom door.

"All the way down and back," she says.

———————

In 1998 Baba's comrade Charlie Cobb began working with him to write *Radical Equations*, a book about their seminal voter registration efforts in Mississippi in the 1960s and the reincarnation of that work through the birth of the Algebra Project. I know him as Uncle Charlie. There are pictures of us with him in Tanzania. In preparation for writing the book, Uncle Charlie interviewed some of the Algebra Project students, teachers, and parents that we'd worked with while in Mississippi.

ALGEBRA PROJECT INTERVIEWS CONDUCTED
BY CHARLIE COBB FOR *RADICAL EQUATIONS* (1998)

UNCLE CHARLIE: OK. Let's start. Just give me your whole name and grade. It's just like a conversation more than an interview. Go ahead. Give me your name and, you know, how you want to be called, and your grade, and your age and grade.

COOKIE: My name is Sammie, Sammie Myers. I'm in the eleventh grade, seventeen. And my nickname is Cookie.

UNCLE CHARLIE: Aha.

COOKIE: Like I'm a cookie.

UNCLE CHARLIE: Because?

COOKIE: Because I used to just walk around the neighborhood eating cookies all the time. And the teachers, they call me Cookie, too, because I used to hide them in my pockets.

UNCLE CHARLIE: Where do you live?

COOKIE: In Georgetown, over by (indiscernible).

UNCLE CHARLIE: And you're in the eleventh grade?

COOKIE: Yeah.

UNCLE CHARLIE: OK. Now, let me pick up on what you were telling that lady there. How come you don't like school?

COOKIE: Well, it's kind of personal. But the neighborhood I live in, there's like a lot of gang violence. If you pay attention to what they say on the news. But it ain't really bad; it's the people that are there. You've got, you've got one gang on this side of the school, and another gang on this side of the school. The school separates the gang. And both gangs go to the school but they don't like each other. They've been around for like a hundred years over there. It's been like that for a long time.

UNCLE CHARLIE: Do those gangs have a name?

COOKIE: Yeah.

UNCLE CHARLIE: What? No? OK. What's the issue? They just don't like each other—

COOKIE: Well, now, it ain't really a gang; it's neighborhood. See, the gang stuff is really dying out. It's just neighborhoods.

UNCLE CHARLIE: So the gang stuff is dying out.

COOKIE: Yeah.

UNCLE CHARLIE: But the neighborhoods are still—

COOKIE: But it's like neighborhood against neighborhood.

UNCLE CHARLIE: Oh. Well, where are the grown-ups in all this?

COOKIE: What you mean?

UNCLE CHARLIE: I mean, how come . . . the conflict is between young people? Or it's not.

COOKIE: Yeah.

UNCLE CHARLIE: It's between grown-ups?

COOKIE: No, no, no. And most of it, there's a lot of—us young boys trying to follow in our big brother, our uncle, whoever—footsteps. And being in that neighborhood and growing up in that neighborhood, we know what's happened in the past. And we just—it really just —They want something to call their own, that we decide, OK, yeah, they can't come over here and shoot basketball on our court. Our (indiscernible) here from their neighborhood, and we can't shoot basketball in our own court. It might be just something like this, something simple.

UNCLE CHARLIE: So that's— Anyway, we were talking about why you didn't like school.

COOKIE: Yeah, because—

UNCLE CHARLIE: So it's because of that.

COOKIE: Yeah.

UNCLE CHARLIE: So how are you doing in school?

COOKIE: All right.

UNCLE CHARLIE: Are your grades up?

COOKIE: No, not really. Ain't where I want them to be. Passing barely, but.

UNCLE CHARLIE: You're not failing anything?

COOKIE: No, I've just got to get it together.

UNCLE CHARLIE: Are you going regularly?

COOKIE: Huh?

UNCLE CHARLIE: Are you going to school every day?

COOKIE: Not every day.

UNCLE CHARLIE: Not every day? Most of the time?

COOKIE: Yeah.

UNCLE CHARLIE: You're sure?

COOKIE: Just give it that "most."

UNCLE CHARLIE: Most of the time, give you that most.

COOKIE: Yeah. My mother's sick.

UNCLE CHARLIE: Sorry to hear that.

COOKIE: Well, that's been a good experience for me, because I had— I took a class at— I don't know what you want to call it. If they want to stay home, like the kids can take them, their son or whatever. I took a class; I can learn how to give her her shot soon. Something goes wrong, how to handle it. I was just learning a whole lot of stuff.

UNCLE CHARLIE: What's she sick with, do you mind? Is it something you want to keep to yourself?

COOKIE: Yeah.

UNCLE CHARLIE: OK. Father?

COOKIE: Huh?

UNCLE CHARLIE: Father? Or, are you the man of the house?

COOKIE: Yeah. My dad he lives overseas somewhere.

UNCLE CHARLIE: You have brothers and sisters?

COOKIE: Yeah.

UNCLE CHARLIE: How many?

COOKIE: I got four brothers and two sisters.

UNCLE CHARLIE: Younger or older?

COOKIE: Older.

UNCLE CHARLIE: So what do you like best in school?

COOKIE: What subject, or what I like?

UNCLE CHARLIE: Yeah.

COOKIE: What you mean?

UNCLE CHARLIE: What subject?

COOKIE: I have to go with English.

UNCLE CHARLIE: English?

COOKIE: Yeah.

UNCLE CHARLIE: Why?

COOKIE: I don't know why. But like in the seventh grade I wanted to be a writer. I started writing some, I'll get to—but I just can't—when I start writing I start getting a headache.

UNCLE CHARLIE: You start getting a headache?

COOKIE: Yeah.

UNCLE CHARLIE: How come you get a headache from writing?

COOKIE: I be trying to think. Now I'm saying on my own. I ain't talking about in school.

UNCLE CHARLIE: And your head starts to hurt?

COOKIE: Yeah. And like when I read, I like reading a lot of stuff. Like *Make Me Wanna Holler*.

UNCLE CHARLIE: *Make Me Wanna Holler*? Yeah, Nathan McCall's book?

COOKIE: McCall, yeah. I want to write a book something like that, like the way I grew up, like I live the longest—like my book going to be more pages.

(*Laughter*)

UNCLE CHARLIE: So let's talk about—when did you first get involved in the Algebra Project?

COOKIE: Well, I went—I didn't get in until sixth grade, but I had met Taba. I was kind of doing something I didn't have no business doing. He's like, "Little man, come here. What grade you in?" I was like, "Fifth grade"—I was in fifth grade.

UNCLE CHARLIE: Mm-hmm.

COOKIE: "What school are you going to next year?" I was like, "Brinkley." See, he had just came down and he wasn't knowing nobody. Now doing—seeing me doing—he knew a little something about that, so he talked to me—

UNCLE CHARLIE: What were you doing?

COOKIE: So he talked to me. I can tell you, but I don't—

UNCLE CHARLIE: It's OK.

COOKIE: Yeah. So, he's like, "Little man, come here." You know how they talk—"Hey, yo, come here." And like, "Well, what you doing?" Like "Man, you know." Like that. I'm just trying to talk all cool to him. And he asked me what school I was going to. I was like, "Oh, (indiscernible) Brinkley—that's (indiscernible), right there."

UNCLE CHARLIE: Mm-hmm.

COOKIE: We've got a choice.

UNCLE CHARLIE: Go to either one?

COOKIE: Yeah, because they was so close to each other. And then he was like— like, come over to Brinkley. I'm going to be working on an Algebra Project in Miss Moss's class. All right. So after a while we had started kicking it with each other on the summer, just kicking it, you know, just having fun, or hanging out.

. . .

The first time I go to pick Cookie up I don't want to go inside his house. Home is a place that struggles to keep him dry and warm. Part of me doesn't want to intrude, part of me is squeamish, doesn't want to touch the insides of his struggle. When the front door opens, I can see the blue flames from an open gas stove beating back the darkness. He lives in what a child of Harvard University students can only describe as a shack on the edge of a nameless strip of dirt that leads to a creek. He smiles. His smile is born from an appreciation of life, of embracing what's been required of him to survive, becomes self-conscious as it grows wide enough to reveal his teeth, which are round in the shape of a cookie, like he'd sucked on his thumb too long.

"That's why they call you Cookie," I want to say. He reminds me of the runt in the Rottweiler litter that Taba and I had raised. The puppy who'd had to fight its way to its mother's tit for what was left of her milk. Cookie's eyes convey that he understands what it means to teeter on and grow from the precipice of life. His mother, who looks like him, is more skin and bones, with somber eyes that convey the weight of life on her body and spirit. She recognizes me as Taba's brother and because of that allows Cookie to come with me. Cookie and Dusty are the first students I kick it with outside of Brinkley.

Taba and Khari and I spend the remainder of the week getting to know students' names, building relationships with them and their teachers. Below the surface of it we are conscientiously confronting, in some ways for the first time, our own relationship with America's classrooms and cotton fields. How that system of economic exploitation and extraction and the culture it produced has materialized in our lives.

"Culture and economy are inseparable," John Mohawk said. "Even spiritual life revolves to a considerable extent around the ways that people see their lives supported. Indeed, it is arguable that people's personal relationships, and their relationships to their environment, are molded by the ways in which they meet their needs."[2]

Each student is a mirror, forcing us to reflect on why we need to rock Timberland boots with shorts sagging from our ass in oven-degree heat. Our style rooted in the articulation of each black generation's journey—from Africa to enslaved to contested citizen in the creation of the spirituals and blues and jazz and rock and roll and soul and now hip-hop. The "sharecropper music" that grew out of the Mississippi Delta and became the blues became the street music that grew from the rubble of the South Bronx, permeating black culture, eventually American culture, eventually global culture, enabling Brinkley students to recognize and embrace our style, which signified that though we were from a different part of the country, from different circumstances, we were coming from the same place.

In the waves of students that rose and fell against us in the hallway I could see versions of the crew of brothers Taba and I had run in and out of the projects with—brothers who, in the shadows of Harvard and MIT, were being educated to drive Cambridge's orange public works department pick-up trucks, to ride on the back of trash trucks, to become meter maids and police officers, to land in the Charles Street jail, omnipresent across the bridge on the Boston side of the Charles River, predestined for America's prisons like the Indians in India born to clean shit for a living.

·   ·   ·

Outside again is blinding heat, stewed chicken and mustard greens, yams and black-eyed peas, peach cobbler and sweet tea from Bully's on the hood of Baba's rental car in the parking lot next to the shotgun shacks. We will do this again and again until the cadence of it, day to day, week to week, turns into years. Baba eats a sandwich from the Rainbow Co-op, the only vegan store in Jackson. We chase the food with ginger beer. It is one of a few rituals that allow Baba and me to relate to each other outside the Algebra Project, as father and son.

Baba and I watch as a wave of Brinkley students spills out of the building through the gymnasium doors after band practice, becomes an impromptu marching band, plastic tubas tucked around waists, trumpets to lips, snare and bass drums, clarinets and saxophones beginning to find a groove. I walk to the edge of the parking lot to see how far they will go. They march a straight shot past a church, an abandoned bar, the parking lot of the adjacent laundry mat and candy store, pausing to drop each other off at each other's stoops until the last instrument arrives in a front yard. Watching them is uplifting. Dusty follows the music on a bicycle and then winds his way back to where we are, grinning. The color of his skin is almost indigo, his nose straight, eyelashes curled, his body wiry.

"What up, yo. Let me get some of that, yo," Dusty says, laughing as he points to the food. "Where Taba and Khari at, yo?"

Taba and Spice have taken the Maxima and are headed to the liquor store to grab a bottle of Paul Masson and a gallon of orange juice to celebrate our first week in Mississippi and to let the dogs out.

"Don't let them shit in the neighbor's yard," I said. In the morning I had walked Tyson and the two puppies to the back of our yard to shit near the creek. Tyson and I had unknowingly ended up in the neighbor's yard. The man looked like some version of the law, shaven like a marine, came out to meet me in the first stages of fixing a tie. I thought he was coming to say hi, and then I noticed he had a heater on his hip. His wife and kids wouldn't speak to us when he was around.

"Hold that dog," he'd said.

"He's OK."

"Hold that dog!" He pointed to a small pole with a flag. "Don't let those dogs in my yard."

"I thought this was my yard."

"I'm just warning you," he said. "I don't want those dogs shitting in my yard."

"Fuck him," Taba had said, when I told him what had happened. "I'm gonna let 'em shit in his yard."

"Where you been?" I ask Dusty.

We'd been looking for him all week. Dusty and Cookie were the type of rebellious students that schools shipped to prison. Baba knew that if we could make Brinkley work for them, then it could work for all those students marching themselves home.

"They suspended me, yo."

"You sound like you're from Boston."

"I am, yo," he says, laughing.

"For what?"

"They got me fucked up, yo, if they think I'm finna alligator-walk that whole goddamn hallway." And then he laughs again. "What you doin' for it? Let me hold somethin'."

"How many days you get?" I ask.

"I don't know."

Baba wants to know if his mama is home.

"Naaa, but my granmama is."

Baba and I walk behind him as he gets on his bike and zigzags the few blocks to his yard.

"That's Dip," he says, "my granmama's boyfriend." Dip's feet poke out from under the belly of the car parked in the dirt between their porch and the curb.

We wait in front of the porch while Dusty goes inside. Dip comes out from under the car, unshaven, big caged-animal eyes, hands and lips black as the Maconde statues in our family home.

"Who you here for?"

"Dusty," I said, then, "Antonio."

"Hole on a minute," he says, then goes in the house.

Dusty returns to the porch with his mother's mother. She is shorter than Dusty; she wears glasses, a Shoney's shirt, her hair different shades of gray, cropped close, maybe a wig.

"Granmama, these are my math teachers," he says.

"How y'all doin'?" she says. Baba stands with one foot on the step, the other in a patch of soot. As I watch him, I feel as if I have been cut and pasted into the books about the Civil Rights Movement that publishers would send to our home on School Street, that Mama and Baba refused to open, that when we were kids we flipped to the back of to search for our parents' names in the index—Bob Moses or Robert Parris Moses. We found Janet Jemmott a few times. We found pictures of Baba when he had hair, was the age I am now. One had a picture of Baba standing in overalls in front of a porch in the Mississippi Delta like he is standing right now, in front of Dusty's grandma.

"I didn't know I was walking into history," he said about his journey into Mississippi.

Dusty pops back inside as we begin to introduce ourselves; the windows are covered with sheets. Baba becomes soft-spoken, intimate, offers to make sure Dusty is caught up with his work before he returns to school. Baba talks about the Algebra 1 test, the need for Dusty and all his classmates to take Algebra in the eighth grade.

"We need to raise the floor," he says sternly, his eyebrows furrowed. Dusty's grandma nods in agreement.

"Mane!" she yells toward the door and Dusty comes out again. "They gonna bring you your schoolwork," she says, "and Oma here can help you do it. I don't want no foolishness." Dusty smiles, attempts to hug her. "I had ten children," she says, "and now I have more than twenty grandchildren and some great grandchildren, and I've stopped tryin' to remember their names."

"Ain't I your favorite?" Dusty says as he manages to wrap his arms around her. "Ain't I?"

"Go on and stop that foolishness," she says.

———————————

W. H. MOSES SERMON

One of the hopeful signs of the times is that folks are cursing preachers. That is the hopeful sign. If you think folks are not cursing preachers you don't know the news. (*Laughter*) And do you think that folks are disloyal to the program of Jesus Christ? No. But they do not think that we are carrying out the principles of Jesus Christ. . . . Let me tell you something. Here in this country we have some five million Negroes organized in the churches. England and France and some white folks, who don't mean to be fair, are no more studying about you and your churches than they are about the winds that blow. And you know why? Because we are not going to do anything but say "Hallelujah." They are not paying any attention. No matter what anybody will tell you, the whole world wakes up to hear more what Marcus Garvey has to say than all the Negro preachers in the world. (*Loud applause*) And why? Because the average preacher is not preaching anything worthwhile. For two thousand years we have been perverting this gospel that Jesus left here and have been preaching lies.

CHAPTER 7

The Wild

The wild was a strip of woods on the other side of the Charles River, across Memorial Drive, across the walking bridge. We were approaching the 1980s, spermless, still missing teeth, unaroused by buoyant breasts, maybe seven and nine, when Taba and I began crossing the water alone. We rode our bikes past Corporal Burns Park, along Harvard's wrought-iron fence to the traffic lights, across the crosswalk and then over the walking bridge. It was the route we took when walking to swim practice, feet dragging then, fingertips scraping the cement railing. The cement railing was where the JDs jumped into the river on hot days like this, bodies scorched and brittle, hell-bent on shattering whatever serenity remained in the water.

We would climb the railing on the other side of the bridge, place our feet in the bridge's ribcage to reach the boysenberries that fell from the tree that grew at the edge of the water and stained its surface.

We rode along the opposite bank, through flocks of geese, moving between the paved road and the goose-shit-quilted grass. There were runners. Mostly bare, stiff white legs. Usually on the dirt path that wiggled parallel with the pavement, sometimes farther into the grass, wide enough for one person, one bike at a time. We continued past two boathouses. There were boats like water bugs, one person and two oars that skirted the surface of the river. There were others that held more people. Each person with one oar, and usually one of those men with a bullhorn who yelled *pull*. Sometimes a woman. Sometimes there were bigger boats with motors. I thought of this body of water as perilous. Not life giving. Life taking. There were dead catfish on slabs of rock at the edge of the water. Clouds of flies, of gnats.

The gnats drifted, hovered above the pavement. We parted the swarms with our fists and faces. Eyes and mouths snapped shut. There were stray gulls. They called to the river. Cans and wires and rubbish, nameless muculent things were regurgitated, gathered at the edges of the water. It had been fertile once. Where the Massachusett[1] people had migrated to from their winter villages, had foraged and hunted and fished for herring, shad, alewife, and Atlantic salmon in the fresh and saltwater marshes where the river and the Atlantic Ocean greet each other. Before the factories. Before the marshes were filled with dirt, the dirt paved. Before the Massachusett were removed from the wild, remembered on the official state seal with an Algonquin man holding a bow and arrow, pointed down, signifying the authority of the state now bearing their name.

· · ·

We rode the bikes that Uncle Greg, Baba's brother, had given us—hand-me-down wheels that had first been our cousins', that had gears and wheels made for paved roads, not the wild. A few years after we'd arrived in America, our whole family had taken the train down to Stamford, Connecticut, to meet Uncle Greg and Aunt Janella and their kids, Marie, Michael, and Val. They were Maisha's age and older. Uncle Greg and Michael picked us up in two gold Cadillacs. The cars were cleaner than we were. Uncle Greg was a bigger version of Baba—more cheeks, more thighs and chest. Less quiet. Baba called him Skeets. Mama called him a Republican. He and Baba greeted each other as if a mountain remained between them. Baba's story about Skeets was that he'd left him to fend for himself when he'd been approached by a gang of boys in high school. *Never the same* is how Skeets described Baba after he returned from his first trip to Mississippi. Uncle Al, who'd made the arrangements for our family to return from Africa, was a friend of both Baba and Uncle Greg, had grown up with them in the Harlem River Houses. He said their apartment had been small, sparse, that they hadn't had much of anything, no money, not enough for food, bought only what was available and cheap, that they ate a lot of Wonder Bread. He said their mother, Louise, had been quiet and sweet. That they'd adored her. That Pop had been a kind and gentle guy, that he'd had problems with alcohol and wasn't functioning, wasn't able to work. That Baba and Uncle Greg always had part-time jobs. Mama said when Pop was drunk he would make Baba and Skeets box each other. I could tell from the way Baba got smaller when they were in the room together that Skeets used to kick his ass. That Skeets kicking Baba's ass was in the distance between us.

Michael took us on a tour of their house, kept us up all night, burst into our rooms with a goblin mask on his head illuminated by a flashlight. He laughed harder than we screamed. His whole body shook. My legs were heavy like his and Baba's and Uncle Greg's and Uncle Roger's.

In the morning we tried to sell Uncle Greg a large envelope of swim-a-thon raffle tickets for our swim team, the Bernal's Gators Swim Club. I'd thought selling the raffle tickets would be easy, like when we'd stood in Central Square in our Cambridge Police baseball uniforms with a can full of nickels, dimes, and quarters. I remember the disbelief on Judy Richardson's face—Mama and Baba's comrade from the movement—when she saw us wearing uniforms sponsored by the Cambridge Police. She was the only person who'd asked what we were going to do with the money.

When we asked Skeets to buy the raffle tickets, he made each of us stand up and explain why we were raising money. Told us the same story Baba had told us, about how they'd grown up selling milk with their mother before going to school, that they'd gotten to keep a bottle for every box they sold. Baba said this was how they'd gotten milk on their table. He said this whenever we complained about cleaning our rooms, washing dishes, sweeping the floor, working at the Cambridge Food Co-op. We'd been four and six and eight when we began stocking shelves and labeling produce in the co-op basement. Our family's co-op membership was how Mama and Baba had kept organic fruits and vegetables on the table. Baba had acted like working at the co-op when we were four, six, and eight wasn't comparable to selling milk before school.

Uncle Greg bought fewer tickets than expected. And then he gifted us Mike and Valerie and Marie's old bikes. His presence was profound. His relationship with America was different than Mama and Baba's. He lived well, seemed to enjoy life. He loved us. He and Baba came from the same womb, through the same white wilderness, the same Harlem River Houses. He had broken through barrier after barrier to become one of the first black partners in a major accounting firm, had gotten a golden parachute when he reached the top of America's corporate ladder.

Baba taught each of us how to ride Mike and Val and Marie's old bikes in the courtyards of Peabody Terrace. He gripped the backs of our seats and ran with us, keeping us steady with his whole hand and then a finger, eventually letting go and catching his breath. I peddled timidly, was in no rush for him to let go. Taba peddled as if his life depended on it, right out of Baba's hands.

"Get out the way," he would say, before crashing on the brick.

. . .

There was a bridge at the second boathouse on the Charles River, and a paved path that curled under it. Under it was always dank, dark, a puddle of water seeping from the walls, fed in drips from the ceiling. Taba's and my voices ricocheted off the walls as we approached top speed—"Seventy-five miles an hour," I said. Our engines were slivers of cardboard we stuck in our bike frames that rubbed against the spokes of the back wheels. The tunnel roared as our tires sliced through the puddle, spit mud on the bottom of our shirts, the back of our socks. On the other side of the tunnel was a wall of light. We busted through it and then woods became visible. We were leaving civilization. Moving beyond our parents', society's gaze. Peabody Terrace erect and gray on the other side of our shoulders.

The wild was a canopy of trees.

More dank and dark. We became still in its shade. Allowed the quiet to envelop our skin, reach our bones. Instinctively we shut down our engines, put the cardboard strips in our back pockets. And then we began peddling again. I felt the urge to urinate, to leave my scent on the bark. As our eyes adjusted to the dim light, a path emerged in the bramble, meandered between trees, around rocks, carved by many feet treading over the same earth, polishing it bald, littered only with rocks and twigs and roots. Our bikes' rims were easily warped—their ten speeds and curved handlebars designed for paved roads. The bramble reached our chains, left burrs on our socks. The path diverged at points, moved in irrational ways, under a broken tree, around an empty patch of grass. The trees became audible—wind and leaves, branches swaying. We trampled what had fallen. And then we stopped to fill our lungs. The air was crisp, laced with dirt and vegetation. Insects hummed in our ears. There was an audible ocean of them. Rising and falling like waves between the canopy of leaves and moist earth, birds serenading, scolding. The shade felt like I could be below the tamarind tree on the dirt road in Tanzania. We reached a clearing in the woods, where it was grass and bush, and the path abruptly ended.

The sun reemerged, struck our eyes.

Our hands became visors.

We surveyed the field.

There was fresh blood on our shins from racing full speed through the bramble, from our feet slipping off the pedals. Our sneakers were nameless, what the kids called bobos. Mama used scissors to cut our hair into beady afros. We didn't comb them. In the wild we could be Africans.

Our bodies were thirsty.

We foraged for raspberries. Some were almost ripe. We juiced them with our molars. There were other berries we couldn't name that smelled bitter. We left them for the crows.

We saw a man there once who grew as tall as the tall grass. After the first sighting he was always there, in our mind's eye. He appeared to be white beneath skin saturated with sun and wind and dirt, as if his days were consumed by foraging and birdwatching. He appeared to be abandoning civilization to grow with the warblers and buttercups and black-eyed Susans, on his way to becoming indigenous.

"It was through her actions of reciprocity, the give and take with the land, that the original immigrant became indigenous," Robin Wall Kimmerer said.[2]

I wasn't sure if he could see or smell us. If he pissed and shit in these woods. If we were trespassing.

He could have been from Vietnam. Not Vietnamese. But a POW MIA. He could have been from Harvard, from the sidewalks of Harvard Square. Our teachers had begun gathering us in the auditorium during school to warn us about kidnappers. It was a thing I thought about. Strange men who hung around parks. If the colored white man tried anything, I told myself, Taba and I would fuck him up, show him that we were too big to be stolen.

·   ·   ·

Mama said that her great-grandmother had been born in Cameroon in the age of Ngang (1788–1830) during the reign of the seventh Fon of the Oku people. That she couldn't remember her name. That her home had been a five-hundred-mile swath of mountain, peaks rising ten thousand feet, valleys of raffia and eucalyptus, craters that became deep lakes; two dozen villages spread across the highlands. That she had arrived in Dominica in chains, been abandoned to fields to chop sugar cane with men. Like most of Dominica's enslaved Africans, she had been allotted a patch of land to grow vegetables, raise chickens. Mama said she became a venerated healer like the legendary medicine men of Oku. That she was freed before slavery was abolished by the British in 1834. That Babu had been raised by his grandmother on five contiguous acres bordering the botanical gardens, with horses and a stable. That she'd owned a dancehall in the city of Roseau.

·   ·   ·

Taba and I removed the cardboard strips from our back pockets as we prepared our bikes to return to civilization. Our engines became a siren as we began racing again, from one side of the woods through the meadow to the other.

"One hundred miles per hour," Taba said as he reached top speed.

I was the first one out. Bunny-hopped into a wall of sunshine. Kept peddling. We were tire to tire. I could hear the cars growling on Storrow Drive. Peabody Terrace not visible yet. We rode adjacent to the Harvard University Athletic Complex. The stadium, built in 1903, was the nation's oldest permanent concrete structure dedicated to college sports, rose on the banks of the Charles like an ancient Roman arena where gladiators battled to the death for their freedom. The Blodgett Pool, which sat at the foot of the stadium, was where the Bernal's Gators swim team practiced. The pool was where Mama and Baba had sent us for basic training, to learn how to swim well enough so that we would not drown in America.

Every day of my life between the ages of eight and twelve was defined by whether I had to return to that building.

·   ·   ·

Maisha was the first of us to integrate the swim team, was approaching ten, was knees and elbows, long joints, short cornrowed hair, thick glasses, eventually braces. With each leap from a starting block, like Uncle Greg climbing corporate America, she shattered the lie on the surface of the water, on the surface of America—that black people were less buoyant and couldn't swim as fast as white people, that people with darker skin were more African and less human.

I joined the team next and then Taba. Six and eight and ten, diving headfirst into America's deep end. Our teammates were from suburbs as far as New Hampshire; "Live Free or Die," the state's motto, scattered among the license plates in the parking lot at the end of practice.

The team was broken into five age groups: 8 and under, 9–10, 11–12, 13–14, and 15 and up. We swam thousands of yards a day. The monotony of practice—going back and forth in the frigid pool a couple hours at a time, five, six, seven days a week, depending on your age group, sometimes twice a day—taught us how to detach our minds from our bodies, how to go beyond our own perceived limitations in an environment that was often hostile to our existence.

I'd begun swimming competitively when I was seven with the Cambridge YMCA Sea Cobras. The first time I tried out for the Gators I was approaching eight and didn't make the team. The laps were longer and the water colder than at the YMCA. Baba wouldn't let me return to being a Sea Cobra and spent the summer working with me on my stroke, building my stamina to be able to race the length of the Blodgett Pool. Some days after we practiced, Baba would give me a couple dollars. Most days I cried in the water. Baba understood the power of the water to shape our minds and bodies to be able to better navigate and not succumb to the perils of white and black America.

Coach Bernal taught us how to envision ourselves moving like dolphins in the pool as he trained each of us as if he was preparing us to stand on an Olympic podium. In the imagining and reimagining, in the detaching and reattaching our minds to and from our muscles, in the duende that was required to overcome and redefine the limits and boundaries of our bodies, in the single-mindedness required to pursue excellence and stand at the top of an Olympic podium, I learned to rise above the cage of expectations circumscribing black life in America.

I practiced the butterfly on the walk home, put on my goggles and practiced my freestyle on the kitchen floor, flip turns against the fridge. I experienced the joy and freedom on the other side of fear and pain when pushing my body past its limits. I oscillated between not wanting to swim at all and wanting to stand at the top of a podium. It became my goal to win the high-point trophy, given to the fastest overall swimmer in each age group in New England. The trophy was made of thick wood and solid metal and felt permanent, like a statue. "That's not what you should swim for," Baba said. But I wanted to be commemorated. Maisha won the high-point trophy first, and then me and then Taba. Taba was a natural. Coach Bernal thought he could be an Olympian. Baba thought swimming could be Taba's ticket to college. Crawl space for Taba's journey through black and white America.

Mama subscribed to *Swimming World* magazine. The magazine arrived monthly and contained the twelve fastest times in each age group of swimmers from around the planet. I decided when I was ten that I wanted my name to appear on those lists. At the beginning of the season I set goals for how fast I would swim in each of my races and wrote them in a notebook that I left under my bed. By the end of the season my name would appear in *Swimming World* twice, which instilled in me the belief that I belonged in the pool with the fastest swimmers my age on the planet and, more importantly, the understanding of what was required of me to get there.

"Don't shit in our toilets," the Harvard students and faculty with whom we shared the pool said. "Don't use all our hot water."

I left my swimsuit on in the Blodgett Pool showers. Wrapped a towel around me before I put on my underwear. Didn't want to be caught naked in their building. Became aware of shitting in their toilets. Of using their hot water.

Baba was familiar with what we were experiencing. His journey—from Harlem River Houses to Stuyvesant High School to Hamilton College to Harvard University to Horace Mann to Mississippi to Tanzania and back to Harvard—straddled the jagged distance between black and white America.

He offered us his gurus to help us navigate America's perilous waters.

"How does he do that?" our teammates asked, as he appeared to fall asleep between and wake up at the beginning of each race.

"He is meditating," we said. He gave us books with stories of men and women who lived in the Himalayas in caves for hundreds of years. Who floated in air, turned themselves into tigers.

Baba thought of himself as a fallen yogi. We would stumble upon him in the living room, seated on the floor, back erect, one eye opening, head turning like a great owl, as he attempted to transcend his body, America's body, return to his creator.

·   ·   ·

Taba and I continued on our bikes past the Blodgett Pool. We stopped to refuel at the walking bridge beneath the boysenberry tree. We stuck our feet in the bridge's ribcage. Pulled ourselves higher so that our bellies grazed the cement, came to rest on the bridge's shoulder. We found our reflections and spat at them, fractured our faces, waited for them to reappear. The river stretched beyond sight, was straddled by other bridges. We were good enough swimmers to do laps in the river, swim from bridge to bridge, or shore to shore, but I was afraid of what had lived and died beneath its surface.

In the dead of winter the surface of the Charles River became ice, covered in tracks. We could see the footprints of people who had attempted to walk from one bank to the other. We could see where they'd lain on their backs to make angels, made snowmen with scarves and pipes. Where they had decided to turn back. Juanma—who was Maisha's age, whose parents had moved to Peabody Terrace from Puerto Rico, who was tall and clumsy (both of his parents were taller than six feet), who was good enough to swim with Bernal's Gators—got halfway across once before the ice cracked. Mama said that if he had fallen in it would have been difficult for him to pull himself out, that his clothes would have become an anchor, that if he'd gone under he would not have been able to break the ice, to find air, that there were currents beneath the ice strong enough to drag him to the ocean, to return him to his creator.

·   ·   ·

After swim practices, the Blodgett Pool parking lot became a maze of red, white, and blue headlights, cars left smoking, civilized suburban moms, bleached blond, running into the lobby to retrieve their children, us huddled like penguins, their hair wet and stringy, our hair wet and woolly, all our bodies drained, drenched in chlorine.

When we were nine and eleven and thirteen, Baba arrived in an evergreen and olive-green two-toned Impala, which was a recent gift from Babu. It was primitive, loud and gassy compared to the foreign engineered Toyota Mini Vans, Volvos, and Mercedes that filled the parking lot. We had just piled in, one in the front seat, two in back, slammed the heavy door shut. The engine was growling, rattling teeth and bones, about to shift into gear when a young Harvard University cop approached, told Baba to move it.

"What did you say?" Baba said detonating a decade of quiet, pushing open his door, standing eye to eye with the cop. The officer froze, became a boy beneath the surface of his uniform. We were also shocked and afraid.

Maisha reached for Baba's arm, returned him to us. It was the first time we saw his anger, pent-up, pent-up, pent-up from his perilous journey through the wilderness of white America, what we felt at times in his quiet, in the tone of his voice, in a glare, the undercurrents of rage his gurus helped to contain, prevented him from drowning in, now spilling into the parking lot, flooding the Impala.

––––––––––––

W. H. MOSES SERMON

You talk about your Universal Negro Improvement Association. It is a fine thing. But as fine as it is your biggest asset is in "G." Don't let anybody fool you. Some may say: "But he has done so many things wrong; he has made mistakes." I tell you he is the biggest asset you have. I don't care how well others can do it. Whatever you may say about Mr. Garvey, his is the voice in the wilderness. When he cries they answer from everywhere in this land. (*Loud applause*) You may talk about you come from Harvard and "I am from Yale," and "I am from Cornell," but the man that speaks to the multitude must come from Heaven. He is not born in a day. No man can make him. He comes out of the groaning and travail of ages. Mr. Garvey is the pent-up feeling of the race that has been in the region of the shadow of death for ages.

CHAPTER 8

The MathLab

ROBERT MOSES'S ACCOUNT OF VOTER
REGISTRATION DRIVE IN MISSISSIPPI IN 1961

00:12:36 Robert P. Moses

Well, I refused to pay the five-dollar cost of court and argued that I shouldn't have been, uh, given anything at all but should have been set free since I was obviously not guilty. I was taken to jail then, this is the first introduction to Mississippi jails. I spent a couple of days in jail and then was finally bailed out. Uh, when the bondman came through via the NAACP we decided to at that point, to appeal the case, though later the appeal was dropped. Well, that was our first introduction to Amite County. Immediately after that we rode out to Steptoe's house, who was a local president of the NAACP in the southern part of the county, and made plans to set up a school at his farm, which we did. And for the last two weeks in August we proceeded to teach people, farmers, down in the southern area of Amite County at the little church there, . . . coming two, three, sometimes five or ten at a time.

00:13:38 Robert P. Moses

Although there had been rumors sort of floating around down near Steptoe's that there might be trouble when people would make another registration attempt down at Liberty, we didn't figure we would have much trouble.

00:13:52 Robert P. Moses

This was a day then that Curtis Dawson and Preacher Knox and I were to go down to try and register. This is the day Curtis Dawson came, drove down by Steptoe's, picked me up and we went into Liberty and we were to meet Knox at the courthouse lawn and instead we had to walk through the town and on our way back were accosted by Billy Jack Caston and some other boys when I was rather severely beaten. I remember very sharply that I didn't want to go immediately back into McComb because my shirt was very bloody and I figured that if we went back in we would probably frighten everybody.

00:14:36 Robert P. Moses

So instead we went out, back out to Steptoe's, where we washed down before we came into, back into McComb. Well that very same day they had had the first sit-in in McComb so that when we got back everybody was excited and a mass meeting was planned for that very night, and Hollis and Curtis had sat in, um, in the Woolworth's lunch counter there in McComb and the town was in a big uproar. We had a mass meeting that night and made plans for two things: one, . . . the kids made plans to continue their sit-in activities, and two, we made plans to go back down to Liberty to try and register some more. We felt that it was extremely important that we go back to Liberty immediately so the people in that county would not feel that we had been frightened off by the beating, and before they could get a chance they had to rally their forces. Accordingly on Thursday, August 31,

00:15:46 Robert P. Moses

there was more activity both in Liberty and McComb. In McComb there were more sit-ins; in Liberty another registration attempt coupled with an attempt by us to find the person who had done the beating and have his trial. Well, it turned out that we did find him, that we did have his trial, but they had a six-man justice of the peace jury; that the courthouse in a twinkling was packed. That is, the trial was scheduled that day. And within two hours, started, and within two hours, farmers, all white, came in from all parts of the county, bearing their guns, sitting in the courthouse. We were advised not to sit in the courthouse while, except while we testified—otherwise we were in a back room. After the testimony was over, the sheriff came back and told us that he didn't think it was safe for us to remain there while the jury gave its decision. Accordingly, escorted us to the county line. We read in the papers the next day that Billy Jack Caston had been acquitted. In the meantime in McComb, the sit-ins, more sit-ins, had taken place.

.   .   .

The science room in Brinkley Middle School looks abandoned. The paint on the walls is chipped; cracked beakers collect dust on large black-topped tables. It reeks of a forgotten, unloved place. The air is damp, contaminated with chemicals whose shelf life has expired. The room is attached to the end of the hallway at the edge of the school building, an unused appendage. In this way it's perfect: a space in the building that needs redeeming, that Baba can redefine, that the Algebra Project, that Khari and Taba and I and the students, can reclaim as our own. Baba calls it the MathLab.

"Crawl space," he says. I understand it as a little wiggle room in the building for us to do what we need to do. Baba thinks about it more broadly. In relationship to the 1957 Civil Rights Act, "It is a space created in the larger political and social world that we can use to our advantage." In relationship to math, "Nations and institutions [are] now making a global transition from reliance upon technology that primarily organizes physical labor to technologies that directly organize mental labor. . . . I see history's broom sweeping us all along a common corridor. As organizers, we can make use of that corridor as a crawl space toward liberation."[1]

Khari and Taba do most of the cleaning—they bought gloves and masks, industrial-strength trash bags. Our Timberland boots feel appropriate now.

"Blue collar!" I call them when I enter the room.

"What up?" Khari says.

"And who the fuck are you?" Taba says.

"White collar."

"Fuck outta here."

"You find Dusty?" Khari asks.

"Yeah, they gave him ten more days."

"In ISS?" Khari asks. In School Suspension.

"Nah, suspension."

"For what?"

"I don't know."

"It's like a jail, yo."

"What are you all gonna do with the closet?" I ask.

"Yo, I caught two kids tryna fuck in there," Khari says.

"Who? Nah, don't tell me. You sent them to ISS?"

"Nah," Khari says, shaking his head, "I told 'em not to do that shit in here. Yo, there was all kinda rotten shit in that closet."

"There still is," I say, peering in.

"Don't remind me," Khari says. "Yo, these heads are crazy. We wasn't thinking about fucking in the closet when we were in eighth grade."

"Speak for yourself," Taba says. "Yo, when I found out this nigga got laid I was tryna get laid as soon as possible."

"When?" Khari says.

"As soon as possible, nigga."

"Not before high school?"

"I was in eighth grade."

"Word?"

"Am I lyin'?" Taba says turning to me. "I got kicked outta camp for that shit."

"Nah," I say.

"You remember that? Mom and Dad sent you to pick me up from the bus station. I was before my time, nigga. Yo, Khari, you was still birdwatchin' when I was gettin' laid."

"You sure about that?"

"You didn't get the bunnies until eleventh grade."

"What do you mean?"

"You had the snow bunnies then."

"I had the snow bunnies? I wasn't the only one with the bunnies."

"No, but you kept the bunnies. You niggas was rockin' X Clan gear, and the only nigga gettin' laid was PJ."

"You sure about that?"

"I'm sure about that," Taba says, "by any means necessary."

The carpentry teacher knocks on the door before entering. He's early for the meeting Baba has organized to discuss his vision for the MathLab. He is under thirty, with untamed curly hair, is from somewhere in the Midwest, has told us his wife and her church are what led them to Mississippi.

"It don't matta'," Taba says, chuckling as the carpentry teacher enters the room. "A yo, Spice, you're crazy."

Baba arrives shortly after the carpentry teacher. He begins talking about painting murals on the walls, putting new colorful tops on the tables, lining the wall with networked computer stations. The carpentry teacher says he can make the seats and create slots for the chairs to hang like fruit underneath the tabletops.

Maisha will say repeatedly that we're in Baba's world now. Brinkley Middle School, the Algebra Project classrooms, and now us in the Math-Lab—all part of a constellation of characters, places, and ideas that Baba imagined could be networked to take advantage of the crawl space this country afforded.

In Baba's world, a student could be a sharecropper. A principal, a plantation owner. A teacher, an overseer. Students in a corridor, a current in an ocean of movement. Sammie and Dusty could become Curtis and Hollis and Brenda Travis and the many others who'd organized with him in the '60s, made demands on themselves and each other for change. A classroom could be a vessel. A jail cell. A school building, a slave ship. Young people, prisoners. A principal, a warden. A postulate, a north star. Mathematics, a trail to freedom. The rails on the Underground Railroad. A farm, a freedom school. Young people, insurgents.

"There's nothing stopping us from inducting ourselves into the We the People class," Baba would say. "We are among the 'We' in 'We the People of the United States of America.'"

The MathLab, a registrar's office. A teacher, a naturalization officer. The preamble to the Constitution, a green card.

"Let us enact an induction for ourselves," he would say and then we repeated after him.

"We the People of the United States,"
"*We the People of the United States,*"
"in Order to form a more perfect Union,"
"*in Order to form a more perfect Union,*"
"establish Justice,"
"*establish Justice,*"
"insure domestic Tranquility,"
"*insure domestic Tranquility,*"
"provide for the common defense,"
"*provide for the common defense,*"
"promote the general Welfare,"
"*promote the general Welfare,*"
"and secure the Blessings of Liberty to ourselves and our Posterity,"
"*and secure the Blessings of Liberty to ourselves and our Posterity,*"

"do ordain and establish"

"do ordain and establish"

"this Constitution"

"this Constitution"

"for the United States of America."

"for the United States of America."

"It doesn't say 'we the citizens, we the whites, we the landowners, we the men,'" he said. "What you need to do is claim it for yourselves."

ALGEBRA PROJECT INTERVIEWS CONDUCTED BY CHARLIE COBB FOR *RADICAL EQUATIONS* (1998)

April (16), Java (16), and Sammie (17)

UNCLE CHARLIE: Let's back up. Talk to me about first getting involved in the Algebra Project. How did . . . different students seem to have gotten in different kinds of ways. So, how did you get involved, Java?

JAVA JACKSON: Well, when I first came to Brinkley, I was unsure if I was going to be at Brinkley, because my name was in the computer system for like three different schools. And I was trying to decide, you know, where to go right at the last minute, and someone said, "Well, stay here at Brinkley." And then I was put in Ms. Moss's math class. And—

UNCLE CHARLIE: Ms. Moss is the lady that jumps on the table, I think, right?

(Java and Sammie and April laugh.)

JAVA JACKSON: After like a couple of weeks—well, I'm not sure how—of the timing, but after a while, Mr. Moses began to come to Ms. Moss's class. And then I made the decision—when he actually started coming to the class, I made the decision that I wanted to stay at Brinkley.

UNCLE CHARLIE: Why were you in three different places in the computer?

JAVA JACKSON: Because I had planned to be in APAC, and I had put on my form to be in APAC—

UNCLE CHARLIE: What's APAC?

JAVA JACKSON: It's like an honor's program. And I had planned to go to Powell for APAC, but they made a mistake and put me to Chastain for APAC, and then they put me for Brinkley because that was my actual zone, so I was trying to, you know, decide where to go. Then when—to be honest with you, I really did stay at Brinkley because I was enjoying Mr. Moses coming to the classes with his games and stuff. I really liked that.

UNCLE CHARLIE: What is he saying? What is interesting about him when he's coming to your class?

JAVA JACKSON: What I found interesting—we didn't have any books, and—

UNCLE CHARLIE: Any books? Any math books?

JAVA JACKSON: We didn't have any math books. If we did, I didn't see them.

UNCLE CHARLIE: Why not?

JAVA JACKSON: When we first started, Ms. Moss—she—let's see, I think the first thing we did was we took the trip.

COOKIE: All we wanted to do was get on that bus, you know. It, it was more hands on. She didn't want to bother about the book.

UNCLE CHARLIE: Now, had you met Bob Moses at this point? Or he was just a name you had heard?

JAVA JACKSON: I didn't even hear his name. I knew—I knew a man was coming.

COOKIE: He came, but he didn't really teach. It was Taba.

JAVA JACKSON: Right.

UNCLE CHARLIE: Well, who came? Bob, Taba, or Omo?

JAVA JACKSON: Omo didn't come 'til later. It was Taba and Bob.

UNCLE CHARLIE: They came together.

JAVA JACKSON: Um-hmm.

UNCLE CHARLIE: And what did they say and do?

JAVA JACKSON: Taba, he taught us that Flagway game.

COOKIE: Yeah.

JAVA JACKSON: He came in, and you know, he was teaching us about the positives and the negatives, and zero, and then he showed us the big mat—floor mat he had out, and he made a game for us, and we—

COOKIE: We did a little something.

UNCLE CHARLIE: Now, let me ask you—let me try and get you to do it this way. Now, imagine explaining this to somebody who you're trying to interest in the Algebra Project, you're trying to explain to them exactly what got you interested in the Algebra Project in the beginning, and you're talking about Taba and Bob coming to class. How would you explain it? What was happening?

JAVA JACKSON: Taba was young. So, that caught everybody's attention.

(*They laugh*)

I'm serious. He was young.

COOKIE: The girls. All those girls.

JAVA JACKSON: The boys too, because they tried to be like him.

UNCLE CHARLIE: What—why is that important, what's going on with that?

COOKIE: Because—

UNCLE CHARLIE: Well, let's have the girls' point of view and then the boys' point of view. OK.

JAVA JACKSON: From the girls' point of view—

(*Laughter*)

APRIL DAVIS: This is on tape, now.

JAVA JACKSON: I know it's on tape. It doesn't apply to me. The girls in general. Taba caught their attention because he was young, he was handsome, and he was like active—I mean, he was so full of energy, so people would tend to pay attention, that they wanted to, you know, get involved and—

UNCLE CHARLIE: Now, what was Taba saying that helped with that?

JAVA JACKSON: He was—he talked to us like he was one of us, for one thing. For example.

UNCLE CHARLIE: For example. Give me an example.

JAVA JACKSON: "Yo, shorty."

(*Laughter*)

APRIL DAVIS: "Sam dog."

JAVA JACKSON: "Come over here," you know, "what's the negative." I mean, you didn't feel uncomfortable too, getting the wrong answer with him. I mean, if it was wrong, it was just—I mean, you know, if you made a mistake, you just made a mistake. He didn't—

COOKIE: He didn't stare at you like—

JAVA JACKSON: He didn't, you know, grade you or anything, all that kind of stuff.

UNCLE CHARLIE: Now, what's the boys' point of view, Sammie?

COOKIE: Well, first, he did the stuff that we couldn't do. Like had his pants sagging, you know what I'm saying, had this attitude, this, you know—

UNCLE CHARLIE: Wait a second. Back up, so he's got—his pants are sagging, you're saying?

COOKIE: Yeah. Not down, but you know what I'm saying. Well, we couldn't wear our pants—

UNCLE CHARLIE: You couldn't do— You couldn't wear your pants like this, right?

COOKIE: Naw.

UNCLE CHARLIE: You couldn't because the school doesn't allow it, is that what you're saying?

COOKIE: Yes. But Taba could.

JAVA JACKSON: Because he was a teacher.

(*Laughter*)

COOKIE: Now, for the boys, you know, he talked to us like— Well, I really can't say, but you know, like the East Coast attitude, about what I'm saying, "yo, brother—"

UNCLE CHARLIE: What's the East Coast attitude?

COOKIE: "Well, yo, dog. You need to do your work, you know what I'm saying, before I smack you." You know what I'm saying? (*Laughter*) After school, see, most of the stuff went on with the boys, it was after school. See, like he might pick us up after practice, whatever, we go to . . . might go to the mall or something, because he just hang out, and we showed him where the mall was so he would take us, you know what I'm saying, just kicking with us. We might go over to the hotel he'd be staying at, you know, just kicking with him.

JAVA JACKSON: And then too, like what he's saying is, Taba did things that they couldn't do. You can look at that in two different ways. Some people may say that maybe that was a bad influence on you, but then again, it could've been a good influence. He could do what he wanted to because of his education. I mean, you know, where he was, he could afford to do what he wanted to.

UNCLE CHARLIE: Was that the lesson—

JAVA JACKSON: You bring yourself. Nobody ran Taba.

•　•　•

When we arrive in the gymnasium for the pep rally, the basketball court is full of boys in football jerseys readying for combat, girls in cheerleading uniforms about to wiggle their hips, students with instruments, some dressed in marching-band uniforms, the rest of the student body in the stands, unleashed, cutting up. The teachers and administrators and parents in the stands don't attempt to constrain them. It's as if the rules have been lifted, as if all that pent-up energy that we could feel in the hallways between classes is readying to explode.

"You have to see it," the carpentry teacher said as Taba and Khari and Baba and I walked with him toward the gym. As if the pep rally alone had warranted his sojourn from middle America to Mississippi.

In the gym, the moment before the first drum is struck, silence gathers like a thundercloud. The football players and musicians and dancers are stoic, some cracking a smile when a name is called from the stands, splitting the silence. And then an arm is raised and a beat is struck on a drum, and then the other instruments take turns getting in on it, repeating what the lead drummer played. In the same way, one cheerleader swings her body in motion and then the rest of the squad follows, duplicating, embellishing her swagger. Batons wave across their bodies, hips swing beyond perpendicular to ankles, and then pandemonium, the boys and girls marching and stomping, the football players running onto the court as their numbers are called, slapping helmets and shoulder pads like gladiators on their way to battle. The electricity in the air leaves goose bumps on my forearm. The parents and teachers cheer like every student on the floor is theirs. The student body keeps yelling names from the stands. The only reference I have for this kind of energy is the duende of Magic City. Which feels inappropriate. To associate this emancipation with black pussy poppin' and big booty clappin'.

"Fire," Taba says, who has been to the pep rally before.

"The MathLab needs to be like this," Baba says.

· · ·

Taba recruits artists from the neighborhood to paint the walls of the Math-Lab. They paint a giant panda, a cheetah, a toucan, and other animals. A corner of the room has become outer space—distant stars and planets with equations and students detached from the forces of gravity, afloat in stardust. They created a portrait of Baba—a regal rendering of Bob Moses, the educator. We thought it would make him happy. But it disturbs him. He is concerned about his image. That he will be revered, like King. That it places him on a pedestal above the principal and teachers and parents and students. He tells us to paint over it, so Taba paints a portrait of Spice—dreads pointing in every direction. It looks and feels like him.

The only thing missing is a phat spliff. Taba paints *Math is what you make it!* above his head.

Spice and Taba and I follow Baba onto the campuses of Jackson State University and Tougaloo College to meet with their professors and others interested in the work of the Algebra Project. The Tougaloo campus feels small, like you could run a lap around it without breaking a sweat. It is gated, its brick buildings dating back to the 1800s, the roads lined with trees draped in Spanish moss. It had been a place of refuge for Mama and Baba in the '60s, a corridor where they'd gathered and organized with members of the Student Nonviolent Coordinating Committee.

We gather now in the library with Professor Fahmy, who is Egyptian, and with college students, their other professors, and a few administrators. These meetings always feel like the beginning of something momentous, as if we are all being transported back into the trenches of the movement. People come from different corners of Baba's world to touch the different parts of him—the philosopher, the organizer, the mathematician, the hero. Some of the college students are interested in activism, some in STEM, some in giving back, some because their parents or aunties or some relative had participated in a sit-in or march. Baba welcomes everyone. Tasks Taba and Khari and me with recruiting the college students to work in the MathLab.

Khari and Taba work with Baba to create a MathLab schedule that includes a class taught by Dr. Fahmy and involves the TI-92 graphing calculator. Which is like a hand-held computer that enables the students to model and animate geometric concepts. Baba is always interested in how technology can inspire and promote what the students know and are capable of. How technology is influencing what the students need to learn and remember.

Mr. Gibbs, who is the father of two Algebra Project students, Mariama and Ayana, is scheduled to teach the African Drums and Ratio curriculum. The students learn how to make drums from cowhide and cardboard tubes. Baba is as Stone Age as he is futuristic, is invested in what can be learned from our earliest human experiences. The beat of a heart, the rhythm of a drum, the rapping of a name, the stomping of feet, all leading to the possibility of dancing while constructing ratios.

Khari and Taba begin training the eighth graders to teach the Flagway game to the students in the younger grades. It is a game that Baba invented that involves learning how to break numbers down into their prime factors. He is determined to plant this game into the topsoil of black culture. Hoping it will grow roots, like the blues grew into hip-hop, that it becomes something that black children identify with. He believes the game can create crawl space, in communities and school buildings across black America, for math to be celebrated. Instead of the students sitting at desks memorizing their times tables, they will gain mastery of multiplication and division while running up and down hallways or outside in the playground or in gymnasiums, sharing all they can about the numbers from one to infinity, demonstrating their desire and ability to learn more and more advanced math. He'd called me in my dorm room when I was in college to tell me about it. He was animated, like he'd discovered black gold. I tried to visualize his inputs and outputs taking a physical form, the idea that math could be something that required our bodies to move. When he came to visit me and Coach Jarvis in DC to sell us on the idea of a math basketball camp, he also took me with him to a presentation he gave to a group of mathematicians. In the presentation he told them that they were important to the planet, which they all appreciated, and which scared the shit out of them—that they shared a responsibility to expand the crawl space that could liberate black and white America.

Baba also developed a three-dimensional version of the Flagway game that involved students building shapes with toothpicks and gumdrops. Eventually the toothpicks and gumdrops were replaced with rods and cubes that Baba had manufactured in New Hampshire. He got a patent for his invention and turned the basement of our house on School Street into a distribution center for rods and cubes. Baba imagined building a math games factory in Jackson, among the bones of factories and mills where the trains had once stopped, now abandoned to wind and rain and weeds, among the cement foundations where buildings had once stood, now sterile patches in feral fields cropped by winding roads.

For two months Khari and Taba lead Flagway practice sessions and then Flagway games, working in the MathLab and in the hallway between the lab and Mrs. Edwards's science room. Khari keeps track of how teams are doing on a giant bed sheet rigged with Velcro that teams stick their names to, that leads to a Final Four bracket that will compete in the gymnasium on the last day of school before Christmas vacation.

On that day the gym is packed, like at the football pep rally, with students and parents. Khari DJs. And then he grabs the mic, and the timer is set. The judges, who are teachers and Tougaloo students, take their places, and kids begin racing around the gym with numbers on cards as the rest of the student body cheers from the stands. Most of the parents and teachers don't know what the hell they're doing but can see that the kids are having fun, that they're playing with numbers, and so they cheer too.

———————

W. H. MOSES SERMON

And what is prayer? Prayer is the soul's sincere desire. Prayer is the dynamo of the soul. Prayer is the creating capacity for enjoying the blessing that life promises. Prayer is not only the creating desire but the dynamo that starts the wheel turning to work out the salvation and get the thing you want. The trouble is we do not ask for anything. Negroes did not ask for anything until Mr. Garvey came. Here we are in this country. Up and down Harlem thousands and thousands of colored people. Shoe stores, grocery stores, hardware stores, drugstores, all sorts of manufacturing concerns. Not only here, but in Washington and Chicago and Philadelphia, miles of mills and mills, miles of factories, all owned by white folks. Thousands of ships in the sea, all owned by the white folks. Thousands of railroads in the world, all owned by white folks. Put you out of business in the morning and your business would not affect the world two hours outside of your own labor. That is true in the West Indies, in Africa, and everywhere. You and I are dead broke, and our ministers and our leaders—the pity of it is not that it is the truth, but our pulpits, our politicians, and public men are willing to stand for it. If a man really gets the desire, he will achieve. Brother, whether you think it or not, if the spirit of God enters in, you will go on. Say to yourself, I am tired living like a dog, I want to be a man like other men. I want to have the privileges that others have. I want to lift my head up and walk with the king's children. I want to have my own buildings, I want to have my own home, I want to have my own government. And if you don't want it, God ought to send you to the uttermost depths of hell. (*Applause*)

CHAPTER 9

American Heroes

The winters of '78, '79, and '80 produced mammoth levels of snow. Imran and Taba and I weaponized it with our palms, stockpiled the freezer for one last snowball fight in the spring. During those years, the snow in the alley became the height of Kilimanjaro, was bulldozed, piled as tall as my bedroom window. The alley became an ivory tunnel. We became Matthew Henson, the first African explorer to land on the North Pole. We returned to school during Black History Month, where the accomplishments of other exceptional Africans were celebrated in the Dr. Martin Luther King Jr. Elementary auditorium. The school building was large, the length of two of Imran's football fields, a lower-level underground and three floors stacked above that, stretching back from Putnam Ave. another whole block. And then outside there was a basketball court where we played dodgeball and kickball, a courtyard that doubled as a parking lot next to the gravel track that inscribed an oval grass field that we played tackle football on, which was littered with dog shit.

The school, formerly called Houghton, had been renamed in 1968, shortly after Dr. Martin Luther King Jr. was assassinated. The Houghton School had been erected in 1904 and named after the publisher Henry O. Houghton, who had polluted the river.

"I am somebody!" Mr. Stead, our vice principal, asserted through the antiquated sound system. We were two hundred pitch-black to off-white first through eighth graders. A melting pot of voluntary and involuntary immigrants. Zero indigenous. The chant an affirmation for burgeoning black identities, a thin layer of blackface for our white classmates. The seats were hard and wooden, left crevices in our legs where the inside of our thighs met our calves. Mr. Stead's voice sprang us to attention.

"I am somebody!" we responded in unison. I would later associate the call and response with Jesse Jackson—"I am somebody!" "Keep hope alive." He had hijacked the media space of Malcolm and Martin. Would run for president twice, in 1984 and 1988. Each time exceeding black and white America's expectations. For a microscopic moment in 1988 he would appear to be the front-runner for the Democratic nomination. This mirage, that his rainbow coalition was a White House contender, that his rainbow coalition had the potential energy to catapult blacks out of the bottom rungs of America's caste system and America into some version of Martin Luther King's dream, turned to smoke when he described New York City as "Hymietown."

We were adrift in the wake of the Civil Rights Movement.

Ronald Reagan, who had been a Democrat at one point, was now president.

When Reagan was running against Jimmy Carter in 1980, he gave a speech in which he advocated for the restoration of states' rights at the Neshoba County Fair in Mississippi, a few miles from where James Chaney, Andrew Goodman, and Michael Schwerner—students Baba had recruited to participate in Freedom Summer—had been murdered nearly two decades before. Reagan's speech about states' rights revived the ghost of Jim Crow, and before that the Black Codes, and before that serving natural life on some white boy's plantation. It was an invitation for America's confederates, its Billy Jack Castons—those Southern white boys violently opposed to black people leaving the bottom rungs of America's caste system—to do the unthinkable and flood what had been the party of Lincoln. When Reagan took office, Mama and Baba reacted as if the grand dragon of the Ku Klux Klan was occupying the White House. As if America was suddenly in danger of returning to what it had been before their tour of duty in Mississippi in the '60s.

Onstage, Mr. Stead was as tall as Dr. J. His hair picked into a conservative afro. He'd been born and raised in Cambridge. Had been a student at the Houghton School. He had a brother who was as tall as him, who was a Cambridge cop, whose beat was Central Square. They had both been basketball and track stars in high school and college. Mr. Stead had graduated from Villanova University. Like Baba, was among the generation of

African Americans who had integrated America's segregated institutions. Had overcome racial adversity with a six-foot-seven frame, trigger-quick muscles, and a quixotic belief in the American Dream. He was the first black man from Cambridge to be hired by Cambridge Public Schools and was a spokesman for the Cambridge Black Community Organization that, in the late '60s, advocated for greater minority representation in city jobs. Mr. Stead's journey through black and white America—which had left him stiff, impenetrable, with a paddle on his desk to straighten out niggas—ended with him on that stage, which was the turf that liberal, white Cambridge conceded, that a black person could be vice principal, eventually principal, eventually superintendent.

The principal, Mr. Caufield, was approaching retirement, sat amused in the front row of the auditorium. Was pliable, swollen red, Harvard by way of Ireland, entitled to his authority. The luck of the Irish had been to be niggers in England and overseers in America. The mustard-colored school building was his plantation. Mr. Stead kept the gears turning. Was responsible for inspiration and discipline. Most of the school's black families were on board for the ass beatings.

I would be summoned to his office once, in seventh grade. A few of my classmates and I were disgruntled; we had suddenly become aware of ass and titties, of our virginity. Of the galactic distance between a vagina and our few inches of penis. We were ready for the eighth-grade boys to graduate so we could mark our territory. We doused our clothes with Polo cologne in hopes of attracting the girls' attention. Their clothes became a boundary. Their flesh now something to reach for. We began intercepting the girls' letters, wanted to know who was or wanted to be kissing who. Danny and I decided to call ourselves the Collecting Information Association. Danny was one of the first friends I'd made in America; his mother was Louise, her partner was Tess, and his father was Jewish. He and I considered blackmail. We scribbled "KHARI THE CIA WANTS YOU" on the bathroom stall. We wanted the company of other disgruntled virgins, harassed other boys in our class on their way home to settle beefs going back to second and third grade, sometimes in response to what we found in the letters. Miguel was one of our targets, towered over us just as much in seventh grade as he had in third grade. Back then he would put on his WWF mask, wrap his python-sized arms around our necks, put us in the sleeper. We waited for him in the shadows at the entrance of the school building as the CIA grew in numbers. We gave him a head start before we began to howl and nip at his heels along Putnam Ave. We chased him every day for a week until his lungs were exhausted.

The parents and administrators of the Open School were alarmed that most of the black boys and Danny had become a wolf pack, that we called ourselves the CIA, were intercepting notes from our classmates, that we'd hunted a few of them on their way home from school. The Open School was the liberal, white, mulatto, lesbian wing of the larger Dr. Martin Luther King Jr. Elementary school building. A true "Rainbow Coalition" (the slogan was the genius of Mel King, Boston's first black mayoral candidate, later adopted by Jesse Jackson's presidential campaign).[1] The Regular School, which was predominately black, was industrial in nature, devoted to order and discipline—kids sat in rows, walked hallways in straight lines, called teachers Mr. and Mrs. something. The Open School was run as a cooperative, was famous for its potlucks, sought to be a model of democratic education—we worked in groups, recognized our teachers by their first names, walked the hallways in broken circles, created class projects to protest other racist institutions.

In sixth grade we'd mailed letters to Anheuser-Busch, the parent company of Budweiser, "the King of Beer," after they launched their Dark Continent theme park in Tampa, Florida. "Welcome to the Dark Continent" was superimposed over a picture of Africa on the cover of their souvenir booklet. "Less than 200 years ago, little was known" about Africa, the booklet read. "Men disappeared into its depths, never to return. Today you can travel into deepest Africa and have no fears. At The Dark Continent—Busch Gardens in Tampa, Florida."

"Entertainingly Wild," "Excitingly Wild," and "Wildly Wild!" were headers on various pages of the booklet.

"Set sail on the African Queen for a journey up the legendary Congo River," the narrative continued. "Steam past thatched roofed villages. Encounter live monkeys, crocodiles, even the dreaded white rhino. Feel the strange, piercing glares of . . . who knows?"

Our righteous indignation ejaculated fifty-plus letters and tape-recorded spoken word, airmailed to the parent company of Budweiser instead of aimed at Mr. Caufield or the school system's superintendent.

In science class we learned that the size and shape of a finch's beak varied from one Galapagos Island to another. Among the test tubes, ceremonial boiling flasks, and out-of-date books was a poster illustrating the progression of us from ape to human. We didn't go into the politics of it, but I knew where Darwin's general theory was headed: to the color of our skin, to the size and shape of our skulls, and ultimately to Africa. He called it *monogenesis.* Which implied that "in each great region of the world the living mammals are closely related to the extinct species of the same region."[2] That "it is probable that Africa was formerly inhabited by extinct apes closely allied to the gorilla and chimpanzee; and as these two species are now man's nearest allies, it is somewhat more probable that our early progenitors lived on the African continent." From which arose a persistent fear: that my humanity could be qualified by the distance bones were excavated from the equator, by the diameter of skulls. That to be African was to be more ape and some human, and to be African American was to be less ape and more human.

Anheuser-Busch eventually changed the name of the theme park from the Dark Continent to Busch Gardens. I wondered how many other classrooms in Cambridge or across the country had been involved in expressing their outrage and if the letters and spoken word we'd airmailed had made a difference. Despite the name change, the features of the park remained the same.

In the Open School we learned to think critically about America within the constructs of liberal, white consciousness. We learned that Columbus had been a tyrant, was not to be celebrated. We learned about the Great Depression, that Roosevelt was a hero. About Pearl Harbor and a lot of Holocaust. Nothing about Hitler modeling the Nazi race laws on America's Jim Crow system. If we, black Americans, were mentioned at all, it was to say that we'd made Uncle Sam proud; that Jesse Owens had outrun Hitler's Aryan man; that we had performed well in the air, at sea; that we could find glory on their battlefields. Nothing about the black men who after fighting for freedom abroad came home and fought for freedom in America. Nothing about Red Summer, the race riots that erupted between blacks and whites during the summer of 1919 in over three dozen cities. "The war is over, Negroes. Stay in your place. If you don't, we'll put you there." This was the notice the Klan posted in black Pittsburgh neighborhoods as signs of black progress—a black man in uniform, Arkansas sharecroppers organizing for better wages, a black child drifting into the white section of Lake Michigan—were confronted with white mob violence. "We are cowards and jackasses if now that the war is over, we do not marshal every ounce of our brain and brawn to fight a sterner, longer, more unbending battle against the forces of hell in our own land. We return. We return from fighting. We return fighting," W. E. B. Du Bois said.[3]

We didn't learn about Reconstruction. Nothing about the thriving black communities that had existed in Seneca Village and Tulsa and so many other Hiroshima'd and Nagasaki'd black places.

We learned about atomic bombs, the power of white consciousness to wipe the "Japs" off the planet, that this possibly saved lives. About the commies, the cursed Kennedy brothers, and the existential threat of nuclear war.

About Gandhi and Martin Luther King Jr. and *I have a Dream*—black and white singing and holding hands—and then Vietnam and then recycling.

Nothing about humanity's miraculous march out of Africa.

Mama, who had made it her life's work to plant our feet in black consciousness, said that Africans had journeyed to the Americas long before Columbus, that Benjamin Banneker was Benjamin Banna-Ka, the descendant of a Dogon prince, that in 1940 Marian Anderson had sung for seventy-five thousand people at the steps of the Lincoln Memorial after being barred from a segregated Constitution Hall, that George Washington Carver had invented more things than Einstein, that the surgeon Charles Drew had died from wounds suffered in a car accident because a hospital refused to treat him, that Langston Hughes had lived a block from her Aunt Ruth, that Father Divine's mansion had been around the corner. "There were always Cadillacs in front of his house," Mama said. "Men escorting him. . . . He had a congregation of blacks and whites, thousands, from the North and South. They owned hotels, shops, restaurants, outposts all over the country. You could get a haircut for a penny, a peace meal for ten cents in Father Divine's shop. He had an economic agenda. What black leader can you name with an economic agenda? He was preaching reparations before the sit-ins. Your grandmother took us to his retreat center in the country once. She would do things like that."

"What was his name?" I asked.

I wanted to know Father Divine's real name. It seemed inconceivable that a character like him could have existed in black and white America.

• • •

"Where's the Beef!?" Danny's father said as we, the members of the soon-to-be-defunct CIA, sat in the cafeteria, on display in front of the Open School's parent body. The line was born from a popular Wendy's commercial. We thought Danny's father was the only parent in our corner. He was a lawyer with an afro bigger than Stead's, except for a bald patch, and he had remarried and was raising his own pack of black Jewish children. The beef at that moment was between white liberalism, black liberation, black tradition, and puberty. There were rumblings of expulsion as the adults discussed the choices we were making with our freedom. The meeting led to in-school suspension, which we served in the school's library. That we'd vandalized the bathroom was under Stead's jurisdiction.

When we were called to his office, Mr. Stead cast his gaze at me from across his large mahogany desk. Eventually I broke eye contact, looked at my hands in my lap, plucked at my fingernails. I began to concoct a scenario for what I would do if he reached for his paddle. He was uncomfortable that we were being raised in the Open School to reject uniforms, to be disruptive (within the school's liberal limits), which conflicted with his no-nonsense approach to straightening out niggas.

Five years later he'd ref one of my basketball games. I was leaving high school and entering college, playing on a local all-star team against kids already in college. Mr. Stead was generous with the fouls he called for me. I scored 30 points, 20 of them free throws. Other than those Martin Luther King Jr. Elementary School Black History Month assemblies (and the time Mr. Stead brought live crabs he'd caught on the Cape into the cafeteria for us to play with at lunch), it was the only time I felt we shared some allegiance.

· · ·

"I am somebody," Mr. Stead said.

"I am somebody," we replied in unison. The call-and-response was African, democratic in nature, an invitation for other voices to participate in a conversation, rooted in work songs sung on plantations, in each evolution of black music, in the pulpit.

We grew silent as Mr. Stead announced that we had a guest speaker: a hero of the Civil Rights Movement. I followed his gaze to the back of the auditorium, watched confused as Baba—all five seven of him—walked slowly down the center aisle. Climbed the half dozen steps and stood next to Mr. Stead on stage. Mr. Stead handed him the microphone.

"Is that your dad?" Danny asked. I had begun to squeeze my body into the seat's crevice.

"Maybe," I said.

I was afraid Baba wasn't worthy of Mr. Stead's stage. That he would fart. That the auditorium would become a gas chamber. That the kids would suffocate, choke on their laughter. He spoke in a frequency I hadn't heard before. His voice was soft, as if his edges had been licked by waves. He was sincere. The sincerity sedated our jittery bodies. We became silent. What I have come to associate with that moment is the story of Jimmy Travis, which Baba told more than any other from his time in Mississippi. He told it as if it had happened to someone else, as if the details remained traumatic.

According to Uncle Charlie, it had happened seven miles outside of Greenwood, Mississippi on pitch-black Highway 82. It was around 10 p.m. on February 28, 1963. Earlier that night, Jimmy Travis, Baba, and Randolph Blackwell, field director of the Southern Regional Council's Voter Education Project, had been meeting with local organizers in Greenwood. During the meeting, Jimmy had spotted three white men in a car outside, so they decided to leave as quickly as possible and head back to Greenville, where Randolph was staying.[4]

"Jimmy Travis was behind the steering wheel," Baba would say, and he'd been in the passenger seat.

"We were coming from a meeting. There were others in the back seat, and two headlights in the rearview mirror. A car sped up and pulled up beside us and sprayed us with a grease gun, an old submachine gun used in World War II. A bullet lodged in Jimmy's head and another in his neck." Baba said that he'd grabbed the steering wheel as the car sped off. Found the brake, pulled into a ditch.

Jimmy survived.

"Jimmy caught a bullet for me," Baba would say. He said that the men who'd shot at them had been trying to take him out. That Jimmy caught a bullet for America.

Mr. Stead said Baba was an American hero.

"We're not heroes," Baba would say. "We're trying very hard to be people."

My classmates cheered as he descended the stage. Baba acknowledged with a glance that he knew I was attempting to teleport through the crack in the seat to anywhere else.

It was my introduction to Bob Moses, the Freedom Fighter.

CHAPTER 10

American Heroes, *Continued*

We were twelve and ten and eight and six when we traveled to Greenwood, Mississippi, for the first time. Mama had baked the bread, made the sandwiches—peanut butter and honey, cheese with a slice of tomato and lettuce—and wrapped them in aluminum foil. We had gone to the department store. Purchased clip-on bow ties. Mama still cut our hair with scissors. Our bodies were streamlined, obsidian, chlorine-licked. We traveled by train. The conductors walkie-talkied each other and eventually found seats for the six of us to sit together. The journey lasted two days. We glided west to Chicago and then down through the cornfields of Illinois into Memphis, and then through the Mississippi Delta into Greenwood, the "cotton capital of the world." Mama and Baba had borrowed the money for the trip from our local "aunts" and "uncles." The train trip was a protracted lurch beyond the concrete and buildings that had become our vantage point into the guts of America. Through the windows, the smokestacks and power lines and telephone lines and freight trains and trucks became redundant, pockmarking and zig-zagging the landscape, making visible the harvesting and distribution of the country's natural resources (in most instances without regard to ecological impact) that our cities required to exist.

We took turns at the window. At night the small towns, patches of civilization, appeared like jars of fireflies. Between them was relatively untampered land, hints of a natural order, the unbound wilderness that still dominated the planet.

We were traveling to Mississippi because Amzie Moore had died. When Fannie Lou Hamer had died five years earlier, in 1977, we had just returned from Tanzania and Baba had been unable to get out of Massachusetts. He'd put us on the phone with Amzie then. We were seven, five, and three and Malaika just out of Mama's belly. Baba had invited Amzie to come up to see us. Amzie didn't have the money to get out of Mississippi. "It was a hard job to stay alive," Amzie said, describing the reality that pursued him to the grave. Amzie's voice was one of a collection of voices that reverberated from the cotton fields and courthouses of Mississippi, the perilous trenches of American democracy, into our consciousness.

"One man, one vote," they said.

"One woman, one vote," they said.

"I am a citizen," they said.

"I am a man," they said.

"Power to the people," they said.

"Freedom now," they said.

When Baba had left Mississippi in 1967, he hadn't thought it would take fifteen years to come back, or that SNCC would no longer exist. At SNCC's height there were only thirty field secretaries on its staff: young people between the ages of eighteen and twenty-six who had "turned away from school, job, family, all the tokens of success in modern America, to take up new lives . . . in the hinterland of the Deep South." "New abolitionists" is how Howard Zinn imagined them.

"We're not heroes," Baba had said of SNCC in 1965. "We're trying very hard just to be people and that is very hard. If anything, what we're trying to do, or have to do, is to see how you can move even though you are afraid."[1]

"They were the little fellows with the tight blue jeans who stood in the courthouses, and marched in the streets and were arrested," Amzie had said, in a 1977 interview reflecting on the movement. "SNCC was a group of young people, moving, had the energy, capability, and didn't want any legal dragging. They didn't want that. They wanted to go into the neighborhoods. . . . When they arrest a line today, another line would form tomorrow, as big, and on and on, where the leadership was produced down to the last lick."[2]

Amzie said he'd never seen energy like that.

·   ·   ·

June Johnson met us at the railroad station in Greenwood. June was as tall as Mr. Stead, towered above us like the Maasai had back on the dirt road in Tanzania. Her skin was onyx like the Maasai too. June hugged us like we were hers, buried us in her breasts. We stayed with her and her son, Hakim, in Greenwood. She called him Keme. He was between Malaika and Taba in age. June had been a middle school student in Mississippi when Baba had first arrived there. She'd become connected to the movement as the voter registration effort that had begun in McComb was then replicated in other towns, cities, and counties. At thirteen she'd been arrested and beaten in a Winona jail with Fannie Lou Hamer. She'd been one of the many young people who filled Mississippi's jails, who'd had their minds set on freedom. When we arrived in Greenwood, she and Baba eased into a conversation about what had and hadn't changed in Mississippi in the last twenty years. Were bound by this, what they had been willing to sacrifice to conjure America.

June fried us chicken. It was the first meat we'd eaten since leaving Tanzania outside of Bibi's kielbasa. There was more fried chicken at the funeral service. We negotiated with Mama the number of pieces we could eat. Everyone respected that number except Taba.

At the funeral service Mama and Baba looked like different people from the parents we knew. Their comrades hugged us like June had. The time that they'd shared with Mama and Baba in Mississippi's jail cells entitled them to claim us as theirs, to project upon us the hope that we would carry the struggle forward. Some said they'd known us when we'd been the height of their palm facing the floor. They took our hands as they braided their arms, planted their feet in the ground, took root, swayed like trees as we joined a chorus of freedom songs.

We became children of the movement at Amzie's funeral.

Baba stood and spoke, said Amzie Moore had been his father in the movement, that Ella Baker had been his mother. We had never met Baba's parents. There wouldn't be pictures of them in our home until we moved from Peabody Terrace, a year later. His mother's death, which had been cataclysmic, in some ways conditioned him to cope with the violence he would endure in Mississippi. His father had died while we were in Tanzania.

A woman approached us after Baba spoke. "Is Amzie some kin to you?"

I was startled by the twenty-one-gun salute, confused by the soldiers in uniform with long rifles, pinned with medals of honor. That they were all black. That they were old. Didn't understand how Amzie, who'd fought in World War II, could have fought for America. Didn't know that they'd been among the men who'd returned from fighting in World War II to fight for freedom at home. "In all of my fighting, and whatever I've done in the years past," Amzie once said, "I haven't done it against anybody, except to try, and through my effort, even as ignorant as I am, to bring together people who will stand for justice and equality, and who will fight anybody, black or white, who attempts to enslave the minds and activities of free people."

Amzie had been the leader of the branch of the NAACP in Cleveland, Mississippi, when Baba arrived in the state, and also the owner of the only service station between Memphis and Vicksburg that served blacks and whites. Despite threats and loss of credit he refused to put up a "colored only" sign. Turned his house into a bunker, well-armed and floodlit.

"He was just here for a while," he'd said, describing Baba's arrival in Mississippi. "He had promised me in Atlanta, when we were up there [to return]. So he came [back] that summer, and we had to get together on what we had in mind. And our whole discussion, I think, in those weeks he was here, was how to improve the economy of the families, how to solve the illiterate problems we had, with public education, what to do about houses that had no windows, smoked inside, had leaks. Our discussion then did not deal in politics, but more or less, we talked about the bare necessities of life that people just didn't have."[3]

Amzie was born September 23, 1911, on the county line of Carroll and Grenada, Mississippi, where he lived with his mother and father and two younger siblings until he was about eight years old. From there, they moved to the Mississippi Valley between Holcomb and Charleston Counties, where his grandfather owned about 640 acres of land. They lived there with Amzie's five uncles and one aunt until his grandfather died in 1922.

"He'd been a slave," Amzie had said of his grandfather, "and was a very interesting character—couldn't read or write, yet he had accumulated more than a section of land and had in the neighborhood of twenty thousand dollars saved when he died . . . at 104. He was unusual, I think. [Each of his children] all had a hundred acres each when he died. . . . They grew cotton, corn, raised hogs until the Depression of the 1920s. . . . All of them lost their land during the Depression." When Amzie's grandfather died, his mother and father separated, and he and his mother and siblings moved back to Mississippi and started sharecropping on the Wilkin Plantation:

> At twelve I began plowing with a mule with a row buster behind it and a
> turn plow. I'd work the land early and plant it in March, then chop it out

and finally try to get around to harvesting beginning in September. We were always through about the first of November. . . . We were always in trouble with our economy. I think that was the biggest problem because a lot of times we couldn't eat. We'd had to wait to receive what we called "the furnish," which began on March first, and go March, April, May, June, July, or June.

Of course, we did learn to grow vegetables and to take corn and grate it for meal. And when the corn was hard enough, take it to the mill to grind for bread. So we did manage to eat. We were much more fortunate in that than we were in clothing. We just didn't have the money to buy clothes for a long time.

The first year we made two bales of cotton. The second year three. Then, my mother, the summer of 1925, my mother took very ill and died in a week. So my father came and picked up the two smaller children, and at about fourteen I was on my own to decide what I could or had to do with my life.

I always had a desire to get some form of education, you know, because at that time we felt like education was the solution to the poverty of the poor and ignorant. . . . We didn't have anything specific in mind. Just to have some knowledge of the history of our country, of our system of exchange, of our heritage. . . . And the leaders . . . in my day, like Booker Washington, R. R. Moat . . . Du Bois . . . and various other people that we knew, George Washington Carver, were idols that kind of came before us as great men. And we kind of looked to them for guidance. . . . I think that their whole concept and their whole program of education had to do with improving people . . . even our local principals were considered great people. . . .

I . . . went to Greenwood, Mississippi, where I attended Stone Street High School in 1926, 1927, 1928, and 1929. The principal found a job for me at a café over on Johnson Street where I cleaned fish, cleaned chickens, washed dishes, and did anything else that was to be done, until I had gone through the years. It meant that I had to work, but it also meant that I could sleep and have food and have a few days of school. When I went into this school, just about two-thirds of the kids were white. And I'd never gone to school with white kids. Then, I began to wonder what in the world was happening. Why were these white kids here? What was happening is that from Carrollton Avenue on the east to McLaurin on the south, from Avenue H to Avenue F, was an area in there where white men had black women. They would build houses for them, they'd build stores for them . . . and they raised families by them. They couldn't send those families to the white school; they had to send them to the black school, and there was quite a few of them . . . and they always had money. In my classroom when I was in the sixth grade, they had money, and if it was necessary to buy me a hamburger or some kind of sandwich, or candy, they would do it willingly. And I think this was the first time I ran into that . . . my first knowledge, and first experience, with what I call integration.

[During] the Depression days in the Delta [in the 1930s] when we had so many banks closing and jobs were so few and the Red Cross was issuing a small piece of meat with some brown flour, I had worked at Byrd's Hotel in Cleveland for eight dollars a week. But the times got so hard until they could not continue employment because they had to eat themselves. It was just that rough. Everybody was hungry. Black men and white men and their families rode all over this country in car boxes, looking for and getting whatever they could find. And if Hoover had served two or three more years everybody would have been integrated. It would have taken that [to survive]. In the hill section of Mississippi they had a lot of potatoes, they had corn, they had beef, they had hogs, you know. They could always grind the meal and have bread. And families of whites and blacks lived together just like a family of children.

I began working with the US Post Office Department in 1935 until I was drafted into the Army of the United States. I spent three years, six months, eighteen days in the United States Army attached to the Tenth Air Force in Myitkyina, Burma, and then I came home from the army in January 1946 and began working again at the post office and was there until 1968.

Now as a child growing up when I would go out and see beautiful homes and bathroom fixtures, I didn't know what they were—I'd know that they were beautiful. People always had houses, automobiles, their kids were always in school, they operated everything from the banks on down. I had the terrible thought that these are special people. . . . On the other hand, I wasn't quite sure why I hadn't been a recipient of the type of things that I saw them with. I just didn't know. And that concept, that belief rather, kind of followed me until I went into the armed forces and traveled around the world and really saw the world at firsthand. And I found that I was wrong! People are just people: some good, some bad. Some rich, some poor. I think our first awakening came April 3, 1940, when we held a meeting at Delta State field, of ten thousand blacks.... That was the beginning of the change. It came in the name of the Cotton Council, but any problem that came up was discussed, like separate but equal, electricity, like accreditation—you couldn't accredit those church schools, you know. We had the world's largest consolidated schools in this Delta, but no blacks went. We had 105 church schools that the blacks went to. I think it was the first serious talk that we held in this county, to talk about change. Change.[4]

Months after Amzie was buried, Baba received a MacArthur Genius Grant for his contributions to the Civil Rights movement. I was ten years old and had begun to think of Baba as a failure—without a job, little money, unconcerned with his appearance. When he was given the grant, Bob Moses the freedom fighter and Baba became one. The award amounted to $225,000 over five years. The MacArthur award enabled him to abandon his PhD a second time, to reenlist in the movement. To do family and movement. He began volunteering at the King Open School and taught math to us and our classmates full-time, which led to the creation of the Algebra Project. The classroom was his way back onto Mississippi's—America's—battlefields.

"The representatives from the MacArthur Foundation called and called" when they were considering Baba, said Uncle Al. "They were nervous. Some saw him as a genius, others saw him as a renegade. They wanted to know how he would use the money."

Uncle Al was a psychiatrist at Harvard. He and Baba had attended commie camps together when they were kids, along with prepubescent feminists and Pete Seeger, whose stories and songs had impressed Baba with how they depicted ordinary people confronting what was going on in the world. Uncle Al and Baba had ended up at Stuyvesant High School together. In high school Uncle Al subbed for Baba at his job at the NYU Medical Library for two years so that Baba could play in his basketball games at the Y. He said Baba and his brothers had always had jobs. That Baba had been serious about basketball. That Baba had gotten a scholarship to play basketball at Bates College but chose to go to Hamilton. The two of them had ended up at Harvard together as graduate students. He said that Baba had been into philosophy then, had had trouble reconciling what he felt would happen if he was not Christian.

Before Baba arrived in Mississippi he had spent half of his life integrating white institutions. He said those experiences had left him bitter, socially crippled. "When I was at Hamilton the white attitude was: 'Well, . . . society has the overall problem, [and our part is] to try and open a door for two or three Negroes, and let's see what happens,'" He said he learned how to be cool, to "pass through unobtrusively" by observing and listening and watching how the dominant society feels, by repressing his feelings. He had experienced the perils of growing in proximity to people who weren't open to him as a person and understood that underneath the liberal white facade was white supremacy.

Uncle Al had been around when Baba's mother died—understood the deep anguish that had propelled Baba to drop out of Harvard and head south. "They all adored her," Uncle Al said. "When Skeets got married [a year after Louise died], Bob made remarks and said that he wished that his mother was there, said how sad he was that his mother wasn't there and began to sob, it was painful, painful to hear him and watch him. My mother also died when I was young and so I knew what it felt like to be torn up like that."

Uncle Al had gone to Mississippi in 1964 when Baba had asked him to help the civil rights workers deal with their mental and physical trauma, and to provide basic medical care. The civil rights workers were battle-fatigued, clinically depressed, shell shocked. It was near the end of Baba's tour of duty—"It felt like twenty years rolled into four," he recalled. Uncle Al said that Baba was a hero in Mississippi. "When he called a meeting, people showed up. They respected him. . . . He was a leader trying to help the have-nots to rise up to be somebody, to be part of the leadership. He had a strong identification with folk, who were poor and excluded from society. Had an ability to reach out and talk to them like nobody else."

Amzie had said in a 1977 interview:

> I don't know whether I can explain Bob Moses, to be honest with you. Quiet, unassuming, a deep thinker, ordinary—you know, when I say "ordinary," just like a common shoe. He'd had a lot of experience in the field of segregation, and all that stuff, and very seldom expressed himself unless asked. . . . I thought maybe the reason he maintained that

attitude was because he had taught in a white institution, [but] I don't know whether that was the reason.

He seemed to have been an individual who was about getting things done. . . . I think he had been concerned, more or less, about the common man.

I think everybody knew, whether he expressed it or not, that Bob Moses was the leader. . . . He didn't project leadership. He didn't say, "I'm the man, you do this, that, and the other." He didn't even argue with you on a point except where people were involved. He was always on the side of the people. Always.

He would much rather have the people in this area do their own thing rather than have SNCC do it. I think that was the whole thing. He felt like it was the people's thing, and other people felt, like the visitors, that it would take years of supervision for it to be a people's thing.[5]

· · ·

When Baba filed assault charges against the sheriff's cousin who had attacked him with the butt of a switchblade as he'd been taking Curtis Dawson and the Reverend Alfred Knox to register to vote, he became the "first African American to challenge white violence" in the history of Amite County. Which led to "alarmed front-page coverage in local white papers," as Baba publicly stated. "The law down here is law made by white people, enforced by white people, for the benefit of white people. It will be that way until the Negroes begin to vote."[6] White men from around the state, carrying guns, filled the courthouse to see who this man was that was challenging their way of life.

"It was guerrilla warfare," Baba said. "That's how I think about it now. So guerrilla warfare you have to have a safe base, right? So we had a base within [the black community]—it's the only time in my life [that] . . . anytime I leave, day or night, doesn't matter what time, I go down the road, I knock on a door, somebody's going to take me in. I'm going to have a bed to sleep in. They're going to feed me. They are going to watch my back. So even the organizing, you're organizing within the black community. So the issue is: when do you decide to go into enemy territory, which is basically the courthouse. I mean, I'm not trying to shop downtown. I'm not doing any shopping, right? So it's when you make your move to take people to the courthouse that you're in danger."[7]

———

W. H. MOSES SERMON

A CHALLENGE

I defy anybody on God's earth to say that Garvey is disloyal to the black people of the world. I defy anybody on earth to say that he is disloyal to the white people of the earth. He is only asking for the black people the same thing that the white folks are willing to die for. . . . No matter what you say, you may have noticed that since Mr. Garvey has been on the scene we preachers have been waking up. (*Loud applause*)

I used to hold revivals and stretch a long face and say: "Where will you spend eternity?" A Negro brought me to my senses, just a plain Negro out of the alley. I was saying, "Where will you spend eternity?" That Negro said to me, "I am interested in where I am going to spend the night." Whether you think it or not, the average black man wants to know where he is going to spend the night, and not only that, but where I am going to spend the day, and he wants to know not only where I am going to spend the day, but where my race is going to spend it.

CHAPTER 11

Building Demand

ROBERT MOSES'S ACCOUNT OF VOTER
REGISTRATION DRIVE IN MISSISSIPPI IN 1961

00:17:05 Robert P. Moses

Brenda Travis had sat in this time; she was a young girl, just sixteen years old, and had been very active with us in voter registration in McComb.

00:17:15 Robert P. Moses

And I mean active. She, with all of us, had walked the streets every day from two to five or from twelve to five as it were, in the hot sun and she had been fed up with the response of the local Negroes there in McComb and the seeming apathy or the fear and the inability to move, the absolute immobility in the face of going down and facing the registrar in Magnolia. Her response was to take some kind of action on her own, so she joined the sit-in group. This infuriated the community, both the white and the Negro community. The Negroes were infuriated that she was so young and should be down there in that jail, and the white people were infuriated that we would send a young girl down like that.

00:18:21 Robert P. Moses

At this point, then, the town was in an uproar. We were having meetings. The white people were having meetings in their section of the town. The Negro people were having meetings in their section of the town.

00:18:36 Robert P. Moses

To top it all off, the next week John Hardy was arrested and put in jail in Walthall County. He had been working there for two weeks and they had been taking people down. And finally one day he had taken some people down to the registrar's office, had walked in. They had been refused the right to register, and he had asked the registrar why. The registrar recognized him, took his gun out of his desk drawer and smacked John aside of his head with the butt of his pistol. John staggered out into the street and was walking down the street when he was accosted by the sheriff and arrested and charged with disturbing the peace.

00:19:22 Robert P. Moses

John wound up in the Magnolia jail in Pike County because it was too hot for him in Walthall County, and they had to transfer him immediately. He was in the cell next to the sit-in kids, and that was the first time that I had gone down and had a chance to see them all in jail down there.

00:19:41 Robert P. Moses

It was pretty hot down there and they told me that they were not being allowed to take baths,

00:19:48 Robert P. Moses

that the food was pretty bad, and their spirits however were good, except that they were obviously losing weight and one of them was very anxious to come out.

ALGEBRA PROJECT INTERVIEWS CONDUCTED BY CHARLIE COBB FOR *RADICAL EQUATIONS* (1998)

April (16), Java (16), and Sammie (17)

APRIL DAVIS: I wasn't living in Mississippi then.

UNCLE CHARLIE: Where were you living?

APRIL DAVIS: On the coast in Bay St. Louis.

UNCLE CHARLIE: Oh, in Bay St. Louis.

APRIL DAVIS: Close to where Bob had the voting—voter registration down south, down by Waveland and—

UNCLE CHARLIE: Yeah. They had a meeting in Waveland.

APRIL DAVIS: Uh-huh.

UNCLE CHARLIE: You know about that Waveland meeting? Bob's talked to you about that meeting?[1]

APRIL DAVIS: I did a report on Bob my ninth-grade year.

UNCLE CHARLIE: Oh, I'd like to see that.

APRIL DAVIS: My teacher won't give it back.

UNCLE CHARLIE: What teacher?

APRIL DAVIS: My English teacher. She didn't really approve—

UNCLE CHARLIE: What's her name?

APRIL DAVIS: Ms. Rose.

UNCLE CHARLIE: Why won't she give it back?

APRIL DAVIS: I think she liked it.

UNCLE CHARLIE: Well, she could copy it. She could keep a copy for herself and give you what you wrote back, don't you think?

APRIL DAVIS: They just have this thing where they don't give back old papers, because they think you might sell them or whatever to the kids that's coming in.

JAVA JACKSON: So, they keep them.

UNCLE CHARLIE: So, they keep them because they think you're going to sell them to the—

APRIL DAVIS: Or give them, something like that.

COOKIE: Give it to the grade before. And they do it all the time.

UNCLE CHARLIE: Well, how do they know that you don't make a copy before you give it to them?

JAVA JACKSON: I know, you could give the rough draft to the kids.

UNCLE CHARLIE: What did you find out about Bob when you did that paper that surprised you, that you didn't know?

APRIL DAVIS: I didn't really know he was involved in the civil rights as much as when I did the paper. He was in a lot. And like, I was shocked when I . . . Like when I was getting books for research, I was like, here goes Bob. Yeah, that's how I'd be. I was like look, here go Bob.

JAVA JACKSON: I was thinking about doing my thesis for my twelfth grade on Mr. Moses, but someone else is doing it. And she told me that when she went to the archives she found like forty-five different things on Mr. Moses. I didn't think . . . I mean, I didn't know there was that much information on Mr. Moses.

UNCLE CHARLIE: Well, there's a lot of stuff on other people from Mississippi's movement that you could do a paper on. Fannie Lou Hamer—you know her name? It's the library across the street. Victoria Gray, lots of things. Anyway, so you—you weren't in the Algebra Project.

APRIL DAVIS: OK. When I first came to Brinkley, I was in Ms. Thigpen's office, and we were doing my schedule. And she looked at my grades from my seventh-grade year, and asked me, did I want to be in the Algebra Project. And I was like, what is that? And she told me that it was like an advanced math class, and I told her I didn't know if I could handle it because math was really not one of my best subjects. But I said I would try it, and if I couldn't handle it I would get out. And so, I tried it and I ended up liking it.

UNCLE CHARLIE: Well, now get me from . . . this work that you're doing in the classroom with Bob to the Young People's Project.

APRIL DAVIS: Well, the first time I started doing anything . . . Well, when Omo came, I was in the eighth grade and he just asked me did I want to help do a workshop with some people from Mali.

UNCLE CHARLIE: Wanted to do a workshop with people from who?

APRIL DAVIS: Mali, Africa.

UNCLE CHARLIE: Uh-huh. In West Africa.

APRIL DAVIS: And I said it would be interesting to meet people from another country, so I decided to go ahead and do it. And like, after that we did a couple of more workshops, then we—

UNCLE CHARLIE: Well, wait a second. This was when? You were in eighth grade, so this was three years ago.

APRIL DAVIS: That's right. And—

UNCLE CHARLIE: And who are these people from Mali?

APRIL DAVIS: I think they were—

UNCLE CHARLIE: Don't worry about it. Don't worry about it. Do you know—who were these people from Mali, Java? Sammie?

COOKIE: They were teachers and people like that, I think.

JAVA JACKSON: There were some teachers, it was some students. I don't know if they were in college or high school. I don't remember, but I do remember that there was more teachers, I think.

UNCLE CHARLIE: And they were visiting Jackson?

JAVA JACKSON: And they were visiting Jackson, and they wanted to—

COOKIE: Learn about the Algebra Project.

JAVA JACKSON: Right. So we did a workshop at downtown, at the Standard Light Building, where— Let's see, part of the workshop was the Flagway game and the other part was, what was another part of it?

COOKIE: I think that was it.

APRIL DAVIS: That was it.

JAVA JACKSON: OK. We just did the Flagway game.

UNCLE CHARLIE: Uh-huh. Were these people older than you for the most part?

APRIL DAVIS: Yeah.

COOKIE: And they didn't speak English.

UNCLE CHARLIE: And they didn't speak—they spoke French?

JAVA JACKSON: There were a few that spoke English.

COOKIE: Yeah.

APRIL DAVIS: Some of them spoke English.

JAVA JACKSON: They were translating.

UNCLE CHARLIE: So there was somebody in the group that could translate from French to the English, and from the English to the French, so that they could—everybody could—understand?

JAVA JACKSON: Um-hmm.

COOKIE: Um-hmm.

UNCLE CHARLIE: Now, what were you thinking as you were doing this with these Africans?

JAVA JACKSON: You know, I really can't remember what I was thinking, but I do remember another student, Dusty. He was like with the—he was acting as if they was like different—

APRIL DAVIS: From a different world.

JAVA JACKSON: Yeah. He was like, what do they eat? And like, when he was talking to them, he was like trying to break down like easy stuff, like the math part of it. And they was standing there, they was like OK. You know, they was already doing the math, you know. It was just the language.

UNCLE CHARLIE: Dusty didn't think they knew anything because they were from Africa?

JAVA JACKSON: Yeah. The language was throwing him off. You know.

COOKIE: When they were playing the Flagway game, they were having a lot of fun playing.

JAVA JACKSON: And they were excited about it. They were. And I remember a lady saying, she was like, she told us that each one of us looked like someone that she knew in Mali at home.

COOKIE: Especially me. They were talking about my nose and my dark skin, how I looked like a—they told me my name and they linked it up with "Gatto."

JAVA JACKSON: Yeah. They told me my name would be Jaba because they didn't have a *V*.

COOKIE: They didn't understand *boo*, if you said *boo*.

UNCLE CHARLIE: And what are you all thinking as you're talking to these Africans?

COOKIE: I was like, wow.

UNCLE CHARLIE: Was any—did anything surprise you?

COOKIE: What surprised me was the way they—they—well, they didn't seem all that different after we got to be around for the first thirty minutes. You know, it was all right.

APRIL DAVIS: Yeah. Before we—before I came in, I thought it was going to be different. I didn't think, you know, they was—

UNCLE CHARLIE: What did you think? Tell me exactly what you thought they would be like before you would come in? Omo has now told you that you're going to teach some Africans. What did you think they were going to be like? April, what did you think they were going to be like?

APRIL DAVIS: I thought they were going to be, you know how a lot of TV shows show Africans with little thin, skimpy—

JAVA JACKSON: Robes.

APRIL DAVIS: —clothing, and robes, and the jewelry, bangles and stuff. I thought they were going to come in like that.

JAVA JACKSON: I didn't think they were going to be communicating with us either. I thought it was just going to be through a translator, them talking to us.

UNCLE CHARLIE: You didn't expect any of them to know any English?

JAVA JACKSON: Any English. No.

COOKIE: I thought they were going to come in and be like, duh.

UNCLE CHARLIE: Like something you saw on *Tarzan?*

COOKIE: Yeah. Like—

APRIL DAVIS: And I didn't think they were going to understand what we were saying. I was like, man, I don't want to do this, because it's going to be hard trying to teach somebody with a different language.

COOKIE: But they were real nice. They were real nice and stuff.

· · ·

Almost forty years separates Baba's reflections on the voter registration efforts in McComb, Mississippi, and Uncle Charlie's interviews with April, Java, and Sammie for *Radical Equations.*

Over four hundred years separates the arrival of the visitors from Mali and the arrival of the first enslaved Africans in what would become Mississippi.

The distance between Sammie, Dusty, April, Java, and me and the visitors from Mali is the distance between African Americans and Africa's children.

The remains of SNCC—the organization that Ella Baker nurtured, that galvanized the energy of the student sit-ins and Freedom Riders, that emboldened local people to make demands on American society—are best embodied in its children: Julian Bond, John Lewis, Chuck McDew, Diane Nash, Courtland Cox, Stokely Carmichael, Rudy Lombard, Jerome Smith, June Johnson, Charlie Cobb, Judy Richardson, Connie Curry, Dave Dennis, Janet Jemmott, Marion Barry, Charles Sherrod, Unita Blackwell, Rap Brown, Margaret Burnham, MacArthur Cotton, Ivanhoe Donaldson, Bettie Mae Fikes, James Forman, Betty Garman, Myrtle Glascoe, Fannie Lou Hamer, Curtis Hayes, Hollis Watkins, Bernice Johnson Reagon, Sharlene Kranz, Dorie Ladner, Joyce Ladner, Staughton Lynd, Fred Mangrum, Charles McLaurin, Charles Neblett, John O'Neal, Willie Ricks, Cleveland Sellers, Ruby Doris Smith, Karen Edmonds, Jane Stembridge, Jimmy Travis, Dorothy Zellner, Bob Zellner, Vincent Harding, and so many others whose work transformed America's social and political landscape, whose life's work, as they continue to recede into the ocean of movement that gave birth to them, has been to keep crashing against America's shores, against those borders restricting the flow of democracy.

"Democracy is life giving and therefore spiritual," Uncle Vincent said.

The organizing efforts that grew out of SNCC—Freedom Summer, the Mississippi Freedom Democratic Party, the Lowndes County Freedom Organization—all celebrated less understood examples of the power of people, both young and old, to make extraordinary demands on themselves and society in an attempt to detangle themselves, and generations to come, from centuries of economic bondage. Those efforts also inspired and informed the Northern Student Movement, the Free Speech Movement, Black and Africana studies departments on college campuses, the Chicano movement, and the feminist movement, and they continue to give life to young people who find themselves gathered in the spirit of love, in the spirit of justice, and in the spirit of protest to confront their generation's challenges.

"The young people need to get their act together," Baba says. He says this often to Taba and Khari and me and with a sense of urgency. As if the young people getting their act together at Brinkley Middle School in Jackson, Mississippi, would conjure in the MathLab the spirit of Brenda Travis and Curtis Hayes and Hollis Watkins and the freedom songs they'd sung in the McComb jail.

Taba and Khari and I aren't clear about what we should do next. How to bottle and pour the duende that had been conjured in the MathLab and unleashed during the Flagway Tournament in the Brinkley gymnasium in other school buildings, on America's black children.

And then what? And then what? I ask myself.

How many more MathLabs?

How many more Flagway tournaments?

How much duende?

How does one thing lead to another?

"You never know what the spark is going to be," Mama says. Implying one thing always leads to another.

"What do you mean I need to get my act together?" is my response to Baba. I am more concerned with my own achievement than with what Taba and Khari and I could do together. "My shit is together."

Baba doesn't know where this is headed, but he knows we must figure it out together.

I believe I'll run on, see where the end's gonna be, sing Sweet Honey in the Rock, some of whose members are Ella's children.

We each have different ideas about getting there, where the end's gonna be.

Khari begins working on a governance structure for the students to run the MathLab. He also has some bourgeoning ideas about doing science and technology workshops. We talk about replicating the MathLab in other schools. We talk about organizing more Flagway tournaments. Taba has one foot in the school building and the other in the music business. He wants to become a version of Puff Daddy, to turn street money into street music. He can rap, can write hip-hop and R&B music. The songs are inside him, the undercurrent, the questions that swirl within him from birth, about society, beneath the uniform, the Timberland boots, the saggy pants:

Why was I put on this earth, what's become of you and me, tryin' to find myself, mistake after mistake, which road should I choose, which path should I use, the life I abuse leaves no tomorrow, yeah, I wanna live forever, never die in sorrow, take me higher, show me the other side of the rainbow, take away my fears, before I disappear, after life, ohhh, I wanna live forever, live forever, after life, ohhh, remember me forever. How can I understand how to become a man, at peace with myself, the world and everyone else, ohh, why have I been chosen to live so I can die, why do I cry, why does life pass me by ooh ooh. . . .

In Mississippi, Taba splits his time between the classroom and the studio. I enjoy hanging out in the studio with him, when he's reciting a verse, making a beat. The rap is raw, necessary, reflects the surface of him—*I get high when I smoke a stack, all this evil that I do make me hold this gat, (something something) on the block where my niggas stay, Mama said there'd be hard times and better days.*

"What are we gonna do?" Taba continues to ask. I don't have a response. It feels like we're doing it.

"How long we gonna stay in Mississippi?" he asks. While the work in the school and in the classroom and with the kids fulfills a need I have to forget who I'd been on the court, to find a new sense of purpose, the answers to the questions Taba is asking himself can't be found in the MathLab.

· · ·

"It felt like there was an opportunity that was calling me, that was calling us," Khari said to me years later. "We went to four-year schools doing the athletics, we were Division 1 athletes, but there was no NBA draft for me, there's no professional swimmers, and so it's not gonna be about continuing to swim competitively beyond this moment. . . .

"The idea of going deeper south, came down to Pops [Baba] talking to me, 'Do you want to come down and support the work in the Delta? . . . Omo's down here, Taba's gonna be down.' . . . Coming down here to live was much different than coming down to help. I had people telling me to come to LA, come to Atlanta—post-college it's about the dream location or the dream job. This place was not on anybody's list, . . . but it felt more important to see progress, the legacy of the work—that felt like what brought me to Mississippi."

.   .   .

Khari and Taba and I begin having dinner regularly with Baba and Dave at the Olive Garden on the outskirts of Jackson. For us, it is a free drink and meal. The conversations center on the work. I get the sense that Dave and Baba love each other and that they are brothers—not how Taba and I love each other or how he and Khari and I are brothers, how our work and personal lives are materially, emotionally, and physically intertwined, but somewhere in the vicinity of how Baba and Uncle Greg, and Baba and Uncle Roger, love each other. It is a love and brotherhood born out of the same womb, born out of Mississippi, of surviving its trenches, born out of the realities of black life in white America. We listen as they update each other, share competing, sometimes conflicting visions of where they are headed and how they are getting there. Dave has created a six-step approach to community development based on the Algebra Project's five-step process for learning math. The Algebra Project's process is less about an order and more about a cyclical approach to unpacking and packing relationships. Baba works with Dave the same way he works with us: he sets the stage, breaks off a digestible chunk of the work, provides some direction, entrusts us with the outcome, even when he knows where our plans are headed. It is in this way that Dave has carved out his turf within the Algebra Project. It's similar to how they'd worked together in the '60s, when Dave was codirector of the Council of Federated Organizations (COFO), which included SNCC and the Mississippi NAACP. COFO was the structural/institutional window dressing responsible for the creation of both Freedom Summer and the Mississippi Freedom Democratic Party (MFDP).

. . .

"Do as I do and not as I say," Dave says, referring to some more personal aspects of his life.

"What I do is supposed to speak louder than what I say," is what Ella Baker said. Which is how I measure the distance between Dave and Baba. Every word that leaves Baba's mouth feels like a manifestation of something he has done, a marker of who he is.

Dave is interested in Taba and Khari and me as people: what makes us wear our shorts so low, why the Timberland boots, how we had grown up in a house with the front door unlocked and a fridge open to friends or whoever else wandered in. Whether or not he can trust us to do business with him. He uses words like *accountability*. Dave is interested in how he could tap into our magnetism, our gravitational pull. He, like Baba, understands that if there is a force capable of transforming America, it resides in young people.

"Being young is a state of mind," Ella Baker says, "young people are the people who want change."

Dave begins organizing a band of students throughout his Southern Initiative of the Algebra Project (SIAP). Baba is wary of this. Wants us to find our own direction, create a space for ourselves, like what SNCC had been for young organizers during the movement. He doesn't want a youth-run wing of the Algebra Project or for us to be co-opted by the SIAP or anyone else.

It isn't clear what the boundaries of the SIAP are. Who has jurisdiction over what. Dave's work focuses on the Delta, which is expanding to include Arkansas. He's responsible for growing the work in Jackson outside of Brinkley Middle School, which is Baba's domain. Baba also is organizing pockets of work in the Mississippi Delta. My sense is that each one wants to move how they want to move, and while Dave will defer to Baba, Baba's solution is to say Dave has his own shop. I begin to understand that when Baba says to Khari and Taba and me that "the young people need to get their act together," he means he wants us to have our own shop too.

. . .

"He could have been there by himself at Brinkley," Khari says, "but he had a vision that included us. He was pretty hands off with the day to day, *I can't do this but you all can do that.* At the core of it people that were a little bit older, that reminded the students of people from their hood, people from their family, were coming into their school. I believed that part of what we were doing at Brinkley could change what happens everywhere."

·   ·   ·

In Baba's mind, "the young people getting their act together" was how one thing would lead to another, in the same way that the sit-ins and freedom rides had led to voter registration, Freedom Summer, the MFDP, and other political organizing and action.

Julian Bond, one of the students at SNCC's founding conference, who eventually ran and won seats in the Georgia House of Representatives and Senate, wrote:

> Freedom Summer brought one thousand, mostly white, volunteers to Mississippi for the summer of 1964. They helped build the new political party SNCC had organized, the Mississippi Freedom Democratic Party (MFDP); registered voters; and staffed twenty-eight "Freedom Schools" intended by their designer, Charles Cobb, "to provide an education which will make it possible for them to challenge the myths of our society, to perceive more clearly its realities, and to find alternatives, and ultimately new directions for action."
>
> The MFDP challenged the seating of the regular, all-white delega-tion from Mississippi at the 1964 Democratic Convention [in Atlantic City] and, in 1965, challenged the seating of Mississippi's congressional delegation in Washington. The convention challenge ended in failure when pressures from President Lyndon Johnson erased promised support from party liberals. An offer was made—and rejected—of two convention seats to be filled by the national party, not the Freedom Democrats, to which Fannie Lou Hamer declared, "We didn't come for no two seats when all of us is tired!"[2]

The MFDP exposed the limits of the liberal wing of the Democratic Party, Mama said.

I met Julian Bond for the first time when I was playing ball at George Washington. I was dribbling the ball up the court and recognized his face in the arena full of fans. I remember wondering if anyone else in the arena knew who he was. I made eye contact. Wanted him to know that I knew who he was. That he was one of Ella Baker's, one of Mississippi's children. I wanted to believe that he was there to watch me, one of Bob Moses's children, play ball.

Judy Richardson, who had been unable to believe that Mama and Baba had let Taba and me play for a baseball team sponsored by the Cambridge Police, who was also one of Ella Baker's children, said, "We left [Atlantic City] understanding that politics wasn't about morality, that politics was about power."

"We learned number one, that the national Democratic Party doesn't care about justice or equality, they just care about power," Stokely Carmichael said. "We went to them, the Freedom Democratic Party, and said: 'Now here we are. We've organized in the state. We haven't shot anybody. We haven't lynched anybody who's tried to vote. We support your platform. We're willing to sign the loyalty oath. And we support your candidates, Johnson and Humphrey.' The white Democratic Party (of Mississippi) came to them and said: 'We don't support your candidates; if Negroes try to vote, we're going to shoot and kill them, we don't support your platform and we ain't going to sign your loyalty oath.' And we said: 'Now, which one will you seat?' And they said: 'We have to seat those white guys, but we'll let two of you go with them so you can become like them.' And we said we didn't want any part of that. No one in the country understood that."[3]

· · ·

Our Jackson apartment gets robbed for the first time while we're all in Boston during the run-up to Christmas. I come back first, the door is open, all our shit is gone: PlayStation, TV, everything else of electronic value. My CDs, the six hundred I'd collected since college, are scattered on the floor, form a trail through the sliding door, the backyard, littering the creek, to where the getaway car must have been parked on the other side of the water.

I go from room to room. Find the Air Jordan shoebox unharmed in the closet. Go outside and then across the street. Don't want to go back inside, sleep there, or call the police. We all have thoughts about who it was—the kids who'd said they were going to college at Alcorn State, who show up every now and then from around the corner to get blazed, or it could have been the landlord. I also have my doubts about the neighbors—no one reported anything.

We never refurnish, except for the PlayStation and TV. I watch as Hot (which is what I call Taba when he's about to do some shit that could lead to him getting arrested) and Spice put on ski masks, prepare for retaliation. Weed first, a shot of something, a heavy object to be catapulted into a window, engine sufficiently warm, double sliding cargo doors cocked, they don't ask me to join them, it was stupid nigga shit, nothing worth getting arrested for. They make it back and we laugh and I wait. For the retaliation for the retaliation. And then a couple weeks later the floor floods. I'm not sure what the cause was or where the water came from—Spice says it was the water boiler—but we spend a couple weeks living in a marsh, walking around the house on wooden planks that become dirt roads on the soggy carpet. Baba doesn't say much to us. The Algebra Project is running out of money and continues to pay rent sporadically. The phone gets shut off. We've been running a phone card hustle and Taba and Spice would spend hours on the pay phone at the gas station on the corner talking to shorties, sending smoke signals to the outside world.

By the time the water dries, we get robbed again. Retaliation for the retaliation. During the day, while we were at school. It had to be the dickheads that Spice gets blazed with because Tyson, our Rottweiler, was there and they locked him in a closet.

Quincy, the landlord's son who manages the property, who in his youth got a scholarship to the Berklee School of Music, who is approaching forty and hasn't made any money from his music, appears at the door one night with tears in his eyes. He looks caked out. I'm the only one home and I open the door cautiously. He's wearing a long trench coat, and I can see another man with a shotgun at the corner of the house. They've come to collect the rent. I tell Dad, who figures out a way to pay him. In the meantime, we all begin searching for another place to live, and Taba and Khari and I ways to get even. We begin making our way to the attic and the air conditioning vents, filling them with piss and all kinds of rotten shit. Dad comes home late, and so we work on the house every day after school until he returns, nails in the roof, etc., etc. He often finds us laughing for no apparent reason—at Spice falling through the attic and landing on his feet in the carport. He keeps telling us that the young people need to get their act together.

We are in "Fuck that!" and "I don't give a fuck" mode. The reality of young black American male life colliding with Baba's aspirations for us, for America. He's concerned that we aren't as concerned about what is happening to black boys in this country as it is happening to us in Mississippi, in real time, in front of his eyes.

He appears unfazed; he has been in worse spots. He projects an aura of calm and confidence. He says that Ella Baker taught him that you could lead a meaningful life in struggle. And then the neighbor who had threatened to shoot our dogs for shitting in his yard runs up on Taba and Khari with his gun drawn.

"It was the middle of the day, early, he had been mad at the dogs for a minute. I don't remember the sequence," Spice tells me.

"I'll shoot your dog."

"You ain't gonna shoot my fuckin' dog," Taba said.

"I'll shoot your dog!" the neighbor said.

"Fuck outta here, shoot the fuckin' fair one."

"What did you say?"

"You heard me. Put the gun away and let's shoot the fair one."

"I'll shoot you and your fuckin' dogs!"

"Stop yellin' and put the gun away so we can shoot the fair one."

"Step in the street! Step in the street!"

Taba walked toward the street and then the neighbor ran in the street waiting for Taba with his gun drawn, and then Taba walked back to the house.

"Shoot the fair one," Taba said.

"Come in the street, come in the street!"

"Put the gun away so I can fuck you up."

"The neighbor would walk back into his front yard and then Taba would walk back toward the street, and then the neighbor would run back into the street and then Taba would walk back to the house," Spice says later.

"Come in the street, come in the street!"

"They did that a couple times," Spice says, "and then when Taba was walking back to the crib the neighbor followed him onto our property and I was outside and Taba slipped inside and locked the sliding door, locking me out. And the dude's waving the gun around talking about he's gonna shoot us. Shit was crazy."

"Yo, bro, you shoulda seen it, the way Spice ran into the glass door with his hands up, I thought he got shot," Taba says.

. . .

The students are disarming. Remediating. They offer the possibility of growing out of something else, growing into something else. I focus on the routine of preparing for and working with them in Mrs. Byrd's eighth-grade math classes. She's my height, bigger boned, chocolate skinned, thin hair that reaches her shoulder. Her voice is soft, can be stern because that is a prerequisite to keeping kids from climbing the walls. After school, when she's with her son, who's about the same age as her students, she is all love, all gentle. She's the type of teacher that has made the Algebra Project possible: not a true believer, not radical in the sense that you could picture her sitting in or marching, but open-minded, willing to give it a shot, wants the kids to do better, the school to do better, is willing to stretch a little and make room for us in her classroom.

Initially, my role in the classroom is to help Baba. He comes up with something he's going to teach, based on where he left off at the last class. If there's time beforehand, he lets me in on his plans; if not I pick it up during the first class of the day and then help with giving instructions to the students the rest of the day. He often breaks the class into groups and I move between as many groups as I can, trying to keep students focused on the question or task at hand, keep the conversations productive. There is an inherent intimacy between student and teacher as the learning process unfolds, a shedding of armor as a student allows who they are, what they are thinking, to be revealed. By the end of each day, Baba lets me run a class. Like Mrs. Byrd, I don't like to raise my voice and spend a good amount of time waiting for the students to be quiet.

By the winter I'm leading my own classes, which coincides with the arrival of the Texas Instruments TI-80 graphing calculators. There is one for every student. Some of the students have worked with them already and they are excited to show the other students and Mrs. Byrd what they remember. The calculator is a version of the one Mama had given me while I was in college. Because I have the most experience with the calculator, Baba begins letting me run the class consistently. During lunch or recess, eventually on Saturdays, I begin working with students who want to help me run the class.

And so, when Dave offers to include me and a group of students in a professional development workshop he's conducting for teachers across the Jackson school district, I accept. I pick a group of students that includes April, Sammie, Java, Chaintain Greer, and Dusty. We begin practicing for the workshop at Dave's office in the Standard Life building. For some of the students it's their first ride in an elevator. Dave is there with us, cooks his version of gumbo, tells stories about what it was like growing up on a plantation. Our workshop presentation involves folding a paper in half and opening it up to see how many sections have been created, then folding it in half twice and doing the same thing, then folding it in half three times and so on. Eventually the paper becomes too thick to fold again and so then we ask a question: If you were able to fold the paper in half a hundred times, how many sections would be created?

When we do it for the teachers, we graph the results and create a program in the calculator that will predict the number of sections for any number of folds. Chaintain, who wrote the program, who took it upon himself to learn how to program the calculator to do all sorts of stuff, who sports an Einstein-like afro, who Java and I are convinced is the coolest nerd on the planet, that he is going to invent something that will make all of us rich, works the main calculator that is being projected onto a screen. Chaintain has stepped into my shoes, attempts to embody what he has learned from me, conjuring what I have learned about teaching from Mrs. Byrd and Baba. As he does, I can see that he has joined me and Taba and Khari and Java and Cookie and Dusty in walking in Bob Moses's footsteps.

These workshops are the spark, the beginning of what we will do together.

W. H. MOSES SERMON

A COMPARISON

Garvey may not expect to live in Africa but his spirit will carry on the work that will be done. I hear a lot of fool people talk about going to Africa. How did Ireland get a measure of freedom? Ireland came here. The Irishmen in Boston, New York, Chicago, and everywhere, they organized and began to create public sentiment that they could not express on British territory, and they made this great America unlock the doors and bring more liberty to Ireland than she has ever had. And just as she was the base of preparations for Irishmen, so God has chosen this America of ours to lay the keel for the ship that shall bring success to the black peoples of the world. America has to stand by. American sentiment has to be loyal to this thing. Do it or deny the faith on which the Government was founded.

CHAPTER 12

In the Distance
Between Us (II)

L ight swung across my legs like a pendulum as the wind gathered in
  the branches, pushed and pulled the curtains to and from the window.

It was a year since Amzie had died, and we were preparing to leave
Peabody Terrace.

Mama and Baba's bedroom was dim despite the sun perched, at the tail
end of summer, in the middle of the sky.

I was ten. I was seated on the floor with tape and scissors, with boxes
ready to be sealed and flat cardboard ready to become boxes. I was alone.
Baba was somewhere else, on the other side of the window getting a U-Haul
and more boxes. I was alone with the memories, some waiting to be packed,
some to be discarded. I sat in the quiet they imposed, in the insurmountable
distance our family had traveled from Tanzania to America.

Taba and Maisha and Malaika had gone with Mama to New York City
to see Bibi, and then to Vineland, New Jersey, to visit Babu. At that point I
had met him once. When they came back, they would tell me stories about
the land he owned and the house he built on it and his dog named Teaser
and his gourmet cooking.

Baba and I had had cornmeal that morning for breakfast. I decided
to reheat the leftovers and wait for him at the kitchen table. It was a dish
we'd eaten in Tanzania. I still enjoyed it, as much for the taste as for the
memories evoked.

Baba was either gathering used produce boxes from the food co-op or
purchasing flat, pristine cardboard that could be folded into boxes at U-Haul.

He'd been surprised when I agreed to stay home and help him move instead of going with Mama to New York and New Jersey. Which surprised me, that his perception of me was so different than my perception of myself. I became aware then that who he saw when he looked at me wasn't who I was.

I'd said yes because it meant we would be alone together. I wanted to return to the relationship we'd shared before we arrived in America. To remember his embrace. I'd said yes because I wanted to show him that I could be who he wanted me to be, that I was more than who he thought I was. I'd said yes because there was a small fortune of stolen bike parts beneath the hallway steps that I needed to get rid of.

I listened for the sound of him in the alley, in branches colliding, the rustling of leaves, in the hum of electricity, the opening and closing of doors in the apartments above and below, the faint chime on the neighbor's balcony beyond.

We had lived here long enough to be remembered, to call the buildings our own. But we couldn't belong to Harvard University, take root in Peabody Terrace's asphalt. Most families lived here a year or two, some a few more. We had managed seven, remained longer than all the kids who had become our acquaintances or friends.

Imran had been the first to leave.

He'd moved to Canada a year ago when his father had finished his PhD. I had wandered the football field, through the courtyard, onto the court, still half expecting to see him, certainly to hear him conjuring his favorite ballplayers. He didn't leave bones like the JDs, who spat on walls, pissed on walls, scraped their names in the concrete.

I had peered into the window of Imran's old room. Where we had watched WWF wrestling matches, seen Hulk Hogan suplex André the Giant. I wanted to be able to see, touch a remnant of him, to acknowledge we had been here, in this place, on this earth together, but the walls and floors had been sanitized.

Our apartment would also be cleared of our bones, our boxes, our memories sandblasted from their concrete.

The boxes in the living room—some taped shut, others still open, some stacked like totems—contained remnants of Mama and Baba's journey out of America and the journey we'd shared out of Tanzania. The sculptures that could fit in the boxes were wrapped in newspaper. The larger Maconde statues remained rooted on the carpet like baobab trees. The boxes also contained some of what we had accomplished and the little we'd accumulated after we'd arrived in America.

I returned to the living room, to my medals and ribbons and the swimming and baseball trophies, too tall to be contained in the cardboard. The books rose like totems too. I had stacked them. A few remained on shelves. The shelves were now bare cliffs. I searched for the book of black men, women, and children getting lynched that had baptized our arrival in America.

·   ·   ·

Taba and I began riding with Frank and Marlon after Imran left. They were also older than us, had recently moved to Peabody Terrace from North Carolina, introduced us to the word *nigga*.

We had new wheels by then, chrome alloy Univega dirt bikes.

Taba and I took the bikes into the wild on their maiden voyage, cut a path through the bramble, and once on the other side we headed out onto the river, across the bridge, bunny-hopping, wheelie-ing, attempting endos as far as we could, farther than we'd ever gone before, and then we turned around and pedaled as fast as we could to the woods again, to reach them before the sun set.

It had taken two years for Baba to save enough money to buy the bikes. The bike store was next-door to Baskin-Robbins, and so each trip for ice cream during those two years resulted in a test drive. We sat on the bikes. Sometimes rode them in the store. Flipped tags. The prices were always the same—too much. And then one day, after Baba won the MacArthur award, they weren't.

Baba made us take courses at the Bicycle Workshop again to re-familiarize ourselves with changing flats, replacing chains, adjusting brakes, removing tires.

We went fishing in the Charles River with Frank and Marlon on weekends. We managed to find worms in the alley's dirt. Each weekend we rode farther and farther out, to where we thought the fish would be. Frank and Marlon were searching for home, told stories about catching fish in North Carolina longer than their forearms. Usually, Taba was the only one who caught anything—never longer than a hand.

Frank and Marlon's father, Big Frank, was also working on his PhD. Big Frank and Baba had traveled the improbable distance from somewhere in black America to the campus of Harvard University.

Mama lamented that Baba had almost finished his PhD, was ABD, that his dissertation was in a box, that he could still get someone to type it.

Big Frank was younger than Baba, made his own French fries. Sometimes we watched boxing with him. It was the golden age of the middle-weight division—Sugar Ray Leonard, Thomas Hearns, Roberto Durán, Marvin Hagler fought epic battles. I rooted for Sugar Ray. Frank and Big Frank rooted for Thomas "Hitman" Hearns. Who we rooted for had everything to do with who we saw when we looked into the eyes of black and white America.

Marlon often wore a shirt that read *Who says we're the minority?* on the front. On the back was the number, in billions, of the world's colored people.

"Where did the white people come from?" is what Mama said I'd asked her, just after we'd arrived in Cambridge from Tanzania, as we rode on a bus for the first time.

"Shhhh," she'd said.

Frank and Marlon said that where they were from was full of black people.

· · ·

When Frank and Marlon began riding with the other black boys from the neighborhood, Taba and I rode along too. Most of their bikes had been patched together. At first Taba and I stood guard as the other boys climbed the fences to the Harvard dormitories and stole bike parts and, if the chain locks allowed it, entire bikes from the Harvard students.

And then Taba and I climbed too, began applying what we had recently learned at the Bicycle Workshop. There was a wheel that I was especially proud of. I'd had to climb the fence at Community Boating (a boathouse along the Charles River where we'd learned to sail its polluted waters) to get to it, unscrew its parts. Then I threw it over the fence without warping the rim and rode with it on my shoulder along the river, over the bridge, and through Peabody Terrace.

From Baba's perspective, the move from Peabody Terrace to the house he'd purchased across the street from the Newtowne Court Housing projects was so that "you wouldn't be afraid of your own people."

From Taba's and my perspective, we were already deeply entrenched in the currency of niggas.

· · ·

When the doorbell rang, it startled me because the house had been a certain kind of quiet for so long. For a moment I thought it was Baba back with more boxes.

"Who is it?" I asked through the intercom. And then static.

"Omowale," Sevie said, calling me by my full name. And then more static.

"I'll be down in a minute." I was wearing shorts. Put on socks, a T-shirt. Skipped down the flight of steps. Let him in from the interior hallway. We slapped five. He was a couple years older than me, taller, huskier. We all had attended Martin Luther King Elementary School. He and Marshall Tyree once had a fight during recess, rolled in the grass that we played football on, in the dog shit that littered it. Both of them had grabbed the dog shit and smeared it on each other's faces.

"What are you doin'?" he asked.

"Packin'," I said.

"Frank and Marlon said you were movin'?"

"Yeah."

"In Cambridge?"

"Yeah, to the Port," I said.

"You still got that bike seat?"

"Yeah." I crawled under the stairwell and began pulling out parts.

"How much for that?" he asked as he fixed his eyes on a Peugeot pump. "What are you gonna do with this? You gonna take this with you?"

"Nah. I'm sellin' it."

"I got fifteen dollars," he said.

"Hold on," I said. And went out to the door that led to the alley. "What time is it?" I asked. The alley was empty.

"Twelve," he said. Baba had been gone since breakfast. It felt longer than that. "What can I get for fifteen?" he asked.

"Whatever you want."

He took the quick-release seat, pump, and handlebars. "I'm gonna come back tomorrow for more." We put everything else back underneath the staircase and then I walked with him back into the alley.

"Put some sneakers on, Omowale, you ain't in Africa." He laughed. Sevie was one of the few people who called me by my full name.

"I'm gonna come see you down the Port," he said.

Alone again in the apartment, I returned to packing and unpacking memories, navigating the distance between Tanzania and America.

I found letters from Hamisi written in Kiswahili. I could hear Mama saying *Omowale, say goodbye. Omowale, say goodbye to Hamisi.* We were about to leave Same. I remember standing on the road outside of our house there, holding Mama's hand, unable to comprehend what she was asking me to do. Hamisi stood with us. Wide smile, gaunt limbs, short fist-tight hair. Baba had taken him into our home on the condition that he continued his studies. He'd become a big brother. Woke and dressed me, kept me from the anthills.

Did he want to come with us? I asked Mama.

Yes, she said.

Why didn't he come with us?

I remember how excited Mama and Baba had gotten when his letters arrived in Peabody Terrace as each page gave birth to an affection that we rarely witnessed in them. They had taken turns reading his letters, at first with ease and then what words they could remember. The letters had come in months and years and then no longer.

Mama said that Baba thought it would be better not to take Hamisi from his home, from the land that had given birth to him. She tried to explain to me that because he had been able to go to secondary school, life would be much better for him there. That after secondary school he would have to serve in the Tanzanian army. I wondered why it was OK for Hamisi to serve in Tanzania's army, but why it wasn't OK for Baba and for us to serve in America's army. I associated leaving Tanzania with leaving Hamisi. But we'd left him before that, in Same when we moved to Kibaha. A sense of him endured. I missed Hamisi like I missed Imran.

. . .

I found the image of Mama and Baba about to leave America, on the deck of the freighter in Red Hook, Brooklyn. The image was soft, slightly out of focus. Baba was incognito, wearing dark glasses. His beard was thick. His hair was thinning. Mama was tall and wiry, sporting an Afro, her body curling into his—they both looked hip, in love, happier than I had ever seen them.

I found an image of me in Baba's arms, seated in his lap.

I found a picture of me holding his hand in the savannah beneath Mount Kilimanjaro.

I found a picture of me balancing on a bike, chewing sugar cane.

Of me and Baba on a basketball court.

Of me holding a chicken, half the size of my body, by its feet.

The images were evidence that the dirt road existed, evidence of a relationship to the planet, of the life we had lost when we had left Tanzania.

The photo album was laid out in front of me, covered two tiles as I sat with my legs spread on the floor. Initially the tiles had been cold but now they were the temperature of my body. Thin plastic film protected each page. Most had two, three photographs on them. I removed the picture of Mama and Baba on the deck of the ship and held it in the palm of my hand. Attempted to remove what looked like dust, sharpen what wasn't clear. But the photo would remain opaque, hazy.

I turned to the pages of pictures of Bibi and her brother and sister traveling through Africa, seated sidesaddle on the backs of camels at the foot of pyramids, dressed as if for Easter. Mama said that Bibi had become the oldest in her family when her older brother, Herman, had died at seven of typhoid fever. That Bibi had buried a notebook of his writing in a trunk when, as a teenager, she'd moved from South Carolina to Cleveland, Ohio, to earn a living working in the homes of more affluent families. That Bibi had exhumed the notebook two decades later to provide Mama with examples of good penmanship. I imagined young Bibi tall as a cornstalk, face long and proud, pressed against the window of a passenger bus taking her to Cleveland; her eyes landing on wide, flat, empty fields, dense patches of palmetto, white lines spit from tires, bridges rising and falling all the way to the edge of Cleveland's Cuyahoga River. Mama said that Bibi's cousins, Annie Fair, Bobbi Jane, and Clyde Lee, had traveled those roads before her. Unlike her cousins, who were on their way to Negro colleges, Bibi was among the nation's first wave of black migrants, 1.6 million between 1910 and 1930, from Mississippi, Louisiana, Georgia, Alabama, the Carolinas, Tennessee, all headed north or west to escape Jim Crow.

Bibi became the summer help for a family that lived in the Shaker Heights neighborhood of Cleveland. The daughter of the family, and then her mother, took a liking to Bibi and kept her on beyond the summer. Helped her enroll at Cleveland Tech to finish high school. Bibi told Mama that in Cleveland she'd met Babu, who she called by his last name, Jemmott.

Mama said Bibi had wanted to be a doctor. There were only a handful of black female medical school graduates then. The mother of the family she worked for helped with her applications to three of the five nursing programs in the country that accepted black people. Bibi moved to New York City to attend the Harlem Hospital School of Nursing, struggled her way to an RN degree. Graduated in 1929. Years later Babu would come looking and find her in Harlem.

When Bibi's father—who had been the deacon of the Greenville Presbyterian Church, who had taught each of his children how to play a musical instrument, who'd driven a taxi, hired himself out as a tinsmith—collapsed one day from heat stroke, fell off a roof, and died, Bibi relocated the rest of the family to live with her in Harlem. They were two sisters and four brothers—Ruth and Ezella, Nat, RB, Richard, and Bliss—and their mother, Miz Minou, as they affectionately called her, and their dog, Frisk.

Five years later, Miz Minou—whose congenitally defective heart had pumped life into eight healthy babies, had borne the premature death of one—died.

Mama, who was just learning to walk, lay in bed with her grandmother in her last days—*Get down baby, your grandma is tired and weak*, Miz Minou would say. Mama said that Miz Minou had been gentle and sweet. That she'd rarely leave the house but that she'd walked her and Bibi to the bus stop the day she would pass. That she'd waited in her nightgown with Frisk by the curb for the bus to arrive, for them to find a seat before raising a hand and waving goodbye.

The last time I saw Bibi, we were celebrating Baba's receipt of an Essence Award. I was in my third year of college; it was six months before she died. I'd borrowed a jacket and tie from my roommate and joined the family on the red carpet extending from the entrance of Madison Square Garden. Baba and Mama, Bibi, Maisha, Malaika and Uncle Roger and his wife, Ralphetta, sat together. Taba and I sat a little closer to the stage.

Jesse Jackson stopped to shake our hands as if he was still running for president; Eddie Murphy stood a few rows behind us and was half the height of his wife; Spike Lee strutted to his seat like Mookie in *Do the Right Thing*; Denzel Washington appeared and every woman in the room stood on their feet and screamed.

A hush fell through the audience as Michael Jackson was escorted to his seat.

Bill Cosby introduced Baba, and Xscape dedicated their hit "Understanding" to him. Baba stood in a batik that had been fashioned into a jacket by an artist from Côte d'Ivoire and dedicated the award to the women, from Ella to Mama to Bibi, who had made him possible.

We cajoled him at the after-party to taste the champagne. He touched the rim of the glass with a lip and sipped as if the alcohol was scalding water. It was the first drink he'd had since Tanzania. Bibi had no such inhibitions and reveled in oysters on the half shell as she stuffed her purse with packets of butter.

"A toast," she said, her wig off center, "to the captain!" who up until that moment, hadn't earned her approval.

. . .

Baba returned with a U-Haul truck. We packed the bikes last and then Baba and I drove our things in batches to the other side of Cambridge to the new house. Each trip took less than ten minutes. Baba parked the U-Haul in our new driveway. The house had been built in 1894, had two front doors. The driveway was in disrepair. Baba's vision for the house started in the basement. He showed me where the ramp would go for our bikes, where we could have a game room (his vision would require six years of construction) and a bathroom, how on the first floor the kitchen would be changed, and then we went outside and back in through the other front door. As we climbed the steps, he pointed to the wall that would be removed, how the two units would become one home, which bedrooms were mine and Maisha and Malaika and Taba's. He said the ceilings would come down and that the attic would become part of our rooms, that our rooms would have lofts, require ladders. And then we went back outside and began moving the rest of the boxes.

Ghetto was outside, loitering on the steps of the apartments across the street with his younger brother Ganzy. They were in high school then. I would learn that they, too, had moved, half a block from the projects to across the street from the projects. I watched Ganzy strut toward the mouth of the projects, arms swinging like a pendulum, knuckles approaching the concrete. A thick iron bar barricaded the entrance, was kept unlocked to allow first responders to enter in the event of an emergency.

"Where you comin' from?" Ghetto asked me.

"What's your name?"

"What is it?"

"What's that, African? For a minute I thought you said Homo."

"Welcome to the neighborhood," he said.

· · ·

We shared the driveway with the Tuttles. The Tuttles had also lived in the projects before buying their own home. The grandmother emerged first. She was short and stout, wore a nightgown and waved. It would be a while before her sons acknowledged us. The flags waving from the pole at their front door indicated they had been to Vietnam. The grandmother's son-in-law had his Roadster parked half on the street, half on the sidewalk in front of their door. The car was familiar from the *Dukes of Hazzard* episodes we used to watch at Imran's. The car had North Carolina plates. A Confederate flag was spread across the rear window. It was the first Confederate flag I'd seen in America. The son-in-law had a haircut like he belonged to the Marines, like he belonged in the images of men pointing at mutilated black bodies, in the book now buried at the bottom of one of the boxes taking root in the basement.

· · ·

Frank and Marlon came to visit us a few days after we'd moved in. They were also leaving Peabody Terrace. We went fishing in the afternoon. We hadn't caught anything the entire summer. Had ridden our bikes as far as we could along the Charles River. We rode over the river on the Boston University bridge and then ten miles along the Emerald Necklace, a chain of parks, parkways, and waterways developed by Frederick Law Olmsted, landing us in Jamaica Pond in Boston.

We spent the rest of the day beneath the trees, next to the water, mobs of turtles sunning on logs.

Taba caught a small sunfish.

We stopped for pizza on the way home.

We left our bikes outside with the bikes of two other kids inside the store.

The kids nodded their heads to acknowledge us as we walked past them to the back of the shop to begin eating our pizza as they finished theirs.

When we came out of the shop, the Univegas were gone. The shock of it felt like getting stopped and frisked when I was a kid, like diving into the Blodgett Pool's frigid water. Like landing in America.

The kids had left their own bikes in place of ours. They were like the BMX bikes the black boys patched together, part by stolen part. We rode until it got dark, Taba and I on the kid's bikes, up and down the neighborhood, into some projects.

I punched a brick in the projects and then we returned to Olmsted's Emerald Necklace, to the Boston University bridge and over the river into Cambridge. All I could think about on the way home was what Baba was gonna to do to us.

"What happened to the Univegas?" Ghetto asked as we pulled into the driveway.

When we told Baba, he gasped and hit something and became visibly upset, like when the cop had said "move it" in the Blodgett Pool parking lot.

The bikes had meant as much, maybe more, to him as they had to us.

In the morning, he took the bikes that the thieves had left and planted them on the other side of the thick iron bar barricading the entrance of Newtowne Court.

It was where Taba and I took root in America.

W. H. MOSES SERMON

WHERE WE STAND

The authorities at first were unwilling to let the black man participate [in World War 1], but God had His way, and black men saved the day. And what was the fight about? The nations of Europe were fighting about the World, and Africa in particular. They were fighting about oil wells, and gold, and land. The white folks were gobbling everything up.

But let me tell you something, justice is not only in the hearts of black men, there are thousands of white men willing to give you justice.

The policy of the world is to hold the black man as the slave of society for time immemorial, but under God I would rather die and go to hell than to live like this. The spirit of the Lord is upon all flesh. . . . The District Attorney prosecuting Garvey said that we have guns, but we haven't a pistol. What we have is truth. . . . We can't do anything at this stage by fighting, but we will convince the world. The British Government has more black subjects than white ones. The British Empire has got less than one hundred million. We have two or three hundred million. . . . France has more black Frenchmen than white. And from now on we want the President to know there are more black ones than white ones. And we have got some scattered all over the world. Not only in our homeland, but everywhere in the world. And not only the black folks of the world are waking up, but in India, too. They may have no guns, but they are saying "Let's go." In India and Japan and China and Australia and in the islands of the sea they are waking up and saying: "We are scattered around and we want to come together." (*Loud applause*)

I am just as sure that it is coming as I am living today. The Negroes here are just Negroes in quarters. The Negroes are out yonder. Tall sons and daughters, broad shoulders, men that can eat men alive. (*Laughter*)

CHAPTER 13

The King of the Port

W e ran the streets.

There were twelve of us—Moke and Fats, Colin and Dana, Dico and Daco, Hector and Alex, Ariel and Nando, me and Taba. Six sets of brothers, each within two years of each other and, within that, three sets of twins.

We were between ten and twelve years old.

We ran from adolescence to the precipice of manhood.

"I know your muthas!" Wolf yelled.

He was short and fat, barreling down the narrow hallway that led to the back door of Topps Donuts, where he made the donuts and was in charge of preventing us from stealing the ones that were cooling on racks. We grabbed them in fistfuls. The honey dip melted in our palms. I stuffed one in my mouth as we turned and bumped into each other on our way in and out.

We raced out the door and across the parking lot, full speed as we turned onto Cherry Street, the sun to our backs. Wolf in the dust, bent over, breathing hard at the edge of the parking lot. We would see him again in the projects—at night or in the morning, on his way home or to work. He wouldn't chase us then, whether in uniform or not. The projects were home base to all of us.

We ran past our house on the corner of School Street. Baba had turned the crib into a construction site. We didn't have a front door for months. He nailed large sheets of plywood together to cover the hole at night as he converted it from a two- to a one-family home. During the day the house was wide open. Baba was somewhere inside, attempting to master another

THE KING OF THE PORT · 175

recipe from the *Moosehead Cookbook*, saddled with the burden of walking in Mama's shoes. He wasted entire days preparing shit we wouldn't touch. When he wasn't cooking, he was renovating the basement. Mama, who spent her days and nights in medical school, came home exhausted. "Your father is stubborn," she said. "I told him to start with the second floor, so that each of you could have a bedroom. But he had a vision of turning that shit pit into a place you could hang out and park your bikes."

We ran past the Tuttles, past the American and POW MIA flags that hung from their front door. Their den flooded with inebriated disfigured Vietnam veterans on weekends. I was always surprised to see black men adrift in the burden of that brotherhood—of fomenting beer and controlled substances, the shared trauma of life and death on America's battlefields—bickering with each other, with their bitches, with the United States of America.

We ran past Paul's, the store that sat across the street from the mouth of the projects. The store was a relic of the plantation economics that enabled America's capitalism—welcomed food stamps, sold overpriced groceries, submarine sandwiches, applied a convenience tax to shit like orange juice for the distance muthafuckas didn't have to travel to Central Square.

Paul and his brother, Ernie, opened and closed the store precisely at 6 a.m. and 6 p.m. every weekday and on Saturday, took regular vacations, raised their families in the suburbs. Their kids sometimes helped on weekends, but they were on their way to college and weren't going to take over the family business. I thought Mama was trippin' when she refused to let us spend any of her money at Paul's. I wouldn't understand until I saw Spike Lee's *Do the Right Thing* why she'd been adamant that we walk to the food co-op in Central Square for orange juice.

I watched the movie a dozen times. Each time as transfixed as the first. Once with Wimbledon at the Harvard Square movie theater.

Put some black people on the wall, Buggin' Out yelled from the screen.

Wake up! Mister Señor Love Daddy implored, perched in the window of the radio station overlooking the block.

One of them was Black! Smiley stuttered, referring to the police officers. *Fuck the police and burn Sal's* was my unequivocal response as we watched Radio Raheem get lynched. Which I assumed was Wimbledon's response too.

KILL HIM! the white woman who sat behind us screamed. She wept as we watched Mookie throw the trash can into the window of Sal's Pizzeria, shattering the glass, instigating a riot.

We ran over and under the iron bar that guarded the projects. Others joined us. We became a tidal wave and crashed in a courtyard. Flooded the concrete with laughter as we caught our breath and reached for the tray of honey buns that Garth—who had just got beaten up by Vernon in the locker room of the YMCA, where we played ball on Saturdays—had grabbed from Topps.

"Hey, Vernon, you're gonna have to kick Garth's ass every Saturday," Moke said.

"Not for nothin'," Daco said. Dico and Daco had been born on the same day at Brigham and Women's Hospital in 1972. They were the last of their mother's ten children. Cambridge Housing had had to break up two apartments so that they could have six bedrooms.

We ran along a river of dirt that cut the projects in half, that doubled as a BMX bike racetrack. "It used to be hills," Daco said, "used to be all dirt." Boys our age and older raced from one end of the projects to the other. Some raced outside the projects. Chris, who lived upstairs from Dico and Daco, "was numba five in the country," Daco said.

We ran to where the dirt became cement, out the projects to the grass lot across the street that was our football field. We split up into teams and began to tackle each other. I was usually the quarterback.

Jim Brown! I could still hear Imran yelling from the courtyard in Peabody Terrace whenever I ran the ball into the end zone. Behind the field were more empty lots and abandoned buildings. "We used to go to abandoned places, half of the abandoned places near MIT, we used to make clubhouses, like the Goonies," Daco said. "Carl introduced us to weed, we used to sleep in the clubhouse, bring our blankets and chill."

We ran from the empty lots and barren fields and abandoned factories, which would become Google and Microsoft and Facebook and Pfizer, back into the projects to turn a rock into chalk, the courtyard into a baseball diamond. We drew a strike zone on the wall below Colin and Dana's window and swung a broom stick at a tennis ball for the windows on the other side of the projects.

We cut the bottom out of milk crates, attached the crates to wood, and hung them on the chain-link fence next to the clothes lines, high enough so we could dunk on each other.

We got a wrench from somebody's toolbox and stole the basketball rim from the Margaret Fuller Neighborhood House playground, around the corner from my house on School Street, ran with it back into the projects and nailed it to a light pole so we could dunk on each other.

We ran for inexhaustible hours in the Newtowne Court gym. The gym was near the mouth of the projects and was part of Cambridge Housing's administrative offices, a small, one-story brick building with a basement. The court was the basement, was half the size of a regular basketball court. The windows stood at street level, were covered by metal mesh grates, didn't let in much light. The lights buzzed inside circular fixtures that hung from the ceiling. It was damp and dark. When it rained, the roof leaked and the court was littered with buckets. The hoops were attached to poles that were attached to metal bases that could be rolled around the gym. We always had enough players for a game, sometimes five on five, or however many against however many, or everyone against each other, it didn't matter, we just played, each collision an embrace. The gym was where we became brothers.

Patrick, whose family was from Jamaica and sold food during Cambridge's Caribbean Festival, ran the gym as part of his job as a YMCA outreach coordinator. He was one of thirteen children. He had recently graduated from Springfield College, where he'd run track and held the record in the 300- and 55-yard dash. During the week we ran and pulled and punched and talked shit and elbowed and pushed and molded each other into good ballplayers. Sometimes Patrick organized a practice to help us learn how to play together and then he took us as far as the Basketball Hall of Fame in Springfield to battle other kids at other YMCAs on weekends. We always won. In Springfield he took us to a pizza spot to celebrate. They sold the biggest pizzas we'd ever seen—one slice was like a small cheese at Stefani's back in Cambridge. Each trip was a journey out of the Port, armed with kicks, with a ball, with our game, the chemistry from all our collisions, into worlds that felt blacker or whiter than ours, against teams who were blacker or whiter than us. The rides to the games were always filled with nervous excitement, laughter, the anticipation of who and what we were going to face and what would happen when we faced it and all the shit we said we were gonna do when we got our hands on the ball. We talked just as much shit on the ride home and during the week about what we had and hadn't done on the weekend, about who had missed what.

We ran through door 23, up the steps past Dico and Daco's door, so we could pitch quarters. To beat each other for whatever change we'd stumbled upon or stolen from our parents. A foot marked the distance from the wall we threw from. We bent our knees; some blew on the coin to bless its journey in the air. We played until everyone was cracked and one of us had more change than he could fit in his pocket.

We ran to the bodega, what we called the Puerto Rican store on the corner of School and Main, half a block from the donut shop, across the street from the candy factory where Daco would work for a few days before they found out his age. We put our change together and one person would buy something and then the rest of us would leave with however much we could get our hands on.

We ran to the brown doors where Moke and Fats and the Garro sisters and Big Titty Wanda lived. We had become aware of what the girls concealed with their clothes. We scattered when Moke came out his door with Pupadeke, his dad's psychotic German shepherd, at the end of a short leash. We flocked back to the yard when Moke returned Pupadeke to the house.

"You already the king of the Port?" Sevie said to me as he glided past us on the bike parts I had sold him. I had Big Twin, who was always trying to wrestle his way up the pecking order, in a headlock he couldn't get out of.

Moke, who talked better shit than all of us, who usually talked his way out of fighting, said, "He ain't no mutherfuckin' king of the Port!"

"Not for nuthin'," Daco would say, "Busy B is the king of the Port, he got the weed and the girls and a piece of the Source, and one of . . . and one of the Graham brothers."

We ran after the older girls that let us chase them. Around the courtyard and up however many flights of steps to their door to trade a punch in the face for a pinch of ass.

We had become aware of our virginity. It loomed like a perilous mountain we each had to conquer on our journey from the precipice of adolescence to the precipice of manhood.

"I ain't a virgin," we would say.

"Who'd you fuck?" we would ask.

"Ask my brother," we would say.

"Yo, you gotta see it," Taba said. By then it felt like every kid in the city was converging on the Orson Welles Cinema next door to 1001 Plays Arcade on Mass. Ave., between Harvard and Central Squares, fleecing their parents for quarters, whatever fell out of pants, was found in washers and dryers, putting the price of admission together, one dime and nickel at a time.

On the screen, within minutes of the beat dropping—*na na na naaaa, da dum dum, na naaa, da dum dum, na naaaa, da dum dum; na na na naaaa, da dum dum, na naaa, da dum dum, na naaaa*—trains were riding the elevated tracks, kids were doing everyday shit in the South Bronx, *Wild Style* was sprayed across the screen. "That's us!" we said.

We returned daily, one of us paying, the rest of us banging on the side door until the one who'd paid let us in, sitting in aisles if necessary, watching with kids we recognized from other parts of the city, a bag of popcorn passed between us, eyes fixed to the screen.

We shed our skin in that theater. Along with the popcorn on the floor, we left pieces of whoever we had been before walking in. Took clothes from the movie's frames, hung them on our bodies. Gave ourselves new names, became breakdancers. Filled gold and silver belt buckles with our new identities—Coco Puff, Mizoke, Sha Blub, Fizzy D, DNice. Practiced break dancing in each other's cribs. Polished our mother's linoleum with our backs. Stole cardboard boxes from U-Haul. Put change together to buy linoleum from the hardware store. Put it on project floors. Kick worming in shell-toe Adidas, suede Pumas, with Kangols we got for our birthdays, nylon Puma suits for Christmas. Took Confederate hats from who knows where. Took silver herringbone chains, hollow gold ropes, gold-plated clovers from the jewelry store in the Square. Rolled linoleum under our arms, clad in short-sleeve collared alligator shirts. Went looking for other kids with linoleum or cardboard. Took the camel walk from our mothers, what we learned on their kitchen floors, and returned it to the streets. Found other kids to battle on street corners, in other project courtyards.

Poppy, Mama's friend who became our aunt, said, "I saw Omo and Taba breakdancing in Harvard Square."

"Not my kids," Mama said. The Square was where we learned how to turn a street corner into a stage. We didn't give a fuck who was watching—they paid good money to see us tick and pop and windmill with two hands on our balls.

"Omo who?" Ghetto said when he saw my name belt. I had wanted my belt to be the biggest.

"Omo Whale?"

"Omowale," I said.

"Who the fuck is that?" Ghetto asked.

"It's the name they gave Malcolm X when he visited Africa," Baba would say.

. . .

We ran a version of Carl and Daco and Fat Daddy's muscular dystrophy hustle. *Would you like to make a donation to Muscular Dystrophy?* they would ask. Carl used to get the Muscular Dystrophy forms, take them to all the colleges—Brandeis, Harvard, Brown.

Taba and I stood in the mouth of the projects and handed out books of King Open School raffle tickets. It was early evening when we made our way to the Square, split up in groups, sold the tickets in bars, in restaurants, at the train station. We rendezvoused in Burger King when it was dark. Bought one cup for soda, one bowl for the salad bar. Took turns refilling both until everyone was full. Placed the money in a pile on the table. It was the most cash I had ever counted and divided. We had enough for each of us to leave with twenty-one dollars.

Mama answered the phone not long after we got home. It was Colin and Dana's mother.

"Not my kids," Mama said. Colin and Dana showed up on the porch ten minutes later with long faces and gave us back some of their money. Mama cried. Said we had to stay in the house until Baba, who was out of town, got home. I was convinced he was gonna beat our asses.

But it wasn't until later, when Taba and I quit swimming without his permission, that he beat our asses. Maybe it was all the delinquent shit, all the time we'd spent roaming the streets, that made us feel like we could make our own decisions. We had no idea of the line we had crossed until Baba busted through the door and snatched whatever independence we thought we'd accumulated and spanked us. We were shocked. The anger we'd seen in him the night he'd confronted the cop in the Blodgett Pool parking lot, now fueling the momentum of his hand, rising and falling, stiff and precise on our backsides. He stayed furious for a week. Huffing and puffing around the house as we cowered in his presence. And then he said that he was sorry, that he would never hit us again. It didn't mat-ter—after the spanking, we knew we could survive the worst of him. I told him I would swim one more season and then I was quitting, that I was going to be a basketball player. He said Taba would quit if I quit. Me quitting the Bernal's Gators to become a basketball player remained in the distance between us.

· · ·

In winter, we ran with fists full of snowballs out of the mouth of the projects and launched them like missiles at every passing car. Occasionally, someone threw their shit in park and got out and chased us as fast as they could as we ran for our lives.

In winter, Taba and I ran after Ghetto and his crew as they drove down Cherry Street on the ice and slush, and then they slowed down so we could grab the bumper. We laid on the ground and held on for our lives for as long as we could as they took off.

We called it mushin'.

We ran from elementary to high school like that, like the brothas in Central Square who ran after buses and jumped on the corner of the buses' back and held on for their lives for as long as they could, from stop to stop.

At night we gathered in empty apartments, bare living rooms, sometimes a couch. Someone brought music, sometimes a strobe light, the girls usually waiting on the couch for us to ask them for a dance. If they were late, we stood around accusing each other of being virgins.

We waited for the slow jams to ask the girls to dance, so we could wrap our arms around their bodies, stuff our hands in their back pockets.

"No French kissing," we said.

· · ·

"Come an' get it," Big Titty Wanda said from her third-floor window as Moke and I stood at the entrance to door number 6 in his courtyard. She looked dangerous.

"I need a rubba," he said, as if that would have saved him from suffocating in all that cleavage.

We ran from pussy, were afraid to let go of our clothes, to get our tongues and dicks wet.

"Don't have too much sex too soon," the photography teacher said.

We ran to the Community Arts Center in the basement beneath door 24 in the projects to roll film in the darkroom with her. The photography teacher was just out of college, with dyed blond hair and a mole on her chin. When the older boys came into the basement, they lied about all the sex they'd had. "Save some sex for later," the photography teacher warned us in a husky voice when the older boys were gone. I wanted to know how much sex she had had. Just the word *sex* in her mouth triggered an erection. I visited the basement religiously. Wanted to learn everything she knew. She taught me how to roll film in pitch blackness, load it in a Pentax K1000 camera, how to take pictures without using a flash, how to turn the negatives into the images we'd captured. It was intimate. Her standing over my shoulder beneath the red light in the dimly lit room, her breath on my neck as we watched the moments I'd captured magically reappear in the bins of chemicals. I wanted to lose my virginity in that dark room.

I don't remember the name of the girl I met in front of 1001 Plays, the arcade next to the Orson Welles Cinema. I was with Thomas Jackson, a classmate at the King Open who had pawned some of his mother's records so we could have quarters. She stood with a friend below the awning. We began a conversation. They said they were from Boston, were already in high school. I came out of my shell long enough to get her phone number.

"Are you a virgin?" I asked, reading from the piece of paper where I had written down questions to confront the inevitable silence.

"Have you had sex before?" she replied.

"Yeah," I lied. "Have you?"

"Yeah," she said.

"Do you want to?" I asked.

"Why?" she said.

"Why not?" I said.

When she came over, Mama and Baba and everyone else was in DC. I had told them I didn't want to miss my basketball game at the Y that weekend. We sat still, shoulder to shoulder on Mama and Baba's bed, and then turned and pressed our lips together. I unbuttoned her shirt. She helped me with her bra. I put my mouth on her titties. We lay down and took off the rest of our clothes. I struggled with the condom. The wrong side was lubricated. I lay on top of her body. She spread her legs. It felt like a lifetime getting inside her. She was warm. I closed my eyes for a minute. She got dressed and left. I don't know what was in it for her. She left a hickey on my neck, which lasted a week, which was the evidence that I needed to release me of that heaviest of burdens, as we ran—

from Freedom Songs,
toward Hip-Hop music,
out of our parents' dreams
into the dreams we harbored,
for ourselves,
and each other.

———————————

ROBERT MOSES C-SPAN INTERVIEW (1986)

Every human being has etched in his personality, and these are King's words, the indelible stamp of the creator. The worth of an individual does not lie in the measure of his intellect, his racial origin, or his social position. Human worth lies in relatedness to God.

And I wanted to pick up from that last sentence.

And ask a question: How are we to understand our relatedness to God? One way to understand that is through a metaphor.

God is an ocean of consciousness and we are individual waves in that ocean of consciousness. And we are to think of ourselves as related to God as the wave is related to the ocean.

And you think about that, it's trying to give you a picture, 'cause we know the ocean and we see the waves and they rise and fall on the bosom of the ocean and . . . so we in that metaphor rise and fall on the bosom of God.

CHAPTER 14

The White Peril

ROBERT MOSES'S ACCOUNT OF VOTER
REGISTRATION DRIVE IN MISSISSIPPI IN 1961

00:21:34 Robert P. Moses

We got there early in the morning and there were people gathering and gathered as soon as we appeared. They sent us up into the buzzard's roost; it's a little sort of sloping, shelf-like extension at the back of the courtroom in Tylertown, which is the county seat of Walthall County. And then all the old farmers and the young ones and the thugs and an all-men, male, chorus gathered downstairs to see if the trial is going to take place.

00:22:09 Robert P. Moses

While we were sitting there, the county prosecuting attorney came in and announced that

00:22:14 Robert P. Moses

The Justice Department had obtained a stay from Judge Reeves in Alabama and that the trial would be continued from term of court to term of court, and that until that time John Hardy was free and not bound to stay in jail. So we left—at least we tried to leave.

00:22:37 Robert P. Moses

The people were rather thick in the card as we were leaving and were grabbing hold of John by the shirt sleeve and making nasty remarks at him as we left. We finally got through to the car and then of all things the car door was stuck, so we couldn't get it open, and finally the local policeman came up and told us that we better hurry up and get out of there because he couldn't hold those people back but for so long. We backed out into the mob and then got on out of town, being very careful to stay under the speed limit . . .

00:23:11 Robert P. Moses

and finally got back into McComb. Well, that was about it. A couple of days before John Hardy was arrested, we had gone back into Amite County, to Liberty.

00:23:25 Robert P. Moses

This time I was not beaten, but Travis Britt was; I think that was around the fifth of September.

00:23:36 Robert P. Moses

And I stood by and watched Travis get pummeled by an old man, tall, reedy, and thin; very, very, very mean, with a lot of hatred in him.

00:23:47 Robert P. Moses

However, he wasn't very, very strong, and luckily he didn't do too much damage to Travis, who suffered from an eye bruise and some head knocking. On that particular occasion Travis and I had been sitting out front on the courthouse and then decided to move around back because the people began to gather out front.

00:24:09 Robert P. Moses

. . . and finally everybody, about fifteen people, gathered around back and began questioning Travis and myself. My own reaction in all those instances to the questioning is to simply, to shut up, to be silent and get very, very depressed.

00:24:27 Robert P. Moses

So the people were talking to Travis and he was answering them some. They were asking him where was he from, and how come a nigger from New York

City could think that he could come down and teach people down here how to register to vote when they had all those problems up there in New York City and problems of white girls going with nigger boys and all such like that.

00:24:49 Robert P. Moses

Finally they began to beat on Travis, and I started going towards the sheriff's office and was cut off. Finally went back and tried to get Travis away from this fellow who was beating on him. We did this and then we walked over to a truck which was nearby and got in it and went on back to McComb. Well, the Travis Britt incident followed by the John Hardy incident and Walthall County just about cleaned us out. The farmers in both those counties was no longer willing to go down.

00:25:22 Robert P. Moses

The people in Pike County in McComb were in an uproar over the sit-in demonstrations and the fact that Brenda Travis, a sixteen-year-old girl, was in jail.

00:25:47 Robert P. Moses

People who were in jail on the sit-in charges had five-thousand-dollar bail over their heads, and the problem was to raise that money and get them out of jail and then to sit down and see if we couldn't collect the pieces together. Well, we got through September, aided in great measure by the presence of some of the lawyers from the Justice Department who finally came in to begin investigating the voting complaints, and they stood in for about a two-week period, and while they were there they give a lot of support and confidence to the Negroes in the community and allowed us to go back out into Walthall and into Amite Counties and interview all the people who have been involved in the voter registration campaign and raise some hope that perhaps something would be done.

00:26:43 Robert P. Moses

And then finally the boom lowered. On September 31, Herbert Lee was killed in Amite County.

ALGEBRA PROJECT INTERVIEWS CONDUCTED
BY CHARLIE COBB FOR *RADICAL EQUATIONS* (1998)

Frank and Laura Figgers,
Parents of Algebra Project Student Fareeda Figgers

MR. FIGGERS: So everything east of the creek to Baylor Avenue was where white people lived. And Blacks moved in there and occupied that all the way to Baylor Avenue, because in '67, white people were living east of the creek to Baylor Avenue on the Woodlawn side. That's kind of how it came to be, I think.

UNCLE CHARLIE: And are both of you from this community?

MRS. FIGGERS: We both grew up, as a matter of fact, our home houses, you can look out, you can almost look out our front door and see both of our houses, and we grew up as childhood sweethearts.

UNCLE CHARLIE: I was going to say, so you've known each other since you were like—

MRS. FIGGERS: We grew up together.

MR. FIGGERS: That's right. And beyond that, we can look out of the back door of this house and see my grandmother and grandfather's house on my father's side. And we can look out the front door of this house and see my wife's grandmother and grandfather's house on her father's side.

UNCLE CHARLIE: Is this typical? I mean, would people of your generation still generally, in Jackson, have stayed, more or less, in the same neighborhood?

MRS. FIGGERS: In the same neighborhood?

UNCLE CHARLIE: Or are you not typical?

MRS. FIGGERS: We're not typical. We are about the only, no, I think it's one other family that's still here.

MR. FIGGERS: There's a few other folk, you know, like—the Colemans, and you know, well, Kenny Stokes grew up in this neighborhood. And his wife grew up in this neighborhood.

UNCLE CHARLIE: Has it always been the inner city?

MRS. FIGGERS: No. I wouldn't say Georgetown was the inner city.

MR. FIGGERS: In the mid to late '50s, the city limits stopped at where now the intersection of Medgar Evers and Martin Luther King is. Just beyond that was outside of the city limits of Jackson.

MRS. FIGGERS: That's called Five Points. That's where the city limits were until, like he said, the late '50s, and then they moved it out to 49 or either Martin Luther King. What was it back then?

UNCLE CHARLIE: Let me interrupt you here. What were those streets called? Because they certainly weren't Medgar Evers and Martin Luther King when I was here in '62.

MRS. FIGGERS: That's what I was trying to think—49? Delta Drive. Medgar Evers was known as Delta Drive. And then it became 49 on up the road. And Martin Luther King was known as Whitfield Mills Road. And after, when Kenny Stokes got in office, he had it changed to Martin Luther King, and I don't know who was responsible for it being named Medgar Evers.

MR. FIGGERS: You don't think he did it?

MRS. FIGGERS: You think he did that too?

MR. FIGGERS: I think he did.

UNCLE CHARLIE: So I'm still trying to get a fix on partly how the neighborhood changes.

MRS. FIGGERS: None of us who lived in (indiscernible) came back, even after the parents died. Even my mamma's house was vacant until we rented it out. My brothers and my sisters had moved into their own homes, so there wasn't anybody to come back to the house. We have our own home, and the same thing with Frank's parents' house. When they died, we had to rent it out. And a lot of times, when you rent houses out, the people that come in, you think you know what you're getting, and you really don't. . . . We had a lot of professionals living there, teachers, and Percival lived there for years, and then they moved farther out into more prominent areas.

MR. FIGGERS: When it was a rural area, it was no school here. The closest school was a elementary school that served all of these people, and that was Mary Jones. So they used to have Rosenwald schools here. And the church that we attend now was in charge of one of the Rosenwald schools. But the people in this area lived primarily, well, a lot of them was still in agriculture, so they used to hire out for the day and go and pick cotton.

UNCLE CHARLIE: They were day workers out in the county?

MR. FIGGERS: See this already was the county. So farther out was the farmland. And they would go out and work on the farms during the day, but then school only went a half a day.

UNCLE CHARLIE: Oh, like up in the Delta.

MR. FIGGERS: Yeah, uh-huh. And certain times of the year. So a number of children went to school in the morning part, and a number went in the afternoon part.

MRS. FIGGERS: That was before us, now.

UNCLE CHARLIE: That would have been your parents' time and your grandparents' time.

MRS. FIGGERS: What happened was, the neighborhood grew so fast, and they couldn't accommodate all the kids, so they did a split shift. Half went, if you live on this side of town, half of you went, but I wasn't involved in that when I went to Mary C. Jones, I was going a full day. But when Catherine and my brother started off, they had to go a half a day, and then the kids who were closer to Mary C. Jones went in the evening time.

MR. FIGGERS: And . . . other church schools, like Ms. Washington's school . . . your cousin went there. And my sister went there, I went there, and my cousin went there. And some children went there all the way through fourth grade before they went to the public school, or to any other school, and it was an all-day school, and that was just right, a block over. And so when the neighborhood changed from a rural—then it went to like a suburban, you know, area, and so they built some new houses. There were old houses like my grandaddy's house. And they might have built a sprinkling of new houses that might be now, 45, 50 years old, you know. And then there's another sprinkling that might be 30 years old. But I think 45 and 50 years old, that's about here. And by then it was kind of suburban, but, . . . when that happened, you know, all through, there might be an apartment here, but then it might be another house here that was single-family. And then somebody that might have worked in the post office, or, then somebody might have worked on the railroad, and somebody might have taught school, and then somebody might have been a factory worker. This area was bustling, too, because just over beyond where Brinkley is, I mean it was just factories that employed as many as 1,000, 1,500 people, you know, during the fifties and sixties.

UNCLE CHARLIE: What kind of factories?

MRS. FIGGERS: Furniture.

MR. FIGGERS: One was a furniture factory.

MRS. FIGGERS: Presto, what is it? Presto, makes pots and pans.

MR. FIGGERS: Uh-uh. That was DeSoto.

MR. FIGGERS: It was Mississippi Products, MP&I, and then DeSoto.

MR. FIGGERS: Then you had—

MRS. FIGGERS: Grocery stores, post office.

MR. FIGGERS: Th— the fertilizer factory was over there. The box factory was over there.

UNCLE CHARLIE: And these are hiring mostly Black people, or all Black?

MR. FIGGERS: Uh-huh, just about all of the labor. Yeah . . . And then the mill works was over there, and the radiator place was over there. G&O was over, not G&O, but G— where Mr. Bill Good worked. I can't think of the name of that place.

MRS. FIGGERS: On Mandy Brook?

MR. FIGGERS: Uh-huh. It was a body shop. He used to hire a lot of people. So, you know, it was bustling, and people was living around there. So, and then, the next wave come through, so these people just grew up, you know, and lived amongst each other, and everything was all right. But as it shifted again, by '67, my generation of folk were leaving, going in the army, you know, '65 maybe to '70, going in the army, going to college, you know, and going for better opportunities. So we got older. And as they kind of faded off, then, you know, these people might take their property and rent it, you know, like that, so you have what we have now, you know. So people, they come in here, and live, and when they save money and can do better, they move on, you know. But Laura and I kind of wanted to stay.

·   ·   ·

"Mr. Moses, Mr. Moses," Mr. Figgers says as he approaches me in the hallway at Brinkley. I understand Mr. Figgers to be the father of Fareeda, a sixth-grader in Mrs. Moss's Algebra Project classroom, as well as a faithful member of the Shady Grove Baptist Church. He'd also been a student at either Tougaloo College or Jackson State when the Freedom Riders had arrived. Mr. Figgers is a vibrant bridge between the generation of young people who'd come of age during the Civil Rights Movement and our generation. He is colorful like a peacock, dresses in flamboyant lime-green, purple shirts, yellow slacks. With a hitch in his step. A snap in his handshake. His style declares a love of life, that his light will shine despite whatever darkness he has had to wade through. It is an act of self-defense, defiance, combating the notion that we need to mute our iridescence to survive black and white America. You can't miss him, peeling his hat from a matted Afro scraped backward as he enters the school building, quickly scoping out who he is sharing space with, greeting everyone with an observation about something he sees in them or sharing what he's heard "on the street" about them or someone they know that will incite a laugh, crack the stiff black facade most of us travel with to create distance between the inside of us and whatever peril lingers in black and white America.

In his exchanges are attempts to commemorate the significance of the moment we've each arrived in, perhaps a moment to lighten the load we're carrying, before we continue on our way, through black and white America.

This is his way. The way of black people instinctively nodding when passing each other in the street—to acknowledge the distance we've traveled, from Africa to America, from enslaved to sharecropping to convict leasing, from southern to northern cotton fields.

His hand grazes his beard as he speaks. A mustache, left to grow feral, curls over his lips, hangs like Spanish moss from his chin, has been left to turn to little naps on his jowls. He is as indigenous to Mississippi as the magnolias, as the bed of cotton scattered on what had been Delta Road, is now Medgar Evers, leading to Highway 49.

.   .   .

Remnants of the Delta litter Jackson's landscape, remain on the horizon, a step beyond a stoplight, markers of when cotton was king, of the centuries when the majority of black life was restricted to plantations. The fields are now on the other side of the city limits, some still dedicated to cotton, others to different crops, others turned into catfish farms, their flat ponds the size of half a football field, reflecting a cultural need to extract the planet's resources, by any means necessary.

"Technologies have always defined cultures," John Mohawk said, "and cultures have always had some impact on environments."[1]

The brown cornrowed dirt marches toward the horizon as I gaze from the passenger seat of Baba's rental car on our first trip to the Delta.

Baba sings like Taba said he would, under his breath at first—"People Get Ready," "We're a Winner," "Keep On Pushing," and other Curtis May-field numbers—and then louder and louder as we move from the urban to farmland and the wind pours in the window, peels tufts of cotton from un-ginned bricks stacked on top of each other by the truck load—each brick up to sixteen un-ginned bales, each bale culled from a half to an acre of field, each ginned bale roughly 480 pounds.

Three hundred to five hundred pounds was what one very productive cotton picker could pick with their bare hands.

In the MathLab, Baba told us the story of the mechanization of cotton picking, how in 1944 hundreds of people had traveled to the Hopson Plantation in Clarksdale, Mississippi—where the blues, what they called sharecropper music, was born—to witness the first mechanical cotton picker pick an entire field of cotton.

"Each machine picked about one thousand pounds in an hour. A good human cotton picker could pick about twenty to thirty pounds an hour."

Baba used the story of the invention of the cotton picker and before that the invention of the cotton gin to talk about displacements, the distance and direction we travel from one place to another, by choice or force, or by necessity—the combination of the two. He talked to us about the role of technology in displacing people, always landing on where the students would end up in the twenty-first century if they didn't get this algebra.

The invention of the cotton gin in 1794 had accelerated the processing of raw cotton and allowed for different types of cotton to be grown, allowed cotton plantations to spread north, south, and west, forcing Native nations from their ancestral lands, transforming America from a minor exporter to the world's dominant economy.

"For this reason, the definition of colonialism needs to be expanded in the consciousness of the peoples of the planet Earth," John Mohawk said. "Colonialism is a process by which indigenous cultures are subverted and ultimately destroyed in the interests of the worldwide market economy."[2]

By the early 1800s, cotton was king—on its way to becoming America's leading export, fueling the growth of textile mills along the banks of Northern rivers, bankrolling financial institutions, launching shipping and insurance companies and countless other individuals and enterprises into prosperity.

By speeding up the processing of raw cotton, the cotton gin increased the profitability of growing cotton, which increased the demand for cotton pickers and launched America's internal slave trade.

Of the 10.5 million Africans who survived the passage across the Atlantic, only about four hundred thousand landed in what became the United States.[3]

The first official United States census (taken in 1790) counted the number of free white males aged under sixteen years, number of free white males aged sixteen years and older, number of free white females, number of other free people (59,150), and number of slaves (697,624).

The first census didn't count the number of Native Americans or distinguish between white and black slaves.

In the years between the invention of the cotton gin (1794) and the doorstep to the Civil War (1859), six slave states became fifteen, America's initial hundreds of thousands of enslaved Africans became four million enslaved African Americans. One million were kidnapped from the North and returned South, rupturing bonds of marriage, family, community. On the doorstep of the Civil War, enslaved Americans were worth more than the country's railroads, factories, and farms combined, valued at 80 percent of the rupturing nation's gross national product. An untold number of Americans bred into bondage.

In Clint Smith's *How the Word Is Passed*, Julia Woodrich recalled, "My ma had fifteen children and not of them had the same pa. Every time she was sold she would get another man. My ma had one boy by her moss that was my missis brother's child."[4]

In the Reverend James Robinson's narrative, published under the name James Roberts, he writes: "From fifty to sixty head of women were kept constantly for breeding. No man was allowed to go there, save white men. From twenty to twenty-five children a year were bred on that plantation. As soon as they are ready for market, they are taken away and sold, as mules or other cattle. Many a man buys his own child. . . .

"On Wade Hamilton's farm the same process went on to a great extent, each planter vieing with the other to see who could raise the greatest number of mulattoes a year for market, (as they bring a higher price than the blacks,) the same as men strive to raise the most stock of any kind, cows, sheep, horses, &c."[5]

Reverend James Robinson's life traveled the distance between hundreds of thousands of enslaved Africans and four million enslaved African Americans. He was born in 1753 and enslaved by Francis De Shields, who he fought beside as a fellow soldier under General Washington in the Revolutionary War. He was sold to a plantation owner in Louisiana and fought alongside General Andrew Jackson in the Battle of New Orleans in 1812. He didn't obtain his freedom until the 1830s. His memoir, *The Narrative of James Roberts*, published in 1858, a few years before his sons fought in the American Civil War. He lived to be 115 years old.

Robinson writes:

MY motives for placing this little Narrative before the public, are the following:

First, to comply with the earnest request of many of my friends, both white and colored, who have strongly solicited me to publish a narrative of my long and eventful life, believing, as they have said, good to the rising generation and to posterity would result therefrom.

Second. I have for many years greatly desired, nay, it has been my earnest prayer to the Father of spirits, that I might live and have an opportunity afforded me to have my narrative written by a colored person, even if it should not be as well written as many white persons could write it; it has been my desire to get one of my own race to do it, that I might have the great satisfaction of knowing and seeing one of my despised race capable of writing a book, however small. For when I was a boy, to have seen a colored person with ability to read and write, would have been not much short of a miracle; it would have been a very great curiosity, so much so, that hundreds would have gone fifty or a hundred miles to see such an one. But I think my God that I have lived to see those days of miracles pass away, and to see, what I desired from my youth, many of my brethren capable of doing, by the aid of education, what other races can do. I have demonstrative proof before me, in this country, that my race is as susceptible of intellectual culture as any other people; and that they are not only susceptible naturally of high mental improvement, but I rejoice with exceeding joy that hundreds of my race have availed themselves of that susceptibility, and are now prepared by education to discharge the duties connected with any station in civilized life, even those which require the highest grade of education.[6]

It was in James Robinson's unimaginable narrative that I found a response to the question I had asked myself when Mama placed the book of black people being lynched on our kitchen table in Peabody Terrace within weeks of our arrival in America: *Why do white mothers take their babies to witness the killing of black children?*

IT is a fact, well known to all, that the mixed race in the slave States is rapidly increasing; that there are thousands now who differ nothing in complexion from the whitest European; and I set it down as true prophecy, that, in the progress of time, this mixed race will make bare their arm, and strike for their freedom. For what I am now going to relate confirms me in the belief of this prophecy.

In the South, where I lived, there are hundreds in that one section of country who, if you were to see the master and the son riding in a carriage together, you could not tell the one from the other. I will instance a case: John Gillespie and his son, Samuel Gillespie, could often be seen riding in the family carriage; Samuel driving, and the father and master sitting on the front seat by his side; and five white children and Mrs.

Gillespie sitting on the back seats. On the carriage, behind, might be seen two servants, the children of the master by a black woman, and two inside, by the same black woman and master; ten in number, five free, five slaves; all children of the same father. Now, these children will all grow up with one common feeling for freedom, and the one class will not be enslaved by the other; for both, feeling a common parentage, will feel an equal right to liberty, and, whichever attempts to oppress the other, there will be war, for they are both of one blood. One child will not give up to the other. The mulatto, feeling himself degraded and outraged by his own brother, will resist unto death, and wade in blood to obtain that liberty which, reason tells him, is as much his right to enjoy as others of his own blood-kind. Then, in that day, Heaven will be on the side of the oppressed, and will nerve their arms with steel and vengeance, and liberty they will have, though it should be at the expense of the life of every white man who should oppose them, and the utter destruction of the Government of these United States.

I saw an illustration of this in Louisiana, where two children got to fighting; the one a child of the planter's wife, a white woman, and the other a child of a black woman, by the master. The white one contended, that the mulatto should submit to him, that he was nothing but a negro and a slave; the mulatto contending, that he was as good as the other, that his master was the father of them both, and he would not submit to his own brother. Fighting ensued, when the two mothers came and took sides with their respective sons; and terrible would have been the result, but for the interference of the father of the two boys, who came and parted them, and sent the women into their respective houses.[7]

In 1936, the Federal Writers' Project began documenting the journeys of formerly enslaved Africans. Their narratives gave voice to millions of people whose bodies had been seized, whose lives had been exhausted, fueling the country's economy, a system where black men became bucks; black women became mammies and wombs; black men, women, and children became hands, coerced by the crack of a whip to march for unimaginable hours in rows, grazing fields like locusts, like mechanized cotton pickers, to extract as many pounds of cotton per hour per hand as possible. The best hands were women, could be children, each hand had a quota. It was up to the enslaved to train their hands to become more efficient, to reach their quotas, the quotas rising as they reached each one, from 100, to 130, to 200, to 300 pounds of cotton per day.

·   ·   ·

As Baba looks out the window on the drive to the Delta, he begins to recognize the students he teaches in the MathLab as the descendants of sharecroppers, recognizes that what had begun in the South and migrated North and taken root in urban "black" America, similar to the blues and sharecropper music, is sharecropper education. That what buttresses America's economic system is its education system. It is from this window that Baba begins concocting his narrative about constitutional property and constitutional people. The story of people from the Mandingo Nation, Congo Nation, Ado Nation, many other nations, who became property, and their struggle for citizenship. He divides American history into constitutional eras, which span the Revolution, the Civil War, and the Civil Rights Movement. This narrative can be dense and convoluted. Requires detangling. Is spun from a mind that can travel with Albert Camus's essays about victims and executioners in his overalls breast pocket, the distance between Harvard and the Mississippi registrar's office in one short step. He searches for grounding metaphors, for ideas to wrap around our skulls like headbands. In the same way that a math class field trip could be a metaphor for adding and subtracting integers, a wave could be a metaphor for movement, for our relationship to our creator.

"All the children in the country are children of the country and have a right to a quality education," he says. He lands on the idea that we need a constitutional amendment to ensure that every child in the country receives a quality public school education. It is an extraordinary distance to travel, from enslaved to sharecropper to Jim Crow to blues to hip-hop to a constitutional amendment.

"I'm gonna die with my boots on," he says.

·   ·   ·

Mr. Figgers had been there in the '60s when Baba and then more students arrived, was among those who'd remained when most of the civil rights workers left and the nation's attention receded, had been one of the founders of the Black and Proud schools that flowered in Jackson in the wake of Black Consciousness. The spirit of the movement was planted firmly in his body. He'd been wary of the Algebra Project at first, had seen the freedom fighters come and go, seen legions of professional activists come and go.

"Mr. Moses, I have something I want you to look at," he says to me now, in the Brinkley hallway. He hands me a book bound in biblically dark maroon cloth, the spine's ends frayed. I can palm it, grip its edges with the tips of my fingers. I'm not sure what to make of it. *The White Peril* is written on the cover in white letters, below it *W. H. Moses*.

"Is William Moses some kin to you?" he asks.

I don't know but instinctively say yes. I open the book and then close it. I'm not sure if I should keep it or hand it back. It feels precious, fragile. The type is dense, the pages yellow and brittle, stained with the passage of time.

"It's for you," Mr. Figgers says as he waits for me to accept it. As if he has fulfilled one of his life's many obligations.

"Thank you," I say.

When I open the book, I am alone, in the front seat of the car, the windows cracked, a breeze wafting in, the night sky like a blanket, sequined with constellations, markers of what had been trails to freedom. Anywhere in Mississippi is relatively flat terrain, the oscillation between day and night a visible metronome of the slow passage of time, what back home is limited to banks of the Charles River, otherwise obscured by the tall buildings. I am entranced by what remains in the distance, regardless of how far we travel, in the same way that I imagine an astronaut floating in space sees earth, has a broader perspective of what it means to be from earth, a part of the universe, the evidence of life beyond us, a reminder that we are part of a natural order, that, from the perspective of the human body, some places and boundaries will always remain unknown.

According to *Who's Who Among the Colored Baptists*, a book edited by Samuel William Bacote, William Henry Moses was a

Farmer and Rail-Splitter—Pastor—Evangelist—Sensational Orator—Author of the Life of Christ—A Man in a Class by Himself. . . . He was born in Charlotte County, Virginia, December 31, 1872, to Thomas and Sarah Moses. William was the eldest of four brothers and comes from a very religious stock.

Mr. Moses was reared by Richard Morton, his grandfather, who was the largest and leading landowner of Charlotte County. Being the favorite of his grandfather, he was allowed a liberal use of his extensive library. . . .

At the early age of fourteen Mr. Moses was performing the difficult task of plowing with two horses; and at fifteen he was able to chop as much wood, maul as many rails and cut as much grain as the average man in his prime. During the same year he made a profession of religion and joined the Morrison Grove Baptist Church, Charlotte Court House. . . . At seventeen he was made overseer of all hands on his grandfather's plantation and received for the same enough money to enable him to enter college.[8]

In the obituary that Grandpa Moses prepared for himself, he wrote that he was unsure of who his parents were. Of meeting his mother once. Of learning that his father had died.

As I begin to read his book, I am struck by what he had to say, by how he saw himself and the planet. The money he'd earned on his grandfather's plantation enabled him to attend Virginia Seminary, from which he became a nationally recognized, radical black Baptist preacher. As I read, I travel beyond Bob Moses the freedom fighter, beyond his journey into Mississippi, toward the black consciousness that he'd emerged from.

"Should it please God," Grandpa Moses wrote to those who would commemorate his death,

> to call us again from cosmic consciousness, into personal existence, to glorify him, as he has done; then so may it be. Or should it please him to glorify us with a glory which we had inseparable from him before the world was then may the future reveal his presence in an ever increasing fullness, is in my prayer. For my life in this world has been so worthwhile to me that I [am] loath to give it up, despite the fact that I'm expecting to live on, ever rolling the past up into the future.

As the oxidized pages of *The White Peril* move from finger to finger, I am struck by how relevant its words feel to what I'm experiencing nearly a century later.

> The Peril is, that the darker races in general, and the black race in particular is in danger of political, industrial, social and economic slavery or extermination by the white Christian nations. . . .
>
> The Negro group, in Africa and America, is being ground to death between the upper and lower mill stones of white organized capital and

labor; both of which have excluded them from their respective groups and made it impossible for them to form a strong political, social, industrial and economic group among themselves.

The white races of the world are in peril from the reaction of their own perverted Christian attitude toward the darker races of the world; both by the numerical strength of the darker races and the disposition of the white races to destroy each other over the spoils from exploited countries of the darker races.

The hope of the world in general, and the darker races in particular, is the propagation of unperverted Christian principles throughout the world; regardless to the names by which the God of justice, mercy and love is called.[9]

. . .

I spend evenings on Mr. Figgers's porch, just talking about things. I enjoy listening to how his words run a marathon around a point, stuff time with his hopes and provocations. I enjoy time passing, with no apparent destination, along the tenor of his voice. If there are fireflies, I enjoy witnessing their call and response.

From his porch we can see the sprawling one-story brick building that had once been a medical center. We share a vision. We imagine it as a supersized MathLab in the heart of the neighborhood. Brick and mortar dedicated to the upliftment and self-determination of every young person in the community. That from its corners and crevices will grow an army of math literacy workers ready to transform the neighborhood and America.

Mama comes up with the term *math literacy worker*.

She is in Jackson for an Algebra Project meeting and to visit Baba, which coincides with Khari and Taba and me and some of the Brinkley students debriefing on the workshop we'd conducted with the brothers and sisters from Mali. We sat in a circle beneath a ream of chart paper. I stand armed with a marker, Java armed with tape. The wall becomes wallpapered with our conversation. Facilitating and debriefing are part of the Algebra Project process, inherited from SNCC organizers who ran meetings that could span days. Each meeting a unit of democratic participation.

"Local people have really begun to find a way they can use a meeting as a tool for running their own lives. For having something to say about it. That's very slow, but it's happening," Baba said. "People learned how to stand up and speak. The meeting itself, or the meetings, became the tools. In these meetings, they were taking the first step toward gaining control over their lives, by making demands on themselves. . . . They were not credentialed people; they did not have high school diplomas for the most part. They were not members of labor unions, or national church associations. Yet through the process, they became leaders."

Baba designed the Algebra Project classrooms to function like a SNCC meeting.

UNCLE CHARLIE: Was there a particular moment at which you recognized the value of the Algebra Project; when you said, "Oh, I really get it, now"?

MR. FIGGERS: I guess, when I saw the children working together with each other, you know, around the problems they were dealing with and sharing that knowledge. I think children learn another way, that maybe when they can get together with, you know, when they can work together with each other in the learning process, and share. I think that they may have something to do with it.

But then I also saw the teacher doing something that I thought was unique; just not standing up, you know, but were right down there with them—you know, not standing up, over them, but was right down there with them. I saw that and I said, maybe it's got merit.

· · ·

"There ain't no best," Cookie says defiantly, as Mama sits down in the circle with us. We have just discussed what did and didn't go well in the workshop with the visitors from Mali, what the best parts of the experience were.

"There ain't no best," he repeats, un-punctuating what I thought was the end of the conversation. Mama seems moved by Cookie's turn away from the mechanics of the workshop and into the philosophical—trying to attach what we are doing, who is doing it, and who we are doing it for to a broader significance. She can see in the infancy of our circle the other circles of young people she was once a part of. When it's her turn to speak, she describes what we are trying to get better at as math literacy work, describes who we are trying to become as math literacy workers.

I struggle with the idea initially—in my mind I am still a basketball player. But Mama and Baba can see it, that the Algebra Project more than anything else is creating the crawl space for young people to become math literacy workers. That math literacy workers can become twenty-first-century freedom fighters.

. . .

Mr. Figgers and I get as far as looking inside the old medical-center building. Imagining what it could be with a new roof and walls gutted. I have scenarios that include Flagway becoming a hit video game, Chaintain becoming the next Bill Gates, a music studio for Taba's PortLife Entertainment to make hit records that will permanently fund the movement, side-by-side rooms to develop graphing calculator workshops.

. . .

As I read *The White Peril*, I initially begin with each word, then flip page to page, and then return again to the first pages. This will be how I digest the book over months and years, finding profound statements and then getting lost in the distance and density of the history it covers, and then rummaging ahead and landing again on something profound. It becomes clear that the book was written by a preacher-professor for his student flock.

Foremost he raises questions:

(1) Are the white nations of the world Christians? (2) Has Christian civilization saved the American Indian? If not; why not? . . . (4) Did Christian nations start to propagating faith by the sword? (5) How does Christian subjugation of Mohammedan nations today differ from the Mohammedan subjugation of the European Nations in the Dark Ages? (6) How does the taking of Africa from the Africans differ from taking of America from the Indians? (7) Are Central and South African natives better off or worse since the coming of Christian nations from Europe among them? (8) Why does the Native welcome Mohammedan Missionaries more readily than white Christian Missionaries? (9) How does segregation in Africa differ in principle from Negro segregation in America and the "Indian reservations" of the West? (10) What hardships

do the labor unions of Africa and the world work on the darker races? (11) How does white control of industry and trade keep the darker race in economic bondage? (12) What diseases have Christian nations carried to Africa? (13) How does the misery and disease of Christian African cities compare with the native villages? (14) What effect is the liquor traffic of the Christian nations having on the Africans and other darker races? (15) What effect will "The White Peril" have on the white nations whose destinies are being bound up more closely with the darker races through the New Internationalism that is sweeping the world?[7]

And then he lays out their program:

MATERIAL ADVANCEMENT

The material advancement of the race in America under the inspiration of the Negro leadership may be judged from the following. The Government statistics show that the Negroes own and rent, primarily in the Southern United States[,] 42,259,247 acres of farm land valued at $1,104,496,287.00. . . .

FORTY THOUSAND BAPTISTS IN COLLEGE

The Third National Baptist goal should be forty thousand Baptist young men and women in Baptist Colleges and Universities and Theological Seminaries by 1925.

NEED OF EDUCATIONAL PASSION

The one great need just now is an educational passion that will inspire every one of our young people to secure the highest possible training. An educational passion like that of our fathers immediately after the Civil War. Statistics indicate that, that Baptists in general and colored Baptists in particular are less interested in the education of their children and their preachers than are most Christians. That ought not to be so. We must wipe it out in the next seven years. Why should not the next generation of colored Baptist[s] be among the best educated people in the world? Baptists are strenuous believers in Democracy; it is the peculiar heritage of the Baptists. If we would increase the efficiency of our democracy and make our due contribution to national and international development, we must have an educated constituency. . . .

MEASURE UP TO THE STANDARD
OF AMERICAN COLLEGES

The Fourth National Baptist goal should be to make our Negro Baptist Colleges and Secondary Schools measure up to the highest American standards.

GOVERNMENT REPORT ON NEGRO COLLEGES

The United States Government's report on Negro education says: "Hardly a colored college meets the standards set by the Carnegie Foundation, and the North Central Association." "Only three institutions, Howard University, Fisk University and Meharry Medical College, have student bodies, teachers' force, and equipment and income sufficient to warrant the characterization of College." That would make us feel humiliated beyond measure, if we happened not to know that but very few white colleges in the whole country measure up to the above standard. But regardless to the standard of the white colleges, our colleges must by all means be made to measure up to the highest American standard of colleges. We can do it and we must do it, we will do it. . . .

COLLEGE EDUCATION

A nation-wide systematic effort should be made to show our young church people the value of a college education. If the war has taught anything, it has taught us the value of a college man, practically trained. And we must insist on as many people as possible out of every church to go to college that we may have not less than 40,000 in our denominational schools by 1925. . . .

EDUCATION

We should promote education on a national scale with the view of creating an educational passion and making our educational institutions efficient in the highest degree.

And then he presents his vision.

———————

W. H. MOSES SERMON

WHERE WE STAND, continued

I see a time when black people everywhere are going to rise and shine, for the lie is given and the Light of God is shining on the books. I see a larger day. I see a city of schools and churches. I see cities everywhere, extending from the Cape of Good Hope to Cairo in Egypt. I see a crowd yonder extending from the Zambezi to the Niger River. I see this race of mine waking up, hand in hand, American and what not, pressing on together, having a home together. Let nobody deceive you. It may take a year. It may take ten thousand years. But under God the hour will come when Ethiopia shall stretch forth her hand unto God and black men shall hold their heads high, and the name of Marcus Garvey shall be embalmed in our memories and our children's through long ages. For if in the future, as in the past, men continue to prize ennobling gifts used for the higher purpose and the advancement of a race, then at Marcus Garvey's tomb generations yet unborn shall pay homage till the stars sink at the day of Judgement. (*Applause*)

ROBERT MOSES C-SPAN INTERVIEW (1986)

Now, metaphors are what we use to help us understand reality.

I remember a very important metaphor in my study of philosophy . . . about the ship of science on the ocean of knowledge, and the ship of science is a ship that's floating on the ocean of knowledge, and the scientist is a little man in the ship who is trying to rebuild it all the time. But he can never come to dock, he can't land at any port. And he has to learn how to keep the ship afloat while he's rebuilding it, and he has to do it on this ocean. And what he was getting at was that the effort of the scientist to create a precise language of science is forever bounded by the ocean of just ordinary language out of which that precise language has to evolve. The scientist is apt to forget that and is apt to get carried away with that precise language.

SNCC is a boat in the middle of an ocean, and we're inside that boat and we're trying to rebuild it, and we have nowhere to dock, and our problem is how can we stay afloat while we're rebuilding it and not sink.

How is the emergence and success of a leader to be explained. Now I want you to consider again the metaphor about God. That god is an ocean of consciousness, and we are the waves on that ocean. And think of that metaphor about a metaphor about the movement. That the movement is an ocean of consciousness, protest, rebellion, organizing, and fill in other things that the movement is an ocean of, and that the people in the movement were the waves on that ocean.

CHAPTER 15

Black Consciousness

Wadleigh Middle School was built in Harlem in 1902 for girls to become "gentlewomen," in addition to or instead of being ladies. It was the first high school of its kind in New York City and aroused fear among the majority that one thing would lead to another: higher learning to expanded identity, social mobility, eliminating white men's monopoly on the right to vote. The building was old, medieval, inspired by architects of the French Renaissance, from a time of kings and queens, peasants and gentry, when society was rigid, when you lived and died in the place you were born. Status set in stone.

"They needed a body in this classroom and I couldn't find work," Mama said. "There weren't that many jobs for black women then. Wadleigh was an opportunity to avoid the post office and nursing—I had just graduated from Hunter two semesters early and went to the Columbia School of Nursing for six weeks. I couldn't stand being in a place where the symptoms of our oppression became the issue. The pervading attitude was your people are like this because they are poor, but no one wants to do anything about poverty. I didn't need to learn about Freud to learn about what was happening in my community.

"When I was teaching I took the bus from my apartment on Central Park West to 115th and 8th Ave. The junkies would be suspended in front of the candy store early in the morning, as if they were sculptures of wax. You'd think, *He's gonna fall*, but they wouldn't. The ones coming off the heroin shook and scratched for a fix. The students would walk between them with small brown paper bags filled with what they could buy with a quarter. There was always a trail of wrappers, empty bags of potato chips from the bus stop to the school. It was not unusual to see used needles on the sidewalk or rats in the garbage, particularly when it was warm. I remember Jessy Gray standing on an old Studebaker holding onto a large cardboard box surrounded by his people. He was organizing them to collect rats to leave on the steps of city hall. Harlem was festering. Everybody, even the junkies were saying something. I couldn't walk a block without *hey, mama* or *hey, sister*—you had guys walking down 125th looking like whoseamawhuchit with Fanon under their arms [Mama described Fanon as a revolutionary who lived what he wrote about, who had a framework for how the oppressed can become whole again by working to liberate themselves, whether through nonviolent or armed struggle.[1]] We'd been starved and were hungry for information, to have a conversation about ourselves.

"The students had already run out two or three teachers and I hadn't taught before. But that didn't matter; we were hired to provide custodial care. It didn't matter if they learned, just as long as we kept the trains running on time.

"There were only a few black teachers [in Wadleigh], the rest of the teachers, all of the administration was white. Most of them were complicit in the student's failure—didn't believe the children could or were interested in learning. There were a few who did. I felt isolated. Sometimes we ate lunch together, but usually I ate by myself or with the students. I wanted them to have agency to deal with what they encountered, to help them learn something about themselves and the world without proselytizing. But I didn't know how to talk about lynching without getting angry. And so I asked a lot of questions. I would ask them to dig deep, to pull out their pearls.

"When Cassius Clay defeated Sonny Liston on February 25, 1964, one of the students, Jimmy Chester, ran through the hallways screaming, *Who's the greatest? I'm the greatest. Who's the greatest? I'm the greatest. Who's the greatest? I'm the greatest.* The teachers were terrified—even before Cassius Clay became Muhammad Ali—and Jimmy ended up sweeping the halls with Mr. Jonesy for a week. Jimmy came to Harlem from Louisiana, was more red than brown, came to school enough not to be expelled. He could be charming, would sing hambone during lunch if you could get him to smile. He knew what it was like to be barefoot and cold, to be lied to, you could see that in his eyes.

"I had spent the last two years picketing Woolworth stores to desegregate lunch counters in the South," Mama said. "I knew segregated lunch counters were just the tip of the iceberg. Had no illusions that America would become something different, vis-à-vis black people, picketing Woolworths. But it was necessary. Or that my presence in the building would do anything to return it to what it had been for young girls throughout the city—mostly Jewish, mostly immigrants, maybe one or two blacks per class. Who got an education that allowed them to step outside the rigid boxes society placed them in. When Jimmy ran through the hallways I felt the building quiver, how those words and his spirit threatened to release, if only for a split second, what the building was designed to contain.

"At the faculty meeting one of the teachers suggested Jimmy should be expelled, suggested that he and the boys that followed him were dangerous. But the principal seemed amused, said that spending a week peeling dirt from cracks would help to straighten him out and prepare him to be of use to the world.

"I met with the principal every few weeks to give him my lesson plans. He approved them without reading a page. Every now and then he would flip through one and say something which he didn't intend me to respond to—*there's generational pathology within the black family that has to be addressed.* When he saw 'Harlem's Poets' as the title to a plan he asked, *Why not Yeats?* And I said, *Why not Harlem?* without thinking about it. And that was the only time I really looked him in the eye and kept looking until he looked away.

"He began each assembly with Yeats—not Dunbar, not Langston . . . in the middle of Harlem. Can you believe that? Unforgettable. It was not possible for me to believe that he wasn't part of some broader conspiracy that began somewhere in America and landed in Harlem and was reinforced by that school. How else does someone like that get to run the building?

"Mr. Jonesy was the chief custodian, like my uncles, legs and arms like sturdy trees, shoe-polish black, it was hard to imagine him being moved in a way he didn't want to. Always pushing a barrel of trash, empty trash bags hanging from the silver flask tucked in his back pocket. A couple days after Jimmy ran through the halls, Mr. Jonesy waited for me in the doorway to my classroom, the arms and legs of his brooms and mops sticking out the trash barrel. He pulled a book out of his pocket, showed me the pages that he had dog-eared. *You keep doing what you're doing, Miz Janet. Help those boys and girls find a spot in the sun.*"

When Mama read Sterling Brown's "The Ballad of Joe Meek" to her class, one of the poems that Mr. Jonesy had dog-eared, it was the first time she got all the students to pay attention at the same time. "The boys who had trouble reading and writing more than their names began reciting verses to Claude McKay's 'If We Must Die,'" she said. The poem was written in July 1919 and became a black anthem during Red Summer—*Like men we'll face the murderous, cowardly pack / Pressed to the wall, dying, but fighting back!*

When Mama asked the students if they wanted to recite the poems at the school assembly, Jimmy's hand shot up out of his seat.

At the next assembly a singular *Right on!* filled the auditorium as Jimmy led his classmates onstage and began to recite "The Ballad of Joe Meek."

> *When he woke up, and knew*
> *What the cops had done,*
> *Went to a hockshop,*
> *Got hisself a gun . . .*

By the time ole boy Joe had stepped outside the police station, got shot in the back, turned to kill the cop who'd caught him with a bullet, died, and requested a glass of water on his way to hell to meet that police chief who was gonna join him there, the auditorium was on its feet, students standing and cheering as if Jimmy was Joe Meek and the cop was Jim Crow.

"*I could die here and the cockroaches wouldn't know it!* is what my aunt Ruth used to say. That's how I felt about Wadleigh," Mama said. "I decided at the end of that semester, in December of 1963, to go to Mississippi. Mississippi provided a handle that teaching school didn't, was a chance to get to the root of something. I was naive and believed that America could be different.

"Bibi didn't say anything when I asked for permission to go to Mississippi. She could see that my mind was made up. Bibi knew what living in the Deep South felt like. She remembered her own mama rushing home with her daddy with his one blind eye because he'd bumped into a white girl on a sidewalk. How they waited in fear at home for someone to show up and shoot through their door. Bibi eventually organized a few women at her church and raised a thousand dollars to support SNCC.

"I would visit my students in their homes, even after Mississippi. Their parents would say *Miz Janet is here*, and would offer me whatever they had in their refrigerators. All of my students went to high school. We'd talk about their classes and what was happening in Harlem. I would tell them about the students they reminded me of in Natchez, Mississippi."

. . .

We banded together as we walked to our first day of high school at Cambridge Rindge and Latin, the city's only public high school. The sneakers and jeans and T-shirts of less fortunate freshmen were already hanging from lampposts, on clotheslines. We were wearing two layers of clothes we didn't care about. Me and Moke and the Twins and Ariel. Moke had older cousins who he said would fuck up anyone up who tried to touch us. The hazing was a ritual—stripping freshmen on their first day of high school of whatever status, security, or pride they had accumulated in the long march from kindergarten to eighth grade. Returning them to some version of being naked in the womb.

By the time we reached Broadway, we had banded together with other groups of freshmen, mostly virgins, innocent-eyed, peach-fuzzed, smothered in Polo cologne. We could see evidence of those who'd gone it alone hanging from a telephone line.

Once in the building we went our separate ways. We didn't have the clairvoyance to embrace, to say goodbye. To acknowledge the end of a journey, the beginning of another.

The school was organized in "houses." House D was for Haitians, other recent immigrants. Houses C, B, and A were for the general population. Fundamental was for students who wanted a traditional education. Pilot was for the children of liberal white progressives. OccEd (occupational education) prepared black and Puerto Rican and poor white boys to become auto mechanics.

The real hazing began inside the building, in the sorting of bodies initiating us into America's economic arrangements. Even Baba said that what we did in the classroom now mattered. As Baba understood it, these classrooms were the catalyst for the perpetuation of America's caste system.

After eight years of Open School, I had decided I wanted the same education as "everyone else," to go to "regular" school, and was placed in House A. It didn't take long for me to recognize and appreciate the difference between a liberal white progressive education and an industrial education. The difference between being able to call a teacher by their first name and not being able to was substantive.

For all the flags waving in the field house celebrating the school's and the city's diversity, the school was segregated. I was the only black kid other than Khari in my honors classes for four years. It would be that way for my sisters and Taba too. When I saw Ariel, Dana, Colin, and Moke it was in the hallways, at lunch, or in the field house.

I made the junior varsity basketball team my freshman year and then broke my ankle in the second scrimmage game of the season. Plodded through winter in crutches. The entire year felt anonymous. I learned how to type and recognized that as valuable. I also learned that I couldn't be a basketball player and continue to steal from the Puerto Rican store, or any store. At least in my mind, those identities were in conflict with each other.

I transferred to the fifth-floor Pilot school at the beginning of my sophomore year. Maisha was a senior there. Like in the Open School, we called our teachers by their first names, came and went as we pleased. There was a school commons where the students from different houses all hung out. There were only a handful of black students in Pilot (most black parents preferred Fundamental because of the tradition and discipline), but we were part of a community.

It was where Khari and his homies became radical, Jamaican, and militant. Chewed root sticks, practiced creole and rapping. Began confronting our minority status. This wave of black consciousness seemed to blossom suddenly, erupting from the cracks in the cement, permeating hip-hop culture. Public Enemy's *It Takes a Nation of Millions to Hold Us Back*, N.W.A's *Straight Outta Compton*, and Boogie Down Production's *By All Means Necessary* were mainstream hip-hop, political, socially conscious, and militant.

The Autobiography of Malcolm X was on the Pilot syllabus.

Posters of Malcolm adorned our walls at home. Audiotapes of Malcolm's speeches were circulated from Walkman to Walkman.

*X*s were emblazoned on clothes. Became shields, armor, amulets for our identities.

Khari and his crew painted a corner of the Pilot common room red, black, and green. Waved the flag like they'd been to Africa. Wallpapered the common room with Malcolm X quotes scribbled on chart paper. Debated loudly enough to draw a white crowd. Got mad love from the snow bunnies. Put what they felt about our black journey through black and white America in Pilot's public square. What we had done with our bodies when breakdancing on corners.

The visual language of Black Power contrasted with the images of freedom singers and marches and sit-ins that had framed my understanding of what was required for oppressed people to liberate themselves. Challenged my perception of nonviolent direct action as the necessary catalyst for transforming black and white America.

When I asked Baba about Malcolm, he didn't say much. And then he said, "*Omowale* was the name that Malcolm was given on his trip to Africa."

"It means the son who comes home," he added, as if I needed reminding.

When I asked him about Black Power, he said, "Ask your mother about that."

· · ·

Mama and Baba met in Natchez, Mississippi. He was married then.[2] It was July 1964, more than a month after Chaney, Goodman, and Schwerner had gone missing, days before their bodies would be dredged from the earthen dam on Olen Burrage's 254-acre Old Jolly Farm. The Klan had gathered in preparation for the arrival of the students on a field, on horse, in robes, among constellations of flames, infiltrated by FBI agents, beneath the hum of crop dusters guarding airspace. Three hundred white knights had prepared for the arrival of northern students into Mississippi, what the Klan's grand dragon described as the "nigger communist" invasion. "Stand back from the main area of conflict," he said. "Be armed," "ready to move" as the "enemy prepares to launch his final push for victory in Mississippi."

Mama and Baba met in Mr. Metcalf's rooming house in Natchez, Mississippi.

"Here's one of our leaders," Mama thought, "who exudes integrity and honesty. The first time I heard about him was from a classmate at Hunter who was going with Roger [Baba's brother], talking about stuff going down in Mississippi, that Roger's brother was in Mississippi."

Mama wrote about her experience in Natchez in Judy Richardson's *Hands on the Freedom Plow*:

> I decided at twenty-two that I would risk my life to stay alive, to walk in the sun without shame or guilt for not doing what in my heart I knew I should do.
>
> I spent my first year in Natchez, which had been pried open by Chuck McDew, George Greene, and Dorie Ladner. We were provided lodging in a rooming house owned by George Metcalf, a local NAACP leader.

He worked at the Armstrong Tire Company and was badly injured in a car bombing. Annie Pearl Avery from Birmingham joined us. . . . By that time, we had established ourselves in the freedom house that Annie Pearl guarded at night with her .22.

I spent a lot of time working with the young people who were becoming increasingly conscious. . . . We would go to pool halls, juke joints—wherever folk were. The community bailed us out when we got arrested.

One time, Annie Pearl was arrested, initially a bystander, she placed herself in the procession being led into the paddy wagon and so was hauled off with the rest of us. At the jail the sheriff insisted that Annie Pearl sit down on one of the benches. When she refused a third time, the sheriff started yelling, threatening to shove his foot up her ass if she didn't sit down. Annie, in a steady voice, asked what he thought *she* would be doing while he was shoving *his* foot up *her* ass!

After weeks of visiting, a woman I knew as "Ms. Crew" and her husband offered us a place to live. They were raising two grandchildren. One of my jobs was to braid their granddaughter's soft, cottony hair—a very uneven exchange in return for biscuits and syrup in the morning and a safe, warm place to lay my head at night.

At some point we were passed onto others, including Mr. Brown. One day I met Mr. Brown and his wife. He listened unemotionally as I told him who I was and why I was there. I knew this was not the first news he had had about voting. I invited myself back—another day, another week—to chat some more. He didn't tell me not to return, so I would go back and he would ask if I had talked to so-and-so. After several months they all agreed, singly, that registering to vote was a good idea and that they would support a voter registration day in Fayette.

I don't remember how the FBI got involved.

On the morning of the demonstration, local people began to gather around the courthouse in clusters. Some stood across the street, and others sat at the side of the courthouse lawn. I moved from group to group, greeting onlookers and those who had indicated that they might try to register. We escorted those ready to take the long walk up the courthouse steps into the registrar's office.

I recall that at some point several white men in a pickup truck drove up in front of the courthouse. I watched them from the courthouse steps as they got out of the truck. As they approached the stairs, several other white men—FBI—intercepted their approach and escorted them to their truck.

Mr. Brown . . . sat on the stone embankment that bordered the side of the courthouse, one among several men with whom we had worked rather closely over the past few months. He wore baggy denim overalls and held a crumpled brown paper bag in his lap. I sat down next to him as instructed and gently asked if he was ready to ascend the courthouse steps. He answered by opening the paper bag in his lap. In it lay a large pistol. "Now, Mizjaunette, don't you worry 'bout a thing. You just keep working," he said.[3]

"Maybe we're not going to get many people registered this summer," Baba said, "Maybe, even, we're not going to get very many people into Freedom Schools. Maybe all we're going to do is live this summer. In Mississippi, that will be so much."

"By the end of Freedom Summer, there had been 6 known murders, 35 known shootings, 4 people critically wounded, at least 80 volunteers beaten, and more than 1,000 people arrested," Uncle Charlie wrote.

Freedom Summer culminated in the MFDP's challenge to the seating of the so-called "regular" state party at the national party's convention in August in Atlantic City, New Jersey. The MFDP was the culmination of parallel precinct, county, and regional meetings that had been organized by SNCC during that perilous summer.

"It was the message of empowerment for grassroots people these meetings generated that was delivered to the entire country on national television at the 1964 convention by the sharecroppers, domestic workers, and farmers who formed the rank and file of the MFDP," Baba said. "They were asking the national Democratic Party whether it would be willing to empower people in their meetings in a similar way. The answer was no."

For SNCC, the MFDP rejection was a turning point in the organization's history. "Never again were we lulled into believing that our task was exposing injustices so that the 'good' people of America could eliminate them," recalled Cleveland Sellers. "After Atlantic City, our struggle was not for civil rights, but for liberation."[4]

"Each challenge served as an object lesson for strengthening black political independence, and the organizing and lobbying efforts for each laid the groundwork for congressional passage of the Voting Rights Act of 1965," Julian Bond wrote. "The MFDP served as a prototype for the model of Black Power advocated and popularized by Stokely Carmichael."[5]

"You got Stokely working in Lowndes [and] Moses [and] his conference and this is how you get Black Power," Ed Brown said.[6]

Movement encourages movement, Baba said. "The civil rights movement of the 1960s was less about challenges and protests against white power than feeling our way toward our own power and possibilities—really a series of challenges by ourselves, and our communities, to ourselves."[7]

· · ·

Uncle Al said that Mama was behind the scenes, helped organize an all-black conference about decolonization called Roots in New Orleans. When I moved to Mississippi, Mama shared, as if some clandestine artifact, a copy of a memo that had been presented to SNCC staff at the opening of the Roots conference. The memo listed as its authors Janet Jemmott, Dona Richards, Doug and Tina Harris, and Bob Parris. Baba, in an attempt to detangle himself from his heroification in Mississippi, had dropped Moses and taken his mother's maiden name. Mama said that even though Baba's name was on it, he wasn't one of its authors. Baba said that Mama had been a driving force behind the conference. That she could have been a thing in the movement but didn't want the attention.

"In history there are no sharp breaks," was the memo's opening line. "There is no place where one may say; here history changes, here an age ends and another begins. . . . Man has constantly searched for his past. For it is his past which he uses as a foundation for his present and future. 'Rootlessness' which grows out of a lack of understanding and misinformation 'strips him naked' by depriving him of a historical frame of reference that comes out of knowing that anthropologists have discovered a 'Negroid' skull dating back to 600,000 B.C. in what may have been the 'Garden of Eden' in the fertile valleys of Kenya in East Africa."

The memo and the conference attempted to plant humanity's feet in African soil.

Mama traveled to Lowndes County, Alabama, where Stokely Carmichael, who had been elected chairman of SNCC, and other SNCC organizers had planted their feet after the National Democratic Party had failed to seat the MFDP at the 1964 convention.

Lowndes County, Alabama, founded in 1830, was part of the Black Belt in the American South. After the federal passage of the Reconstruction Acts in 1867, four thousand black citizens registered to vote in the county. Freedmen held local offices and were elected to the state legislature.

In 1960, at the doorstep of the Civil Rights Movement, after the rise of Jim Crow laws and white terrorism, the number of registered black voters in what became known as "Bloody Lowndes" was zero.

The Lowndes County Freedom Organization, the first independent black political party in the county since Reconstruction, was founded in 1965 by John Hulett and other local community members with the support of SNCC organizers. The organization adopted the black panther as their logo.

The Alabama Democratic Party's logo was a white rooster, its slogan "White Supremacy."

In 1970 John Hulett became the first black sheriff to be elected in the county since Reconstruction.

Stokely spoke with *National Guardian* reporter William A. Price about the evolution of the organization.

WILLIAM A. PRICE: Are there lessons you have learned from the MFDP?

STOKELY: We certainly have. . . . For the six years we've been in business we've always had mock power, we've had mock elections, mock votes, mock freedom. This is the first year that we've had real power. And that's reflected in the Lowndes County Freedom Organization. What the [SNCC] staff was doing was [asking] how do you deal with this real power? For example in Mississippi we had several mock elections, mock votes which were just pressure tactics to demonstrate to the country that black people weren't really apathetic, that black people really wanted the right to vote. . . . The idea was to get Negroes to start thinking politically. We finally got real power in 1966 in Alabama in terms of being able to vote and to form political parties.[8]

· · ·

What do we want?
Black power!
Was the call and response that originated in Bloody Lowndes.

What do we want?
Black Power!
What do we want?
Black power for Black people!

Was the call and response that reverberated in the spirit of Freedom Riders, in the spirit of freedom songs, in the spirit of sit-ins, in the spirit of the MFDP, in the spirit of love, in the spirit of justice, in the spirit of protest that rose and fell, becoming a wave in an ocean of organizing, of rebellion, of consciousness. That rose and fell on the bosom of Mississippi. Crashing onto black America's shores. Adopted in Oakland. Igniting the flames that swept through Chicago, Harlem, Newark in the '70s. Rising from the ashes and rubble of the South Bronx in the '80s, in the spirit of hip-hop, blasted from boom boxes amplifying mostly young black and Puerto Rican male voices teetering on the precipice of manhood, now rolling up into Khari's fist, erect in the Pilot school common room, among a chorus of snow bunnies.

———————

ROBERT MOSES C-SPAN INTERVIEW (1986)

That's how I always thought about the movement and my relationship to it, and SNCC and other people's relationship to it. It was the movement that was this ocean, and we were the waves on the ocean. Now when you think about the movement in that way, you can ask a question different from the one that Alden asked. Alden's question is, "How is the emergence and success of such a leader to be explained?" And we can ask, rather, . . . how is the emergence and the repression, the success and the failure, of such a movement to be explained? You want to shift our attention from the wave to the ocean. Because the wave is not the ocean. No matter, even if it's a tidal wave. It has no meaning apart from that ocean.

The idea is that the history, any history of the movement—when we talk about it, we have to also talk about its failures, its false starts, as well as its successes. We have to offer to our young people an understanding of why King was assassinated, as well as why he became a Nobel Peace Prize winner. But not only King—we have to offer them an understanding of why Medgar Evers, Herbert Lee, Louis Allen, Goodman, Cheney, Schwerner, Malcolm X, those two Kennedy brothers—why all those people were assassinated from 1961 to 1971. And the point is that King's assassination has no meaning apart from the assassination of all those people—*you cannot* understand it as an isolated event. And they belong to the ocean that was the movement. That's what has to be studied to get a deeper understanding about who and what Dr. King was.

That really is my major point. That we can ask and should ask other historians that they offer us a history of the movement. And that through that history of the movement, we can understand the relationship of Dr. King to the movement. But without that history of the movement, it's as meaningless as trying to understand the wave without the concept of the ocean. There just is no understanding to be had.

And what we're left with is frustration. It's a frustration that Dr. King's sister expressed in the press room in connection with young people that don't know how to relate to Dr. King because they see him as a God. So they have no concept of how they, too, can be like him. And that's what happens when the focus is wrong, is misplaced.

CHAPTER 16

In the Distance
Between Us (III)

Newtowne Court, constructed in 1938 for white residents, and Washington Elms, built next to it in 1942 for black residents, were the first housing projects in Cambridge and among the first in America. Segregated housing was in the distance between black and white America. There were other projects—big brick bunkers built in other Cambridge neighborhoods—many of whose residents, a combination of American born and recent immigrant families, sought to emerge from these segregated communities and achieve some semblance of the American Dream. The Tuttles, whose fathers and sons had fought in America's wars and landed jobs at the post office, were among the families who were able to move out of Newtowne Court and purchase a home in the neighborhood.

When Baba decided to purchase a house next door to Newtowne Court, he was concerned, primarily, with how we, his sons, would grow up in proximity to black and white life in America. It meant in part that who Taba and I would become, and want to become, would grow out of running in and out of Newtowne Court with Moke and Fats, Colin and Dana, Dico and Daco, Ariel and Nando, and Hector and Alex. He understood from his own journey that our spirit—and thus our minds and our bodies—would be safer growing in closer proximity to what imperils black life in America.

In Cambridge, more so than in most communities, what imperiled black America and what imperiled white America—like the once-segregated Newtowne Court and Washington Elms—could be neighbors.

. . .

"Too many niggers," the Tuttle brothers said—in the neighborhood, in America—and it was the point of view of the majority of white America. One of the brothers walked in parabolas along School Street as I stood on our porch, unable to sleep in the heat. He was returning home from a bar in Central Square, struggling with gravity, with the weight of his journey.

"This neighbahood's goin' to the shitta'," he said as he approached our porch, "too many niggas." And then he stopped and invited me to join him in the street. His face red, bloated, and porous from the heat, from whatever substances he was abusing.

"There's four of us left you know, . . . they all killed for me. I took a hundred in Nam, . . . I went into the pits, . . . I was the first one in, . . . I had to get the General, . . . , he looked me in the eye and took it like a man. Some of my brothers believed in God. They stood up straight when the chinks was aimin' for our heads. Me, I was up and down." He put a hand above his head as he ducked. "I got over two hundred bodies, most as a civilian, you know what I mean." And then he stumbled into the shadows of our shared driveway, through his backyard and into his crack den.

Drugs were beginning to tear at the fabric of the neighborhood, upend the city's progressive social order. Tidal waves of cocaine, like the heroin that had flooded Harlem in the '60s and '70s, landed on the sidewalks of the Port. By 1990, crack was king, creating an economic incentive to hang on corners. Corners became drive-throughs. Brothas became drug dealers. Parents became fiends. Chicks became chicken heads. Conscious hip-hop drowned in an ocean of gangsta rap, became underground music. Movies like *New Jack City, Boyz in the Hood, Menace to Society* eclipsed *Do the Right Thing* in the hearts and minds of the majority of brothers and sisters on the streets. The red, black, and green flag that had begun to flower, to plant adolescent black feet in African soil, was replaced with colors that claimed a block or a neighborhood.

"Niggas is marchin' because a white boy died?" Ghetto asked when Jesse McKie and Rigoberto Carrion were stabbed to death in front of Newtowne Court. Jesse was a soon-to-be father, former Pilot student, breakdancer, and painter, Rigoberto a father of two five-year-old boys. Their murders drew attention to the perils of white life growing in close proximity to black life in Cambridge. Their murders drew attention to the Port and the perils of what felt like a regular part of black life anywhere, in the same way that the deaths of Chaney, Goodman, and Schwerner had drawn America's attention to the perils of black life in Mississippi.

Khari and other students in the high school organized Students Against Violence and for Equality and marched from the Port to city hall.

I didn't attend the march. I felt like I didn't belong there, could only see myself on a basketball court.

In the distance between black and white life in Cambridge were concerns that the murders of Jesse and Rigoberto had been drug or gang related. MIT reported the impact of the murders on their community as ambiguous, that more students were requesting the night escort service. The *Harvard Crimson* described the Port as a haven for drug dealers that other Cantabrigians were afraid to walk through.[1] According to Ghetto, kids from Boston had come over the bridge and tried to rob Jesse for his jacket and he'd refused to give it. The murderers stabbed Jesse in the heart and head, stabbed Rigoberto in the heart. Rigoberto's story didn't carry the same local significance as Jesse's. In the same way that the death of James Chaney hadn't been planted, like Goodman's and Schwerner's, in the nation's consciousness.

When asked why he'd organized white college students to converge on Mississippi in the '60s, Baba said, "I wanted to force the country to look at itself through the eyes of the people it recognized as its children." With Jesse's death, the city mourned the loss of one of its children, as it attempted to also recognize Rigoberto as one of its own.

. . .

When Baba bought the house next door to Newtowne Court, he wanted Taba and me to be able to see America through Ghetto's eyes. Like the Tuttles, Ghetto's family had moved out of Newtowne Court and into the apartment across the street a couple years before we moved into the neighborhood. "The Port back then had a mixture, a real diversity of people," Ghetto said. "Not made-up diversity, the white boys that lived there were just like black folk and Spanish folk, we all got along, we were like brothers growing up, we were all broke, we had a lot of fun together—kick the can, hide-an'-go-seek, cops and robbers, stickball, all that stuff. Portuguese, Irish, Italian, to us they were just whites—Budroes, Gomes, Carpelos, Parmazano, when you got older you figured it out. If you saw a person of color, they were black. If they spoke Spanish, you thought they were Puerto Rican."

Ghetto understood that some version of getting jumped was a rite of passage for kids in neighborhoods like the Port. Growing up, crews of kids from one neighborhood would meet crews of kids from other projects, from another neighborhood, to battle. It could lead to a gang tackle on a football field, broken ankles on a basketball court, head spinning on stiff concrete, sometimes to throwing fists and elbows. Which led to wounds, festering resentments, so that being somewhere without your crew could lead to a group of niggas kicking your ass. In Cambridge the niggas could be Portuguese, or African American, or Puerto Rican, or Irish. The gangs could be mulatto.

The Boston version of this had happened to me and Taba when we were kids, after Baba had handed me $160 and we'd taken the train from Central Square over the bridge to Crystal's Sneakers at Downtown Crossing, where we each bought a pair of shell-toe Adidas and Nike Air Force Ones. It felt like Taba and I had been waiting our whole American lives for some fresh kicks, instead of the bobos that we had haggled with Mama and Baba about, that brothas would never rob you of.

A thin, hollow, gold rope chain hung from my neck. A gold-plated crab the size of a silver dollar hung from it. I was born in April on the cusp of Taurus and Aries and would have preferred a bull to a ram or a crab, but the crab was fat and the girls would ask me if my sign was Cancer, which would begin a conversation.

I could feel the brothas' eyes on my neck as we approached the store-front—suddenly the crab felt conspicuous. Some of the boys were taller than us, others appeared our age and younger, like they could be a gang of kids who'd grown up on the same block. Once we entered the store it didn't take us long to forget, among the towering shoeboxes, that they were waiting for us outside. I found a pair of shell-toe Adidas with navy-blue stripes and Nike Airs with a maroon swoosh. Taba's were white on white.

As soon as we left the store I could feel their eyes again, now on our bags. I took a right out the store instead of walking toward them, which led us away from the train station. They began to follow us, some jogging as we walked faster. Within a block they were reaching for the bags in our hands, the chain on my neck. Taba and I swung the bags like fists, Taba trying to pull them off me as I began dragging a couple of them, as they tried to wrestle me to the ground. The security booth at the edge of a parking lot loomed like a divine goalpost.

"What's going on?" the guard said as he stepped out of his cage. His badge and gunless uniform enough to get the brothas off our backs and necks and wrists. Taba and I looked each other over to make sure we weren't bleeding and then plotted a course back to the train station. We sat next to each other on the train in silence. They'd gotten the gold, but we had our kicks. Which was all that mattered. That we held onto the bags, to each other. We smiled as the train rattled over the bridge back into Cambridge. Where all of a sudden I felt safe. I certainly appreciated the river and the bridge and the distance they provided between niggas in Cambridge and niggas in Boston.

· · ·

"When your dad was trying to get us to go to do math at the King School on Saturdays I wasn't trying to hear it. I had already made up my mind to go this way," Fat Daddy said.

Daco and then Fat Daddy were the first among us to hustle. "I made six hundred on Thursdays, Fridays, and Saturdays," Daco said. "I made six hundred in an hour," Fat Daddy said. "I'll never forget. D gave me some weed. I smoked all the weed. And then he gave me a bag of coke and was like, smoke that. He said we're doing half and half and I made six hundred in a hour. I never looked back after that. We'd take the shuttle to New York and bring the coke back in shoes, underwear. We was young. I wasn't fifteen yet. When I got locked up, it took years and years to be able to think about going another way."

The first time Taba was arrested, I was in the loft on the mattress in my bedroom with Wimbledon. She had just come back from the Square with a couple slices of pizza. The lofts had been Baba's idea. It had taken him six years to rehab the house. He'd converted the attic into bedrooms last. We helped to gut the ceiling and held the beams as he added another level to our rooms, extended their height and sovereignty. We sanded and polyurethaned the floors and door moldings and painted the ladders that lead to our mattresses. My and Taba's rooms were conjoined by a passage that led to the skylights we shared, which gave us a bird's eye view of the first and second floor hallways. If we had girls over, we could hear or see if Mama or Baba were climbing the steps, and if they tried to enter one of our rooms, the girls could move unnoticed from one room to the other.

When Taba called, Wimbledon and I had just peeled our bodies apart. I wanted to remain skin to skin. Had begun to grow attached to her heart. To like is to spit, to love is to swallow she said. She waited in the loft as I walked to the police station in Central Square to bail him out. I was told that I couldn't and needed to show up in court the next day. I struggled with whether to tell Baba then. The next morning he and Mama wanted to know where Taba was. I told them he was OK. In the courtroom I saw brothas I had forgotten existed. The judge spoke another language. The lawyers spoke another language. The language they spoke resulted in see you later. Everyone pleaded out and accepted whatever the judge offered. Taba was the first one, in the hours I was there, who pleaded not guilty.

He'd been arrested by Mr. Stead's brother. The charge was disorderly conduct for letting his pants sag low in the square.

Baba told me that my word wasn't good anymore when he found out what happened. He marched the entire family up to the police station to talk to the police chief, as if he could protect us from what was coming—the resurrection of Jim Crow laws that gave the police the right to put their hands on our bodies. Taba getting arrested for letting his pants sag low was in the distance between us.

Mama would ask if Taba was OK. I said yes. I believed yes. That he and I were different from the rest. That the Twins, who went to church, who still hadn't gotten laid, were different from the rest. Eventually, we all found out he was hustling. I was speechless. Mama and Baba cried, argued with each other about what to do. That was when Baba sent him to Tanzania. Taba came back with pictures and stories—about the market on the beach, how he'd been welcomed like a long-lost son, how men held his hand and walked him around villages, how boys drove him around on their mopeds and made him promise to send them the latest hip-hop albums, how the other African Americans were treated like strangers. And then he went back to hustling. Baba began taking him with him around the country to Chicago and Mississippi as he grew the Algebra Project. Taba would come to visit me at George Washington, sometimes on his way to Virginia, where

Moke and the Twins had landed at Norfolk State University. We'd eat. Hit the club. Sometimes he'd get on the court with the team. Play video games. Watch a movie. In those moments we returned to who we'd been when we'd first roamed the earth together. He told me stories from the world he was living in. I would laugh and say, "Yo, that shit's crazy," but never said what I felt—that I wanted to erase the distance between civilian and soldier.

. . .

In the distance between civilian and soldier was the dream that we inherited from Mama and Baba. That was a yardstick for whatever we were doing with our lives, that we would be part of a wave of young people working to transform America through the realization of our individual and collective gifts. A dream that mutated in each of us. That Taba and I shared. A black boy's prayer. That the bounce of a ball, the hook of a song, would deliver us, together, to the other side of America's cages. That was reflected, in whatever disappointment or anger I felt, as Taba and I stood eye-to-eye whenever we confronted each other. "One looks into the eyes of another to find oneself," John Mohawk said. "Each of us finds an identity through the reflections of ourselves that we see in others. . . . Such are the ways by which human beings place values upon themselves and upon others."[2]

. . .

Taba and Khari and I are trying to plan a MathLab lesson in the Brinkley Middle School library when Taba and I confront each other. I am unable to tell him what I am afraid of, that I have dreams of him getting shot and thrown in jail. I am unable to tell him that I love him. In that way I am crippled. In the end, I call him a drug dealer. Mrs. Jefferson, the English teacher, tiptoes out of the library, back into the hallway. Taba begins crying. We don't speak for a couple of weeks.

"When are you gonna work that shit out?" Khari says.

When *Radical Equations* is published, Baba writes notes to each of us as he signs our hardcover copies. "To my beloved son," Baba writes to Taba,

> who appeared one night on his own to announce his coming appearance, silently sitting as if in a stone, who loved his movies on the floor behind his closed and non sleepy eyes before he was 2, who walked with

me to get the morning milk up the long flight of stairs and down them holding my hand, who woke up after dinner when the others went to sleep and played to greet the night before he was 3, who played day and night with his brother tumbling in and out of fun and tears, who took to the water and swam smooth for the joy of the feel for the water, who faced me down, swallowed a hurt when I forgot how a father is to a son, who loved me in his hurt as a son can love his father, who drifted to the streets in search of life, who took the streets into his understandings to make for himself an education, who took the movies of his early years to learn the music of his years to come, who I love and who taught me how to love him, Baba, 1/18/01.

———————

ROBERT MOSES C-SPAN INTERVIEW (1986)

There was always within the movement a tension between organizing and leading. Or organizing and mobilizing. And you can trace the history of the movement in terms of certain great mobilizations, yes. There was Albany, Georgia, there was Birmingham, there was Selma, Alabama. . . . But you can also trace the history of the movement in terms of certain real organizing efforts. . . . There was the organization of SCLC. There was the organization of SNCC. There was the organization of the Nashville Sit-In Movement. There was the organization of the [1963] March on Washington. And you can trace in the movement the tension between people in their roles as organizers and as leaders. And try to get some sense of what that meant. I think of Ella Baker. She was a great organizer and she was a leader too. But one of the characteristics of the organizer is that their work emerges and they subside. I mean, if you think of the wave and ocean, at a certain point they subside back into the ocean and what you see is what they organized, or their work. SNCC is a work of Ella Baker. But it was SNCC that emerged and not Ella. The March on Washington was a work of Bayard Rustin, but it was Martin Luther King that emerged, not Bayard. And the point is that Bayard never organized that march so that he should himself personally emerge; it was organized in a setting where someone like King could emerge. And Bayard knew that. And he set out to do just that. And that's the mark of the organizer. Ella didn't set up SNCC in a way that she could possibly emerge as the leader of it. Quite the contrary, Ella organized SNCC in such a way that she could never possibly be the leader of it. And in doing that she taught us about organizing.

So there is in the movement these great examples of organizers and their organizing efforts. And I miss that. It seems like it doesn't make good copy, right? But it really helped—it made the movement. It was the tissue and the bone and inner structure of the movement.

. . . Amzie Moore was a leader in Cleveland and would not be broached. He was the civil rights leader in Cleveland, Mississippi, but he was an organizer in Mississippi and never a leader. In the state as a whole he moved like an organizer, never out front, working with people to set up certain plans—the voting plan, for example—but in his own town, in his community he was a leader. Now, civil rights workers got in trouble when they didn't understand that and tried to organize in Amzie's territory.

They asked me to write a paper, and I had two problems: one I'm not a scholar and I don't write papers, usually, and the other, I don't think about the movement in terms of King. And . . . I understood that this was a conference about King and the movement. And I have no qualms with that. But I never thought about the movement—it never occurred to me to think about the movement in terms of King. I lived and breathed the movement. So I couldn't have written a paper that focused on the movement in terms of King. And so I want to point out that that other question seems to me more important. Not the emergence and success of an individual. But first the emergence and success of, the failure and the repression of the movement. And study its false starts as well as its successes. Its failures as well as where it won out.

OK, thanks.

(*Applause*)

CHAPTER 17

A Wave

ROBERT MOSES'S ACCOUNT OF VOTER REGISTRATION DRIVE IN MISSISSIPPI IN 1961

00:26:53 Robert P. Moses

The Sunday before he was killed, I was down at Steptoe's with John Doerr from the Justice Department, and we asked Steptoe, was there any danger in that area, who was causing the trouble, and who were the people in danger? Steptoe told us Thaddeus Church, who lived across from him, had been threatening people, and that, specifically, people said that he, Steptoe, and Herbert Lee and George Reese were in danger of losing their lives.

00:27:36 Robert P. Moses

We went out but didn't see Lee that afternoon. That night John Doerr and the other lawyers from the Justice Department left. The following morning about twelve o'clock noon, Dr. Anderson came by the voter registration office, said a man had been shot in Amite County. They brought him over to McComb, and he was lying on the table in a funeral home in McComb, and he asked me if I might have known him. I went down to take a look at the body, and it was Herbert Lee. There was a bullet hole in the left side of his head just above the ear. He had on his farm clothes, and I was told he had been shot that morning. Well, there wasn't much to do. We waited until nightfall and then went out to Amite County, and then for the next four or five nights we rode the roads every night from the time it got dark 'til about three or four in the morning, 'til it was light again. The first object

231

was to try and track down those people, Negroes who had been at the shooting, and trying to get their stories, and there were three such people who had been at the shooting, had seen the whole incident and essentially they told the same story.

00:29:17 Robert P. Moses

Essentially their story was this:

00:29:21 Robert P. Moses

They were standing at the cotton gin early in the morning and they saw Herbert Lee drive up in his truck with a load of cotton, and E. H. Hurst following directly behind him in an empty truck. Hurst got out of his truck and came to the cab on the driver's side of Lee's, and began arguing with Lee. He began gesticulating towards Lee and pulled out a gun which he had under his shirt and began threatening Lee with it. One of the people who was close by said that Hurst was telling Lee, "I'm not fooling around this time. I really mean business." And that Lee told him, "Put the gun down."

00:30:07 Robert P. Moses

"I won't talk to you unless you put the gun down."

00:30:12 Robert P. Moses

Hurst put the gun back under his coat and then Lee slid out on the other side, on the off side of the cab. As he got out Hurst ran around the front of the cab, took his gun out again, pointed at Lee, and shot him.

00:30:28 Robert P. Moses

This was a story that three Negro witnesses told us on three separate nights as we went out in Amite County tracking them down, knocking on their doors, waking them up in the middle of the night.

00:30:44 Robert P. Moses

They also told us another story.

00:30:47 Robert P. Moses

Two of them admitted that they had been pressured by the local authorities—the sheriff and the deputy sheriff and some of the white people in town—to tell that there had been a fight, that Lee had had a tire tool and that he had tried to hit Hurst with the tire tool and that Hurst had shot Lee in self-defense.

00:32:13 Robert P. Moses

Lee's body lay on the ground that morning for two hours uncovered, until they finally got a funeral home in McComb to take it in. No one in Liberty would touch it. They had a coroner's jury that very same afternoon. Hurst was acquitted. He never spent a moment in jail. In fact, the sheriff had whisked him away very shortly after the crime was committed. I remember reading very bitterly in the papers the next morning a little short article on the front page of the *McComb Enterprise Journal*, said that a Negro had been shot in self-defense as he was trying to attack E. H. Hurst, and that was it. Might've thought he'd been a bum; there was no mention that Lee was a farmer, that he had a family, nine kids, beautiful kids, and that he had farmed all his life in Amite County and that he had been a very substantial citizen.

00:33:21 Robert P. Moses

It was as if he had been drunk or something and gotten into a fight and gotten shot.

00:35:24 Robert P. Moses

That wasn't the end. About a month later, one of the witnesses came back over to McComb. He told us that they were going to have the grand jury hearing, that he had told a lie at the coroner's jury, that he wanted to know if he told the truth at the grand jury hearing would it be possible to provide him with protection. We called the Justice Department. We talked to responsible officials in that department.

00:35:53 Robert P. Moses

They told us that there was no way possible to provide protection for a witness at such a hearing and that probably in any case it didn't matter what he testified and that Lee, that Hurst, would be found innocent.

00:36:11 Robert P. Moses

So this man went back and told the story he told the coroner's jury to the grand jury and they did obviously fail to indict Hurst. For this man, that wasn't the end of his troubles. And about six or eight months later his jaw was broken by the deputy sheriff

00:36:33 Robert P. Moses

who knew that he had told the FBI that he had been forced to tell a lie to the grand jury and to the coroner's jury, because a deputy sheriff told him exactly what he had told the FBI.

00:36:48 Robert P. Moses

It's for reasons like these that we believe that the local FBI are sometimes in collusion with the local sheriffs and chiefs of police, and that Negro witnesses aren't safe in telling inside information to local agents of the FBI.

· · ·

The wave began with birth—and before that, and before that. The painful, miraculous journey from the ocean in Mama's womb to the surface of her body. The rising and falling on the bosom of the earth. The gathering of moments collectively rolling toward some distant shore. We share a similar journey. Out of eternity and onto the surface of the planet. Catapulted from a declaration of independence—*we hold these truths to be self-evident that all men are created equal, that they are endowed by their Creator with certain unalienable rights*—out of America's womb and onto the surface of America's body. We are struggling to be born again. To rise from the ocean of hatred, in the distance between black and white America, drowning America's body. We have come a long way to be together: 1,300 miles from Cambridge to Mississippi. 7,300 miles from Tanzania to Cambridge. Astronomical miles from generation to generation. 136 miles from Jackson to Shelby.

Taba and I and eight Brinkley students make the trip. Khari doesn't make it; he had planned a trip back home. He will leave Mississippi first. I am relieved by this, as we continue to struggle with the direction we think our work should take.

Taba rents a car. I take the Maxima, figure it will save us a couple dollars, is good for one more journey.

Cookie, Dusty, Durrell, and Melvin sleep over the night before we depart. Durrell is one of two. He has a twin brother, Durrone, who is a musical genius, who can turn anything into a beat, and a sister named Punkin, who has a different father. Durrell's father is a mechanic. I haven't met him, but he wants Durrell to follow in his footsteps and learn how to fix cars. Melvin lives with his mother. He is an only child, tall, with a taller fade, will become a Division 1 basketball player, has a slow game and a decent jump shot, is good with the graphing calculators.

In the morning we pick up Nate first. His father is the phys-ed teacher at Brinkley and coaches the football team. Nate and his brother Jeremy are the only boys at Brinkley I'm aware of who are living with their father.

We pick up April, her mother is appreciative, readies the lecture on Jehovah, hands me a copy of the *Watchtower*, and then we get Java, who lives with her sister and brother.

It is my first time driving into the Delta without Baba.

We are traveling to the Delta because Thelma McGee, a teacher in the Mississippi Delta for twenty years and now an administrator in the North Bolivar County School District, was impressed with the graphing calculator workshop we'd facilitated for her and other Algebra Project trainers. She looked strong, in the mold of Fannie Lou Hamer. Gold framed a front tooth. She said she had some money and would like to pay us to do some work with her students in Shelby.

Shelby is a small town with a couple thousand black people, a handful of white people. It sits on the banks of the Mississippi River, in the heart of the Delta, a few miles from Cleveland, where Baba had first been introduced to Amzie Moore.

There are no markers of the historic struggle that enable us to now move up and down the highway relatively uninhibited. When we took this drive with Baba, it was when he seemed the happiest.

"Keep on pushin'," he sang.

The Delta is flat and vast, the fields stretching to the horizon, the dirt brown and red like the savannah beneath Mount Kilimanjaro. The cotton has been planted, still commandeers the land. In the coming months will blanket the Delta, litter the road. We pass catfish ponds. They sit in the ground like mirrors, reflect an attempt to diversify the local economy. We cross the railroad tracks into Tchula, a town along a strip of railroad, remnant of another time, another place. We return to one-lane strips of highway, cutting through vast fields. There is a shack that leans against the back of a lone tree. Like Tchula, it feels like a marker of another time, another place. I watch it grow in detail as we near it, turn as we pass it—suspended between standing and falling, branches growing out of the roof—then watch it shrink until it fits into the rearview mirror. It feels like it could have been there when Mama and Baba drove on those roads in the '60s and before that, and before that. In its suspended state I see what history has flattened, placed on a shelf, what couldn't be peeled from a book, how life decomposes in three dimensions, how when it is said and done, Mother Earth will reclaim us.

We stay in a hotel in Cleveland. The proprietor, a man from India, is concerned, wants to know who is in charge. Taba and I are twenty-one and twenty-three, and the students are entering high school.

In the morning we drive into Shelby. It is our first time teaching students outside of Brinkley. The town is still segregated, with blacks on one side of the tracks and whites on the other. The classroom is like a one-room schoolhouse, adjacent to the larger school building. One of the girls finds a snakeskin in a desk and the classroom is evacuated before we can introduce ourselves.

Dusty breaks the ice. Says, "What up, yo?" like he's from New England, and everyone starts laughing. He is creating space for us to be something other than strangers. We are creating space for young people to learn from and teach each other. In that classroom in the Delta it becomes easy to imagine that much more is possible.

During the week that we're in Shelby, we use the calculators to model a line of best fit. Cities between Jackson and Shelby become points on a graph within the calculator. We work with the students to find the straight line that runs closest to each of the cities. We calculate the total distance between the line and each of the cities. The mathematical term for what we're doing is a *linear regression*. Mama will say the only regression line for black children in America is predestined for prison. If a path exists, to prosperity, to self-determination, it bends like a parabola, is discontinuous, requires leaps of faith, requires luck, is a maze littered with storm troopers. My hope is that we, the young people from Cambridge, from Jackson, from the Delta, will learn to move in proximity to each other. That we can stitch together a path to self-determination through uplifting each other.

The week ends with the students saying that they learned something, that they want to come live with us in Jackson, with the hotel owner demanding that we leave a night early because of the slamming doors, because of Dusty skinny-dipping in the pool.

We get kicked out on Thursday night. Have to pack up and drive home. The trip back to Jackson is indicative of my larger struggle to help Dusty find a path through America that won't lead to his destruction. The road is pitch black like a tunnel, except for the moon and stars and sporadic headlights. The music is a murmur as the students sleep, four in the back seat, two in the front. In the pitch-black silence is galactic love, a deep feeling of responsibility to make sure that the students reach their mothers and grandmothers safely. It is what I once felt in Baba's arms along the dirt road in Tanzania. What I have felt whenever Taba and I do something together.

In the morning, I go to pick up Java and April and Sammie and Melvin and Durrell, who we'd just dropped off the night before, who want to return to Shelby for the last day of the workshop. All of us fit in the Maxima. The Maxima cuts a long straight line through brown, empty fields. Taba, in the passenger seat, says something about us being a young people's project.

In the naming of us, it becomes immediately clear. That I can become a math literacy worker. That math literacy workers can become a Young People's Project. That a Young People's Project could become a wave in an ocean of Bob Moses, Baba, Janet Jemmott, Mama, Uncle Al, Amzie, Ella, Mr. Figgers, June Johnson, Julian Bond, Uncle Vincent, Dave, Uncle Charlie, Judy Richardson, Chuck McDew, Fannie Lou Hamer, Thelma McGee, Grandpa Moses, and untold millions of human beings who cast their precious lives—in the spirit of love, in the spirit of justice, in the spirit of protest—onto the jagged shores of American democracy.

I decide then to plant my feet in Mississippi, to become one of its children.

The Young People's Project

ROBERT MOSES'S ACCOUNT OF VOTER
REGISTRATION DRIVE IN MISSISSIPPI IN 1961

00:37:10 Robert P. Moses

Well, for some time after that,

00:37:16 Robert P. Moses

I suppose we would have been very, very, very deep down, 'cept that we didn't have the time.

00:37:24 Robert P. Moses

Shortly after Lee was killed, the kids were released from jail who had been in jail for a month on the sit-in cases [in Pike County], including Brenda. Brenda was not allowed to go back into school, and early in October she and 115 students marched out and marched downtown. There's no doubt in my mind that part of the reason for the march, and part of the reason for the willingness of so many students to go, was the whole series of beatings culminating in the killing that had taken place in that area.

00:38:01 Robert P. Moses

Well, needless to say, the white community was completely on edge by this time, and by the time the 115 students stopped in front of the city hall to begin praying one by one, Brenda first, and then Curtis, and then Hollis, and then Bobby Talbot, and then finally all of us herded up the steps and into the city courthouse, and Bob Zellner, who was the only white participant, attacked on the steps as he went up, and then the mob outside: waiting, milling around, threatening, and inside the police brought the people down. The white people, the so-called good citizens of the town, one by one to take a look at this Moses guy. And they will come down and stand at the front of the jail and say, "Where is Moses?" And then the kids would point me out and I was again very, very quiet and all the way down.

00:39:04 Robert P. Moses

And the people would stand up. Just look at them and say one word maybe, or two, and that went on the rest of that day.

00:39:17 Robert P. Moses

We were finally taken up one by one into a kind of kangaroo court which they held upstairs, which was crowded with citizens from the town: the sheriff, the local county attorneys, the local judges. The purpose of the court was to gain information about the planning of the demonstration so that they could prepare their case. We, of course, didn't have to answer any of their questions; nevertheless, we did. One by one we went up and told our story. I remember when I went in, the room was very tense. All the people were sort of sitting around on the edges on benches in the dark and the sheriff was standing. And at one point threatened me about saying "yes sir" and "no sir." And I remember that I finally just

00:40:09 Robert P. Moses

answered the questions without either a yes or no.

00:40:14 Robert P. Moses

Well they let all the kids who are under eighteen years off and took those who are over eighteen years down to the county jail and we stayed in jail for several days.

00:40:27 Robert P. Moses

First we were in, all the boys were piled into a concrete bunker. A room with a concrete bunker, where we had to sleep on the bunker and on the floor and finally were taken into the various cells in the jails.

00:40:46 Robert P. Moses

We were let out for a while.

00:40:59 Robert P. Moses

The spirit in jail is very high.

00:41:03 Robert P. Moses

We sang songs. McDew and I made a chessboard on the floor, took cigarette butts and made pieces and played chess.

00:41:14 Robert P. Moses

Guys swapped their favorite stories and told their jokes. We were let out a few days later on a bail bond and swept back into the problems in McComb, where the balance of the hundred students who had marched out were now being required to fill out a slip saying that they would not participate in any more demonstrations in order to get back into school. Most of them were refusing to do so and the community was again in an uproar.

00:41:48 Robert P. Moses

Every day they were going to school and every day when they got there they would be asked to sign the slips and every day they would march back out.

00:42:00 Robert P. Moses

There was TV coverage, newspaper men. Everybody was around to see what the kids from McComb would do. Finally we decided to set up makeshift classes for them, and we opened up Nonviolent High in Burglund in Mc-Comb. It was pretty funny. We had about fifty to seventy-five kids in [. . .] a large room trying to break them down and give them elements of algebra and geometry and a little English and even a little French and a little history. I think Dion taught physics and chemistry, and McDew took charge of history, and I did something with math. And then in the morning when we would meet, we'd try to meet in the little church there and we'd all do a little singing together and I guess the kids liked that part best. Well, under the circumstances and the conditions and extreme emotional tensions in the town they did pretty well, and we carried on our classes for a week or two weeks, until finally we got word from Campbell College in Jackson that they would accept them all and that they would make provisions for them immediately. The word came none too soon because a few days after all the kids had gone up to Jackson to study at Campbell College, we were back in jail and were spending out the first of thirty-nine to forty days while we waited to see if the fourteen thousand dollars appeal bond money could be raised to set us free. Characteristic of the Mississippi jails is that you sit and rot. There's no program if you're not working, which they wouldn't let us do, because they weren't going to have those uppity niggers out there on the line with a chance for causing trouble. It's nothing to do inside. They give you your meals two or three times a day and give you your showers one or two times a week. They give you silence or nasty words otherwise. We played chess quite a bit. Hollis and Curtis and I were in the same cell and I taught Hollis and Curtis how to play, and we wrote home and got a couple of books. People would come down and they treated us very well; the Negro people in McComb, while we were in jail, they baked chicken and pies and they would come down at first every day with something to give us and they finally cut that out and would only let them down once or twice a week. When they came they would smuggle in letters and we would smuggle out letters and we had a little underground of information passing back and forth between us and the people in town. Well, we spent most of the month of November and on into early December in jail. We were finally released and the kids, high school kids who were seniors, went on to Campbell to school, and the rest of us then we grew to decide what could be done and what projects we needed to carry out next and how we could pick up the pieces.

00:45:46 Robert P. Moses

We had, to put it mildly, got our feet wet.

00:45:50 Robert P. Moses

We now knew something of what it took to run a voter registration campaign in Mississippi. We knew some of the obstacles we would have to face. We had some general idea of what had to be done to get such a campaign started.

00:46:05 Robert P. Moses

First, there were very few agencies available in the Negro community to act as a vehicle for any sort of campaign. The Negro churches could not in general be counted on. The Negro business leaders could also not in general be counted on, except for under-the-cover help, and in general anybody who had a specific economic tie-in with the white community could not be counted on when pressure got hot. Therefore our feeling was that the only way to run these campaigns was to begin to build a group of young people who would not be responsible economically to any sector of the white community, and who would be able to act as free agents. And we began to set about doing this. In most cases it was a conjunction between the young people and some indigenous farmers, independent people, or some courageous businessman able to stick his neck out, or willing to stick his neck out, which was a combination which worked in voter registration drives.

01:05:54 Robert P. Moses

People always want to know why do you do this. . . . People always want to say, "Well, aren't you getting so very little for having to put out so very much?" And the answer always seems to be, "Well, somebody has to do it, and it's got to be done some time." The thing that keeps hitting back home is that you, you're talking about real people, and real lives, and you're trying to effect a change for them. I remember a newspaperman down McComb after the kids had walked out and were fiddle-faddling around, walking out of school every day, and he said, "Well, won't they be better off if they go back in the school? I mean, don't they need their education?" And I looked at him and I said, "Education for what? Each one of these kids, if they get out of this high school here in McComb, they have about one or two opportunities open for them. If they're girls, they can go down there and be domestics in some white folks' home. If they're boys, then they can be unskilled laborers digging ditches and hauling around stuff in their trucks, or a few of them of course they can become teachers. And in this case they simply become, by and large, tools of the system, perpetuating it."

· · ·

On December 22, 2023, Boston's GBH News published an article titled "Minorities and Women Have Been Largely Locked Out of Cambridge City Contracts, Study Shows."[1] The article was based on a study commissioned by the Cambridge-Somerville Black Business Network and conducted by Griffin & Strong, a black-founded and black-led law firm based in Atlanta.[2] The report, completed in October 2023, featured on its cover a mural of an Afro-Indigenous woman reigning over Central Square that had been painted by Victor "Marka 27" Quiñonez. What is left of the Central Square we grew up in are a few iconic businesses—Cheapo Records, Teddy Shoes, the Dance Complex, Brookline Lunch, and the Middle East—and newer spaces like Graffiti Alley and Starlight Square that attempt to preserve (like a museum, like a reservation) the grungy punk rock, hip-hop energy that once roamed wild in what has now been branded Cambridge's Cultural District. The report—released by the city in December of that year but buried in the avalanche of the Christmas frenzy—stated that of the $260 million that Cambridge had spent on goods and services from 2016 to 2021, less than $60,000 had gone to black-owned businesses.

I emailed the article to Moke, Mama, Maisha, and Taba.

"Crazy! Let's talk," Maisha replied.

Maisha is now running the Young People's Project (YPP), an organization that emerged out of the Brinkley Middle School MathLab, the trip the Algebra Project students and Taba and I took into the Mississippi Delta. She arrived in Mississippi about two years after Taba and Khari and me, had been instrumental in the development of the Algebra Project's Train the Trainer program. Baba had wanted her to work with YPP to develop a training program for math literacy workers. "I went to Mississippi because my dad kept inviting me to check out his work in the classroom and because he thought I could help my brothers," she said. We hadn't asked for her help, and I resented Baba meddling in our business, but we needed her—to train middle and high school students to teach math to their younger peers, and to help YPP grow out of something other than the locker-room culture that Taba and I had grown out of.

"THIS IS NUTS!!!!!!!!" Moke wrote, when he saw the GBH article I had sent. He had just gotten reelected to the Cambridge School Committee. It was his fourth or fifth term in office—he probably won all those terms by a combined fifty votes. He still had enough cousins in the city to get elected to the school committee, but not to the city council, which would have automatically put him in the running for mayor (in Cambridge, the city council elects the mayor from among its own members). I imagine that would have fulfilled an unspoken childhood dream. Moke was Ivy League smart, could talk better shit than anyone on a corner. He used to hold down the corner of Mass. Ave. and Brookline Street, in front of what had been Hi-Fi Pizza, like he was Dave Chappelle. He'd be surrounded by an ever-widening circle of people holding onto their slices and laughing hysterically as he and whoever was brave enough to step inside the circle with him talked shit about each other. He and Taba founded a company called Green Soul Organics that grows and sells weed. Articles have been written about them in national and local publications such as "Longtime Friends Set Out to Transform Cannabis Industry," from the *Cambridge Chronicle*:

> As Cambridge natives Richard Harding and Taba Moses watched the cannabis industry emerge in Massachusetts, they noticed two things: White men dominated the businesses, and communities disproportionately affected by the country's War on Drugs received no benefits from legalized marijuana.
>
> "All of a sudden they're making hundreds of millions of dollars selling the same product that the Cambridge Police Department used to harass us and chase us around for," Moses said.
>
> Moses and Harding have set out to change the cannabis industry. Along with planning to open their own marijuana businesses, the childhood friends who grew up in The Port have started a nonprofit foundation to help people of color enter the field.
>
> "The conversation about how these big companies enter into our community needs to change, and it's not just an empowerment thing," Moses said. "Let's rethink how big companies—and how we ourselves as well—enter the community."[3]

Their efforts led to Cambridge passing a two-year moratorium on noneconomic empowerment applicants (applicants who weren't from economically distressed communities) opening retail cannabis shops.

"Part of our mission is to look at people affected by the fake War on Drugs, give a kid with humble beginnings a chance," Moke said.[4]

A few weeks after the GBH article broke, Mr. Figgers called me from Mississippi wanting to know if I still had the book. He described it as if saying its name would conjure the Klan burning a cross in his front yard. He was distressed, weary from decades of fighting in Mississippi's trenches. The Republican-led state legislature was returning to Reconstruction Era tactics, was forming a Capital Complex Improvement District in the city of Jackson—which was 83 percent black and majority Democrat—to subvert local control over resources (like water) and the criminal justice system.

"We are finding ourselves jumping back to days of Jim Crow, days of apartheid," said Rukia Lumumba, daughter of former Jackson mayor Chokwe Lumumba and sister of current Jackson mayor Chokwe Antar Lumumba. "We're seeing this theory that Black people can't govern, that Black people can't make decisions for themselves around who is best suited to represent them in governing processes, and that Black people can't create their own safety." Rukia described this as part of a national backlash to the calls for criminal justice reform, for equity in education and housing and healthcare, that had swept the nation in 2020 after the murder of George Floyd in Minneapolis. "What we're seeing is opponents to those successes figuring out how to tap into municipal control and county control and use the legislature as a source to literally deprive municipalities and counties of the power that they have to govern," Lumumba said, "to engage in systems that are more accountable to the people."[5]

Mr. Figgers was calling because he'd found out that the lawsuit that the NAACP filed in federal court to prevent the "state takeover" of local resources through the formation of the Capital Complex Improvement District had been unsuccessful. He was also calling because the Morris Memorial Building in Nashville, Tennessee—which had housed the Sunday School Publishing Board and the printing press that Grandpa Moses had invested in, which had published *The White Peril* and a number of other books—had been sold by the National Baptist Convention, despite his and others' protests. I could sense his sadness, the feeling of loss, that something was slipping away, that what the building stood for—the ideas the building had protected, the hope and wisdom it had harbored, the struggle for black life in America reflected in its construction, the prayers and pages it had produced for the upliftment of black people—were all being uprooted. I could sense that my voice was connecting him to Baba's, to the moments they'd shared. To "You can lead a meaningful life in struggle." To "Keep on pushin'." *I just wanted to hear your voice*, Mr. Figgers said.

I didn't tell him that I was writing a book of my own called *The White Peril*, and that I carried the book he'd given me every day. I could sense, in light of these most recent losses, that the book had taken on new meaning for him. That these artifacts, whether a book or a building, that represented the point of view and struggle of men and women who'd known firsthand what it was like to begin life on America's plantations, to transcend America's plantations, were priceless seeds that needed to be preserved and replanted in the backlash to whatever progress we've made and will make.

I told Mr. Figgers that I still had the book, and that there were some other books and speeches that my great-grandfather had written that I would send his way. I told him that I remembered the day he'd given *The White Peril* to me and began to describe that moment in the hallway of Brinkley Middle School.

"There's more to the story," he said. "One night I brought your dad over to Shady Grove [Church] to let him look at the space to see if it was adequate for what the young people needed. I can see him coming down the hall.

"'My grandfather was a preacher,' your father said. 'His name was W. H. Moses.'

"'Ohh,' I said, 'I know him.'

"'Frank, you couldn't have known him,' your father said."

"So then we toured the church and I dropped him off at home. I come on home and I begin to look through stuff of mine. And low and behold I found a speech that I had given a few years earlier. I saw where I gave a report to our church on the Sunday School Publishing Board and the building and I quoted a report that W. H. Moses as general secretary had given to people on the building and the significance of the building. And that next morning when I found that, I also put my hand on the book. That next morning I carried the book that I quoted from and the speech that I had given to the Shady Grove Church and showed it to your father.

"The other time, when it came up again, we were at another church, it was me, your father, you, and you brought some young people. And I introduced your father through his grandfather. And your father said, 'Frank has introduced a line of Moses, and I'm going to introduce another Moses in that line.' And he introduced you and you got up and spoke and then you said, 'and I'm going to introduce some others in that line,' and you introduced the young people of the Young People's Project."

· · ·

We incorporated the Young People's Project in Jackson, Mississippi, in 2002. I was its founding executive director and spent the next ten years attempting to build it into a national organization. I began turning things over to Maisha in 2012, when Johari, my first child, was born. She seemed ambivalent about it, and I tried my best to reduce the burden and baggage she would inherit from my almost two decades of leadership. She asked me about my dreams for YPP. I told her that I hoped it would continue to be around so that one day Johari could become a math literacy worker. This seemed to resonate with her.

About a year ago I asked Maisha to help write the epilogue for this book. I told her the title of the epilogue would be "The Young People's Project" and gave her the portion of Baba's interview that opened this chapter, which began with Herbert Lee's murder and ended with my dad's question, "Education for what?" I had hoped she would write about her journey into Mississippi and her role in helping YPP grow out of something other than what Taba and I had grown out of. About how, in many ways, she'd become YPP's mother, had created space for the spirit of love to flourish and eventually overpower that locker room culture. Instead, she wrote a love letter:

> Many may have helped birth YPP, but YPP is Omo's baby; in the words of Dave Chappelle, he was its most powerful dreamer. He translated his formidable state-champion-level basketball skills, his experiences becoming a Black young African American man, and our family movement legacy into the improbable mission of marshaling resources to enable young people to build an organization about the serious business of Black struggle, focused on mathematics, imbued with joy and play, as only children might do. YPP is imprinted with Omo's unique signature, birthed through the force of his will and the sensibilities of his spirit. It is a manifestation of the movement wisdom lessons we absorbed during our childhood; it is a beautiful extension of the Algebra Project and its legacy in the Mississippi movement. I am grateful to Omo, Taba, Khari, and the children who started YPP, and all who have moved it along over the years. I am grateful that somehow it fell to me to become the dreamer to keep YPP going once Omo left.

My dream for YPP was that it could be a space for young people to nurture whatever gifts they'd brought into this world, to challenge them to make good use of their gifts—like the basketball court and swimming pool had for me. A space that encouraged young people to be invested in each other's success, to practice winning and losing together. Some crawl space to become conscious of and perhaps confront the challenges of their generation. I dreamt, like Baba, that math could be a catalyst for learning, teaching, leading, and organizing, for the self-realization and self-determination required to transcend, to perhaps deconstruct America's cages. I hoped that the space that YPP emerged from and created in the Brinkley Middle School MathLab would be replicated, networked, and inherited from generation to generation.

I used to say, naively, that if this space could take root and flourish any-where—as a classroom for participatory democracy, perhaps a catalyst for an equitable society—it would be in Cambridge. It now feels like America's ideals have a better shot of being realized in places like Mississippi than in the shadows of Harvard and MIT and Google and Microsoft and Face-book. It's hard to not get seduced by the window dressing of the city's first black openly gay mayor, its first Muslim mayor, the black police chiefs, the black superintendents, the Black Lives Matter flag flapping above the front lawn of city hall, adorning still segregated public school classrooms, with their probably biased, predominately white female teachers. The facade of black leadership is window dressing for the displacement of working-class families, and the less than $60,000 (a fraction of a fraction of a percent) moving through the city's procurement office to black businesses.[6] In this way, there is absolutely no distance between Mississippi's conservative white agenda to control local resources and Cambridge's liberal status quo. Which deserves national attention. On the national stage, in the run-up to the sixtieth presidential election, what's the distance (besides Trump's ninety-one federal and state felony charges) between Biden, the savior of democracy, and Trump, the threat to democracy? And before that, and before that, what was the difference between eight years of Clintons and twelve years of Bushes for black America?

·   ·   ·

Mama keeps herself busy since Baba passed, establishing the Bob Moses Fund and leading the Bob Moses Conference. In February 2024, she gives the MLK speech at MIT's Fiftieth Annual MLK Celebration. She walks slowly to the stage with a cane, with a limp. A bone from her car accident in Egypt back in the '60s has recently worked its way up through her skin, and the wound refuses to heal. She takes a moment to thank Paul Parravano, who recently passed and was a pillar in the Cambridge and MIT community, before beginning her speech. She starts by describing the view of the 3rd

Avenue elevated train from the bedroom window of her childhood home in the South Bronx, and then pans out for a bird's-eye view of the nation 250 years after its founding.

I'm joined at my table by Maisha and the recently named mayor of Cambridge, E. Denise Simmons, who happens to be black and lesbian and has been elected to the city council and voted mayor by the city council way too many times. I couldn't help but think that she had her hand on some part of the steering wheel as the city doled out a fraction of a fraction of a percent of its dollars to black businesses.

Mama presents a few slides to go along with her speech. The first features a red silhouette of a proposed three-hundred-foot skyscraper to be erected in New York City's Chinatown that will extend two to three city blocks in every direction, that will cost $2 billion and house up to nine hundred inmates, that was ginned up by the deputy director of criminal justice in former mayor Bill de Blasio's administration—who happens to be a graduate of the same liberal wing of the same Cambridge Rindge and Latin High School I graduated from.

"For all the money it has, Cambridge doesn't really do anything well," Moke reflects. This commitment to mediocrity has been on full display during the Cambridge Rindge and Latin basketball season. I am back in the gym to watch Taba's son Parris play with the boys' basketball team in the first round of the state tournament. I stand in one corner of the gym, Moke and Taba in the opposite corner. In some ways Parris's presence on the court is the culmination of the basketball journey that Taba and I shared. Parris wears number 44, which is the same number I wore when we won a state championship. He has Division 1 potential, is a bigger, more offensively skilled version of the player I had been. If it wasn't for Parris, the team would be .500. I've been complaining about the head coach's lack of leadership and vision, about the city's inability to create a quality basketball program for kids. It bothers me because it was this tradition of basketball excellence that helped shape who I was, that I had hoped my son would inherit. But basketball players are no longer made on playgrounds. The courts at Corporal Burns Park and Columbia Terrace and Hoyt Field are empty—evidence of all the descendants of enslaved Africans, the Irish, Italian, Portuguese, Caribbean, Puerto Rican, Dominican, Cape Verdean, and Haitian families that have been pushed out of the city. Basketball players are now made through programs, and it's painful to watch the remnants of the city's legendary basketball talent, all those generations of hopes and dreams, fed into this shitty-ass system.

I still think of the court as the safest place for a black boy to grow up in America. As a little crawl space to develop their minds and bodies and spirits, to learn how to work together, to learn how to lead, to apply these lessons toward becoming whoever they dream of becoming. Johari and I have been playing ball together since he was two. He is now eleven. I worry about how much of my dream is his dream. How much of Parris's dream is the extension of the dream that Taba and I shared.

"Black people are the pot," Toni Morrison said.[7] She understood what we've meant, literally and figuratively, to this "melting pot" we call America. James Baldwin understood. What would America be without black people? Who would white people be without black people? Dave Chappelle understands. Maisha and her partner, Shelby, and I attended his show in the fall of 2023 in the Boston Garden. It was the culmination of one of my dreams, to witness him do his thing live and in the flesh. His ability to move from hinged to unhinged, scripted to unscripted is like the very best of our trumpet players and rappers. In the end he talked about his dream, the dream that had led him to that stage, about the community of big dreamers that he was a part of. What particularly resonated with me was his story about his encounter with Lil Nas X and the realization that he, Dave Chappelle, had been a part of Lil Nas X's dream, that we live in each other's dreams.

After the show I wondered how we black people show up in white people's dreams, what role we play in their sleep, what that has to do with the society we live in.

In the end, we held onto our hoop dreams and weed dreams and movement dreams. Maybe the white peril is that: the Holocaust of black dreams . . . in as much as our dreams have survived this four-hundred-year onslaught to their existence. Maybe the white peril is that: the Big Bang, the inflator of black dreams.

During the summer of 2022, I watched Johari walk with a crew of students twice his size through the Port to teach math games at the Margaret Fuller House. I smiled. At ten, he became YPP's youngest math literacy worker. It was Maisha's doing, her response to my prayer—that in addition to the bounce of a ball, some crawl space exists. In this instance it's a classroom on MIT's campus where YPP has hosted a Summer Math Institute for twenty years. And if you were to stumble upon it, within the labyrinth of numbered buildings swelling with some of the world's most gifted students, you would see and hear what I saw and heard over two decades ago in a classroom in the Mississippi Delta as Dusty broke the ice with "What up, yo?" Young people creating space for young people to be something other than strangers. Young people, through learning and teaching math, trying on the shoes of Ella Baker, June Johnson, Amzie Moore, and Bob Moses. And so many others, as they take their first steps in the footsteps of their ancestors. A path that has the potential to deliver Johari to the other side of America's fences. To stand on his grandpa's and his great-great-grandpa's shoulders. To continue the struggle to dismantle America's cages.

ACKNOWLEDGMENTS

T hank you, Mama, for the gift of words, for nurturing my desire to write, for helping me find my voice. Thank you for your unconditional love. For acknowledging, midwifing, and celebrating every smidgen of a gift we ever had.

Thank you Baba, for loving us, for doing movement, for doing family, for doing family and movement. For keep on pushin', for you can live a meaningful life in struggle, for Ella Baker and Amzie Moore, for Tanzania, for Mississippi, for your gurus, for the seeds you planted all over the planet, for being on time, for coming back to us, for holding onto your body for as long as you could, for giving each of us the time and space to navigate the distance between us, to make our peace with our journey together in this time, in this place, on this planet. You are loved, you are loved, you are loved . . . by Mama and Maisha and Omowale Johari Moses and Tabasuri and Malaika and Zuri and Parris and Krishna and Johari and Kamara and Yohana and Yahra . . . and will continue to be loved by the untold generations of Moseses wiggling their way into the future. For if in the future, as in the past, men and women continue to prize ennobling gifts used for the higher purpose and the advancement of humanity, then generations yet unborn shall pay homage to Bob Moses the Freedom Fighter till the stars sink at the day of judgment.

Thank you, Grandpa Moses, for the past rolling up into the future, for the spirit of Love, the Spirit of Justice, the Spirit of Protest. For cosmic consciousness.

Thank you, Babu! and Bibi! I LOVE YOU!

Thank you, to the Village! for raising us.

Thank you, Kathy and Jon and Ella and Jaja, for family, for sanctuary, for sacred earth.

Thank you, Liberty and Pops, for Huckabuck Village and Pine Isle.

Thank you, Uncle Charlie, for recording and reporting the struggle, for those precious boxes of interviews.

Thank you, Issac Byrd, for your unwavering support of my dad, for keeping us outta jail, for the 930 Blues Cafe, for "what Mississippi needs is a Medgar Evers with money."

Thank you, Uncle Al, for being my dad's best friend, for making it possible for Mama and Baba to come home, for keeping Taba outta jail, for all that you have done for our family.

Thank you, Rudy Lombard, for wrapping your arms around me and Taba. For you don't owe anyone anything, you owe your kids everything. Thank you for Uncle Fred.

Thank you, Fred Johnson, for brotherhood, for friendship, for the Black Men of Labor, for keeping the tradition alive and on the streets.

Thank you, Chris Adagbonyin—for your belief in me, for the time we walked the earth together, for the miles of highway we drove together, for YPP, for Chicago State and the chateau and the hostel, for Finding Our Folk, for becoming a math literacy worker, for becoming a leader and an organizer, for being a devoted father, for Albert Sykes.

Thank you, Albert, for stepping into Bob Moses's shoes and into the shoes of Mississippi's legendary and unheralded freedom fighters, for continuing to struggle to realize your potential and apply it to improving the conditions of our lives, for becoming a pillar in your community, for the blood, sweat, and tears, for healing our wounds, for Big Bun, for Finding Our Folk, for the Hot 8.

Thank you, Bennie Pete, for your friendship, leadership, and brotherhood. Thank you, Soul, Alvarez Huntley, Harry Cook, Terrell Batiste, Jerome Jones, Wendell Stewart, Keith Anderson, Dinerral Shavers, Gregory Veals, John Gilbert, Raymond Williams, and Sammy Cyrus for showing up, for some of the best moments of my life, for keeping the spirituals and blues and jazz and soul and hip-hop on the streets.

Thank you, Khari, aka Spice, for our journey together—in the pool, on the Atari 2600, on the PlayStation, in the Open School, in Pilot, in Dearborn Elementary, in Brinkley Middle School. For leading the way into fatherhood, for when are you all gonna work that shit out, for always finding a way to close the distance between us.

Thank you, Maisha, for being my big sister, for your vision, for watching over me, for always being there for all of us, for the spirit of love, for YPP, for Shelby.

Thank you, Malaika, for being my little sister, for Baba's bracelet, for continuing to share Baba's gurus with us, for Krishna, for bringing us back to Pine Isle, for your love and your willingness to work it out.

Thank you, London, you already know, for giving birth to YPP, for all the long nights at 99 Bishop and in Cleeta's basement, for the distance we traveled, for all the students you fathered, for holding your family down, for being an unheralded pillar in our community, for finding a way out of no way, hoping you continue to realize your dreams as you build a foundation for your kids to realize theirs.

Thank you, Lekecia Tyce, for HOLDIN' ME DOWN!!!

Thank you, Dico and Daco, for all the time we've spent living together.

Thank you, Danny Rice, for reading all of the ugly versions of this, for friendship and brotherhood, for being there when I needed you, for being there since KINDERGARTEN!

Thank you, Craig Dottin, Bobby Mickle, and BEEMA! aka Bruce Martin for all the chips we won together!

Thank you, Dennis Benzan, for your friendship and leadership.

Thank you, Ice, for sharing this journey of fatherhood.

Thank you, Javier, for your belief in our family, for your family, for the work we continue to do together.

Thank you, Laura Yorke, for taking the leap, for reading everything I sent your way, for your editing and encouragement, for your belief in me and this story, for fighting for years to get this book sold.

Thank you, to the team at Beacon Press, for championing my dad's work, and thank you, Gayatri, for picking up the baton and getting this over the finish line.

Thank you, Joan Soble, for reading and rereading and encouraging and re-encouraging.

Thank you, Danny, for Freedom Song, for your commitment to my dad and the Algebra Project, for your commitment to movement.

Thank you, Margaret and Max, for all that you've done for our family.

Thank you, esperanza, for your uncompromising voice, for Formwela 8, for colliding somewhere between 1:15 and 1:30 PST, August 6, 2022, for Life Force.

Thank you, Nilsa Yvette Toledo, for your existence.

Thank you, Moke, Richard Harding, and Fats, Russell Harding, Colin and Dana Gardinier, Alex and Hector Colon, Ariel and Nando Colon, Dico and Daco (Anthony and Jose Garcia) for the Port, for brotherhood, for the precious memories, as we ran the streets, as we ran . . .

Thank you, Moke, for holding Taba down.

Thank you, Rumeal, for opening your arms to me and Taba, for showing us what it took to become a pro and what that life could be.

Thank you, Lizzy Cooper Davis, for the most precious gifts, Johari Cooper Davis Moses, for Kamara Susannah Elizabeth Moses.

Thank you, Tabasuri Watabiri Moses, for Zuri and Parris, for Saba and Yo-Yo and Ya-Ya, for fifty-plus years of friendship, for discovering and making meaning of life together, for shared dreams, for hustle to eat, for PortLife, for new year's @ the Westin, for new year's @ DREAM, for Mississippi, for unconditional love, for conditional love, for returning from all of your miraculous adventures, for forgiving us, for guiding Baba on his journey into the cosmos, for all of the moments ahead of us. I love you.

NOTES

CHAPTER 1: IN THE DISTANCE BETWEEN US (I)

1. Columbus was born in what is now Italy, lived in Portugal, and moved to Spain, where he lived for the remainder of his life.

2. Columbus's voyage was funded by the Spanish monarchs after they'd recaptured Granada in 1492, ending Moorish rule in Spain.

CHAPTER 2: THE KING OF THE COURT

1. Jose Barreiro, ed., *Thinking in Indian: A John Mohawk Reader* (Golden, CO: Fulcrum Publishing, 2010), 3.

CHAPTER 3: OUT OF AFRICA

1. Robert P. Moses and Charles E. Cobb Jr., *Radical Equations: Civil Rights from Mississippi to the Algebra Project* (Boston: Beacon Press, 2001), 293.

CHAPTER 4: FREEDOM FIGHTERS

1. Jose Barreiro, ed., *Thinking in Indian: A John Mohawk Reader* (Golden, CO: Fulcrum Publishing, 2010), 3.

2. Paul Jay, *The Mississippi Freedom Summer: Bob Moses on Reality Asserts Itself*, Real News Network, June 20, 2014, https://therealnews.com/rmoses 140600raipt1.

3. Laura Visser-Maessen, *Robert Parris Moses: A Life in Civil Rights and Leadership at the Grassroots* (Chapel Hill: University of North Carolina Press, 2016), 32–33.

4. Tom LoBianco, "Report: Aide Says Nixon's War on Drugs Targeted Blacks, Hippies," CNN, updated March 24, 2016, https://www.cnn.com/2016 /03/23/politics/john-ehrlichman-richard-nixon-drug-war-blacks-hippie.

5. Barreiro, *Thinking in Indian*, 69.

6. Paul Jay, "Founding SNCC and Taking On Mississippi—Bob Moses on Reality Asserts Itself (4/9)," video, Real News Network, June 22, 2014, https:// www.youtube.com/watch?v=H2BRalmedWs.

CHAPTER 6: COOKIE AND THE DUST

1. "The Freedom Rides really opened up the movement in Mississippi. I mean it was dramatic in the sense that I was there the summer before the

Freedom Rides in 1960 and came back in the summer of '61 after the rides had landed. And the difference in how a young kid would look at me walking the street, right, they knew I wasn't from their little town, right, but in the summer of '60 I was just some stranger who was comin' to their little town; in the summer of '61, I was a Freedom Rider. So, the Freedom Rides had really penetrated the consciousness of the black population in Mississippi." Robert Moses, "Robert P. Moses, the Mississippi Freedom Movement in the 1960s," October 25, 2012, video, NYU Steinhardt, https://www.youtube.com/watch?v=uaGW x7PxD4k&t=1024s.

 2. Jose Barreiro, ed., *Thinking in Indian: A John Mohawk Reader* (Golden, CO: Fulcrum Publishing, 2010), 85.

CHAPTER 7: THE WILD

 1. Algonquin word "Massadchu-es-et" meaning "Great-hill-small-place." "Origin of Names of US States," Indian Affairs, US Department of the Interior, January 4, 1974, https://www.bia.gov/as-ia/opa/online-press-release /origin-names-us-states.

 2. Robin Wall Kimmerer, *Braiding Sweetgrass: Indigenous Wisdom, Scientific Knowledge, and the Teachings of Plants* (Minneapolis: Milkweed Editions, 2013), 9.

CHAPTER 8: THE MATHLAB

 1. Robert P. Moses and Charles E. Cobb Jr., *Radical Equations: Civil Rights from Mississippi to the Algebra Project* (Boston: Beacon Press, 2001), 94.

CHAPTER 9: AMERICAN HEROES

 1. Melvin Herbert King was an American politician, community organizer, and educator. In 1973, King was elected to the Massachusetts House of Representatives' Ninth Suffolk district, where he served until early 1983, and he was the runner-up in the 1983 Boston mayoral election, against Raymond Flynn. King founded the Rainbow Coalition Party in Massachusetts in 1997. The term "rainbow coalition" refers to a political coalition that brings together a variety of demographic groups (including multiple ethnicities). King used it to describe his supporters during his 1983 mayoral campaign, preceding the Jesse Jackson presidential campaign the next year.

 2. Charles Darwin, *The Descent of Man* (London: John Murray, Albemarle Street, 1871), 173.

 3. W. E. B. Du Bois, "Returning Soldiers," editorial, *The Crisis*, 1919, BlackPast.org, https://www.blackpast.org/african-american-history/w-e-b -dubois-returning-soldiers-editorial-from-the-crisis-may-1919.

 4. "February 1963: Jimmy Travis Shot in Greenwood," SNCC Digital Gateway, https://snccdigital.org/events/jimmy-travis-shot-greenwood.

CHAPTER 10: AMERICAN HEROES, *CONTINUED*

 1. Robert Moses, "Questions Regarding the Implications of the Chaney-Schwerner-Goodman Lynching, Bob Moses, 1965," Civil Rights Movement Archive, https://www.crmvet.org/info/mosesq.htm.

2. Amzie Moore, "Oral History with Mr. Amzie Moore Transcript; 1977," Digital Collections at the University of Southern Mississippi, https://usm.access .preservica.com/uncategorized/SO_a1f30051-060f-49de-80da-dd19e9401f5c.

3. Moore transcript.

4. Moore transcript.

5. Moore transcript.

6. Laura Visser-Maessen, *Robert Parris Moses: A Life in Civil Rights and Leadership at the Grassroots* (Chapel Hill: University of North Carolina Press, 2016), 73.

7. Paul Jay, "An Earned Insurgency—Bob Moses on Reality Asserts Itself Pt. 7/9," video, Real News Network, July 26, 2021, https://www.youtube.com /watch?v=VRSGJV4ZMbQ.

CHAPTER 11: BUILDING DEMAND

1. SNCC was struggling with how best to move forward, and in November 1964, field staff and others working with the organization gathered in Waveland, Mississippi, for a week-long "reassessment" conference. "We are a boat in the middle of the ocean," wrote Bob Moses, SNCC's Mississippi project director. The boat "has to be rebuilt in order to stay afloat. It also has to stay afloat in order to be rebuilt." "November 1964: SNCC's Waveland Conference," SNCC Digital Gateway, https://snccdigital.org/events/snccs -waveland-conference.

2. Julian Bond, "SNCC: What We Did," SNCC Legacy Project, https:// sncclegacyproject.org/sncc-what-we-did, accessed April 24, 2024.

3. William A. Price, "SNCC Charts a Course, Interview with Stokely Carmichael, Chairman, Student Nonviolent Coordinating Committee," May 1966, Civil Rights Movement Archive, https://www.crmvet.org/info/6605_stokely.pdf.

CHAPTER 14: THE WHITE PERIL

1. Jose Barreiro, ed., *Thinking in Indian: A John Mohawk Reader* (Golden, CO: Fulcrum Publishing, 2010), 98.

2. Clint Smith, *How the Word Is Passed: A Reckoning with the History of Slavery Across America* (New York: Little, Brown, 2021), 66.

3. Henry Louis Gates Jr., "How Many Slaves Landed in the U.S.?" *The African American: Many Rivers to Cross*, PBS, https://www.pbs.org/wnet/african -americans-many-rivers-to-cross/history/how-many-slaves-landed-in-the-us/, accessed September 9, 2024.

4. James Robinson (as James Roberts), *The Narrative of James Roberts, a Soldier Under Gen. Washington in the Revolutionary War, and Under Gen. Jackson at the Battle of New Orleans, in the War of 1812: "a Battle Which Cost Me a Limb, Some Blood, and Almost My Life"* (Chicago: Printed for the Author, 1858), available at Documenting the American South, https://docsouth.unc.edu/neh /roberts/roberts.html, accessed April 24, 2024.

5. Robinson, *The Narrative of James Roberts*.

6. Robinson, *The Narrative of James Roberts*.

7. Samuel William Bacote, *Who's Who Among the Colored Baptists of the United States* (Kansas City: Franklin Hudson Publishing, 1913), 224.

8. W. H. Moses, *The White Peril* (Philadelphia: Lisle-Carey Press, 1919), available at https://babel.hathitrust.org/cgi/pt?id=emu.010000212007&seq=1.

9. Moses, *The White Peril.*

CHAPTER 15: BLACK CONSCIOUSNESS

1. Frantz Fanon was an Afro-Caribbean psychiatrist and philosopher from Martinique who was born in 1925 and died in 1961, who wrote a book entitled *The Wretched of The Earth*, and who fought to liberate Algeria from the French.

2. We found out that Baba had been married before he married Mama when we were four, six, eight, and ten on a family trip to Pendle Hill to visit Uncle Vincent (who helped to write MLK's "I Have a Dream" speech) and his wife, Rosemary Harding, and their children, Rachel and Jonathan. Uncle Vincent married Mama and Baba for the third and final time under a large oak tree—the first time they were married, Baba had to use someone else's name; the second time was in Tanzania and Mama was unsure of its validity, and so they did it again with us as witnesses. The thought of Baba with another woman added to his mystique and intensified my curiosity about him and the lives he had lived.

3. Janet Jemmott Moses, "If We Must Die," in *Hands on the Freedom Plow: Personal Accounts by Women in SNCC*, ed. Faith S. Holsaert et al. (Urbana: University of Illinois Press, 2010), 266–69.

4. "August 1964: MFDP Challenge at Democratic National Convention," SNCC Digital Gateway, https://snccdigital.org/events/mfdp-challenge-at-democratic-national-convention, accessed April 24, 2024.

5. Julian Bond, "SNCC: What We Did," SNCC Legacy Project, https://sncclegacyproject.org/sncc-what-we-did, accessed April 24, 2024.

6. Laura Visser-Maessen, *Robert Parris Moses: A Life in Civil Rights and Leadership at the Grassroots* (Chapel Hill: University of North Carolina Press, 2016), 290.

7. Robert P. Moses and Charles E. Cobb Jr., *Radical Equations: Civil Rights from Mississippi to the Algebra Project* (Boston: Beacon Press, 2001), 125.

8. William A. Price, "SNCC Charts a Course, Interview with Stokely Carmichael, Chairman, Student Nonviolent Coordinating Committee," May 1966, Civil Rights Movement Archive, https://www.crmvet.org/info/6605_stokely.pdf.

CHAPTER 16: IN THE DISTANCE BETWEEN US (III)

1. Eun S. Shin, "Jury Indicts Five for Murders of Two Men Near MIT," The Tech, February 13, 1990, available at https://archive.org/details/mit_the_tech_newspaper-v110-i3/page/n1/mode/2up; Michael K. Mayo, "Two Men Get Life in Prison," *Harvard Crimson*, February 14, 1992, https://www.thecrimson.com/article/1992/2/14/two-men-get-life-in-prison/.

2. Jose Barreiro, ed., *Thinking in Indian: A John Mohawk Reader* (Golden, CO: Fulcrum Publishing, 2010), 3.

EPILOGUE: THE YOUNG PEOPLE'S PROJECT

1. Meredith Nierman, "Minorities and Women Have Been Largely Locked Out of Cambridge City Contracts, Study Shows," GBH News, December 22,

2023, https://www.wgbh.org/news/local/2023-12-22/minorities-and-women-have-been-largely-locked-out-of-cambridge-city-contracts-study-shows

2. Griffin & Strong, *City of Cambridge, Massachusetts, Disparity Study Report*, October 2023, https://www.cambridgema.gov/-/media/Files/CDD/EconDev/disparitystudy/cambridgemafulldisparitystudyfinalreport_122023.pdf.

3. Diane McLaughlin, "Longtime Friends Set Out to Transform Cannabis Industry," *Cambridge Chronicle*, July 18, 2019, https://www.wickedlocal.com/story/cambridge-chronicle-tab/2019/07/18/longtime-friends-set-out-to/4631730007.

4. McLaughlin, "Longtime Friends Set Out to Transform Cannabis Industry."

5. Akela Lacy, "Mississippi to Create Special Justice System for Just One City: Majority Black Jackson," *The Intercept*, April 20, 2023, https://theintercept.com/2023/04/20/mississippi-jackson-black-court.

6. Diti Kohli, "In Cambridge, Women and People of Color Get Few City Contracts, Study Finds," *Boston Globe*, updated December 29, 2023, https://www.bostonglobe.com/2023/12/29/business/cambridge-city-contracts-study/.

7. Timothy Greenfield-Sanders, dir., *Toni Morrison: The Pieces I Am*, documentary, Magnolia Pictures, 2019.

ABOUT THE AUTHOR

Omo Moses was born in Tanzania, East Africa, in 1972. He is the former executive director and founding member of the Young People's Project (YPP), a national nonprofit organization with programs in over ten US cities that utilize mathematics to prepare students to succeed in school and in life. YPP evolved out of the Algebra Project, which grew out of the civil rights activism of the Algebra Project's founder and MacArthur Genius Grant winner Bob Moses, Omo's father. Omo founded MathTalk, a community-based ed-tech startup, in 2019. MathTalk products make math fun, meaningful, and valuable for kids and families everywhere. One of four siblings, Omo grew up in Cambridge, Massachusetts, attended the University of Pittsburgh and George Washington University on basketball scholarships, where he majored in mathematics and minored in creative writing. Omo is the producer of *Finding Our Folk*, an award-winning student-filmed documentary featuring the Grammy-nominated Hot 8 Brass Band, which tells the story of members of YPP who organized themselves and others to respond to the devastation caused by Hurricane Katrina in 2005. Omo is the proud father of Johari, eleven, and Kamara, nine.